## Books by Nicholas von Hoffman

*Fiction*

Organized Crimes

Two, Three, Many More

*Nonfiction*

Citizen Cohn

Make-Believe Presidents

Tales from the Margaret Mead Taproom
(with Garry Trudeau)

The Fireside Watergate (with Garry Trudeau)

Left at the Post

We Are the People Our Parents Warned Us Against

The Multiversity

Mississippi Notebook

# CAPITALIST FOOLS

# Nicholas von Hoffman

# CAPITALIST

# FOOLS

## Tales of American Business, from Carnegie to Forbes to the Milken Gang

**DOUBLEDAY**
New York London Toronto Sydney Auckland

PUBLISHED BY DOUBLEDAY
a division of Bantam Doubleday Dell Publishing Group, Inc.
666 Fifth Avenue, New York, New York 10103

DOUBLEDAY and the portrayal of an anchor with a dolphin
are trademarks of Doubleday, a division of
Bantam Doubleday Dell Publishing Group, Inc.

Library of Congress Cataloging-in-Publication Data

von Hoffman, Nicholas.
Capitalist fools: tales of American business, from Carnegie to
Forbes to the Milken gang/Nicholas von Hoffman.
p.   cm.
Includes bibliographical references and index.
1. Capitalists and financiers—United States—History.
2. Executives—United States—History.   3. Capitalism—United
States—History.   4. Chief executive officers—United States—
History.   I. Title.
HG172.A2V66   1992
338.7′092′273—dc20
[B]   92-11597
CIP

To the Hundreds of Thousands of Business Executives
Who Do Their Jobs Superlatively Well
and
to Whom the Rest of Us Owe So Much

# ACKNOWLEDGMENTS

Many thanks to Pat Aufderheide, Wayne Barrett, Richard Behar, Margaret M. Bertelson, Mervin Block, Marie Brenner, Maxine Champion, Elizabeth Coleman, Michael Conroy, John Cooney, Sally Denton, Lisa Dubrul, Mary Evans, Patrick Filley, Muriel Freeman, David Gernert, Bonnie Goldstein, Anita Gotlieb, Kitty Kelley, Mark Kramer, Susan Lee and Ken Weisshaar, Stephanie Mansfield, Gretchen Morganson, Julia Nichols, Luvie Pearson, Alexandra Penney, Barbara Rice, Richard Sasanow, Walter Shapiro, John Stickney, Sandy Stuart, Alexander von Hoffman, Les Whitten.

Special thanks to Virginia Barber, who, as per usual, went above and beyond the duties of a literary agent, in her suggestions, counsel and detailed review of the manuscript. (The errors and stupidities are all her fault; the good stuff is mine.) Thanks are owing also to Susan Dooley for her editing and reviewing and helping in ways too numerous to list; to Bill Boon for chasing down people and information and for his enthusiasm; to Valerie du Laney for her resourcefulness, accuracy and follow-through.

# CONTENTS

# Contents

# PREFACE

I BEGAN THIS BOOK intending it to be a conventional biography, a chronological story of a life. Famous and famously glamorous, Malcolm Forbes, the successful publisher, celebrated for his yachts, palaces and parties, seemed to be a suitable candidate for compression between hard covers. He wasn't.

Famous while alive and famous after death are not the same. The dead don't have full-time publicists. Publishing owner-proprietors of greater importance than Malcolm, men like Henry Luce, the founder of *Time, Life* and *Fortune*, lie in graves unmarked save by a diminishing band of contemporaries. Even living with the publicity department going full bore, a person can slip from public view. A generation is growing up to whom the name Hugh Hefner is a fuzzy noise, yet Hefner was as much a symbol of America in the 1960s as Forbes was in the 1980s. Hefner's celebrityhood began slipping away from him during his lifetime. He is still alive at this writing but, as a public figure, he is a cryogenic specimen, a body frozen in ice.

Whatever their accomplishments as publishers, Malcolm's fame and Hefner's were as egregious consumers. The artifacts associated with Hefner were the same kinds of things Malcolm Forbes would be famous for twenty years later. Forbes had the château in France, and the town house in London, Hef—and every middle-class male in America once knew who that was— Hef had the Playboy Mansions, the one in Chicago, the other in Los Angeles. Malcolm had his yacht, Hefner had his airplane, and his bunnies. Malcolm lacked bunnies.

Hefner promised a new way of life for everybody, but particularly for the young men of the post-World War II time. Besides the sex, the first issue of *Playboy* in 1953 carried a declara-

tion: "We want to make it clear from the start, we aren't a 'family magazine' . . . We enjoy mixing up cocktails and an hors d'oeuvre or two, putting a little mood music on the phonograph and inviting in a female for a quiet discussion on Picasso, Nietzsche, jazz, sex."[1] This was the vision of the attainable, cool life—the small bachelor pad, a little Danish modern, an instrument to play some records on, a Braque exhibition poster from Barcelona, a bottle of California wine, and a girl, maybe not a certifiable cottontail, but a right-enough girl.

This magazine was written for the first generation of young men with enough money to leave home before marriage and set up housekeeping as bachelors. They believed things would continue to get better for them, and they were correct. They were ripe for a magazine which told them how they could enjoy this new life, unattainable for their parents in their premarital years. *Playboy*, at its height, was more than the American *Kama Sutra*, it was a manual for better living within your price range. Besides the millions who paid a stiff price for it every month, more millions read it for ideas on life and living. It was the magazine for a generation, white collar and blue, who never had it so good and figured it was going to keep on getting better.

Hefner began his glide path off the screen of national attention about the time Malcolm was claiming his coast-to-coast. The switchover seems to have occurred in the mid-1970s as something else was happening. The good times were ending. After the first couple of years of that decade the standard of living for most Americans eased off its upward climb, trembled in uncertain level flight and then began the slow degradations downward which have not ceased from that time to this.

If one could no longer afford to live the good life, one could at least watch Malcolm live it. The opinion everybody shared about Malcolm was, "Boy, he knew how to live! Jay-sus! Did that guy ever know what to do with his money." Malcolm, of course, hyped the idea by boasting the epitaph on his headstone would read, "While Alive, He Lived."

The multitudes knew Malcolm, the happy spender, drifting about the sky, leaning over the side of the gondola under a hot air balloon, a smile plastered on his face; they knew him as the sunny days millionaire ripping through the sky in his gold jet

named *Capitalist Tool*. The title of the movie he starred in was *If You Got It, Spend It*. He was the platinum-plated Good Time Charlie vrooming over hill and dale on his chromium Hog with the purple-eyed movie queen seated behind him, pushing one of the twentieth century's most famous chests into the back of his leather biker jacket.

The millions did not read his magazine; they did not associate Malcolm with much other than good food, good drink and good sex with the film goddess, performed in palaces filled with expensive toys. Hefner was for mass culture's good livers, Malcolm was for mass culture's good watchers. They got a kick out of hearing how Malcolm was spending his money.

As time went on, conditions changed, life got harder: Hefner didn't make sense anymore. Who has time for three days of sex with five people? While holding down two jobs? Though stricken with heart trouble, modern medicine saved Hefner to live past his moment. When the world learned that he had wedded the ten thousandth and first chick and conceived a child, it was for tabloid TV. Former Horny-Porny can still get it up, Ex-Free Love King on heart drugs but still potent. Hope for cardiac patients everywhere.

Like Hefner's, Malcolm's act was a thin one, for basically what both did was stand around in public and be rich. There were pictures of Malcolm being rich in the air, on the sea and on the ground in China, in Brazil, hither and yon, properly dressed for whatever well-heeled occasion. Malcolm in his balloon suit, in his motorcycle suit, his yacht suit, his party suit and, for a smaller circle in Manhattan, Far Hills, New Jersey, and Morocco, discourteous rumors about him in his birthday suit.

Malcolm got off the globe just in time. His homosexual half-life was close to bursting open in the newspapers, and he was in danger of getting hit by decade change. Americans are taken with the decimal theory of history, which has it that every year ending with a zero inaugurates a new epoch, a new time line which must be given a name and moralized about. Had he lived, Malcolm would have been dismissed as too rich, too eighties, too much the friend of the beady-eyed greedies. He was lucky to exit when he did. They might have started hooting and laughing at him if he'd stayed around. A soft touch, a decent man who always made a small donation, and sometimes

hefty ones, the owner of a magazine read by investors more than anyone else, he wasn't enough of a heavyweight to have been accorded villain status. The last year or so, though still getting ink in *People* magazine, he was on his way toward half-life, toward the faint recognition accorded the previously famous.

Even at his zenith, looking golden, spending money, sailing on his yacht, he was not unique; the publishing industry has given the world more than its share of flamboyant executives. For eccentricity and all-around colorfulness Joseph Pulitzer and the James Gordon Bennetts, father and son, would finish ahead of Malcolm, and William Randolph Hearst outdistanced him by every measure.

Malcolm had one yacht, Willie Hearst had two; Malcolm had one château in France and a splendid town house in London, Hearst had seven castles, not counting the two medieval monasteries he had taken apart, crated and shipped to the United States where they stayed in their boxes because the master of San Simeon didn't get around to deciding what he would do with them. Both were maniacal collectors but Malcolm's hoardings—toy soldiers, Americana, so-so artifacts—were as nothing compared to the mansions and warehouses stuffed to the overflowing by Hearst with old masters, statuary, rare books, priceless decorative objects and furniture. If it were true that Malcolm knew how to live, Willie knew how to live better.

Not right for the nineties, Malcolm was a fast-vanishing subject, a man not six months' dead and already less of a name than an echo of a party everyone wants to forget, a stabbing reverberation in an aching head. A suitable biography for such a subject could not be conventional. The book could not be Malcolm Forbes and his times, but had to be the reverse, his times and Malcolm Forbes. What may endure about Malcolm is not his possessions, the collections of an arrested development, not his parties, which were the prosaic and pompous being important and dull together, but the world of business which he strove to make himself a symbol and spokesman for. Not a mover, not a shaker, but a reflector, nevertheless, Malcolm, for his brief hour, was Mr. Business, an emblem of the private sector and the nation's enterprise.

In the years of Malcolm's highest visibility, business came

back into its own on a scale and with an intensity not seen in America since F. Scott Fitzgerald described the sun falling golden on the lawns of great Long Island estates. The glamorous men of money and power, whom the nonbusiness public took to be represented by Malcolm, were lionized and praised as the companies, whose prosperity they were entrusted with, faltered and failed. The moguls, the tycoons and the magnates were delivering the goods for themselves, but not for the society. They grew richer but America did not.

The majority of young and middle-aged people, the hardcore employed, are divided between the millions who run harder to stay in place and millions more who gradually fall behind. As for the bottom quartile, we step over more and more of them, as we pick our way to the office swatting away the fear that we may wind up on the streets ourselves.[2]

In fact, while the rich got richer, they didn't get as rich as the rich used to get. The big money is not as big as the big money of a hundred years ago. In 1918 Malcolm's father estimated that John D. Rockefeller was worth something like a billion and a quarter dollars.[3] Depending how you figure it, in modern greenbacks that translates into at least fifteen billion, maybe thirty billion dollars. Nobody in the *Forbes 400* list of today begins to have that kind of money. Malcolm, who died regarded as the epitome of deluxe living, didn't enjoy the extravagant enormities of plutocrats past.

The richest man in America, according to *Forbes*, is an old pal of Malcolm's, John Kluge. His fortune is estimated to be somewhere between a sixth and a third of Rockefeller's in 1918. Beyond that nobody's heard of Kluge and nobody wants to because he is, with all the money he's gotten, a pedestrian man. His business career has left him infinitely the richer, but his adopted country has shared little of his wealth. Kluge, a German immigrant, made his pile by finagling, cheapskating and deal making.

By 1918 Rockefeller, founder of the gigantic Standard Oil Trust, may have been the most hated man in America for his monopolistic ambitions, his stealthy commercial treachery and his heartless reach for absolute business dominance, yet his sins must be balanced against his contribution to America as a businessman. Rockefeller invented a vast organization to refine and

market kerosene lamp oil at a price the millions could pay. "Give the poor man his cheap light, gentlemen," Rockefeller would say, and what that meant was described in 1864 by a contemporary who saw the benefits of cheap lamp oil: "Kerosene has, in one sense, increased the length of life among the agricultural population . . . Those who, on account of the dearness or inefficiency of whale oil, were accustomed to go to bed soon after the sunset and spend almost half their time in sleep, now occupy a portion of the night in reading and other amusements; and this is more particularly true of the winter seasons."[4] Adding three or four hours on to the day is a contribution more valuable than the personal computer, once miraculous IBM's last gift to America before it started into its decline. Rockefeller's Standard Oil later developed the gasoline refining and distribution system without which the automobile would have remained a form of transportation reserved for the few.

Kluge got much and gave little in return. Rockefeller got much more but gave back, not counting his philanthropies, much, much more. Rockefeller was present at the sunrise of American enterprise, Kluge at what may prove to be its sunset. How and why American business and businessmen have changed between the time of the young Rockefeller and the old Kluge is a major theme of this non-biography.

In 1947 B. C. Forbes, Malcolm's father and the founder of *Forbes* magazine, threw a thirtieth birthday party for the publication. Guests at the Waldorf-Astoria in New York City were there to see "Today's 50 Foremost Business Leaders" given scrolls. Even then people commented on how different the foremost businessmen were from those B.C. wrote about before World War I. There were still some pioneers at the 1947 affair, founding businessmen like Eddie Rickenbacker, of Eastern Airlines (now bankrupt) and David Sarnoff of the Radio Corporation of America (now sold off to General Electric), but the list and the times were already dominated by caretaker-managers. The dynamism was waning.[5]

In the succeeding half-century American enterprise began to be progressively less able to lift the nation onto higher plateaus of prosperity until upward motion stopped. The theme of this book is the story of business from B. C. Forbes' youth to his son's old age, the long arc from the beginnings, through the

decades of supernal accomplishment and national enrichment to the painful katabasis of our own times.

The Forbeses, father and son, had at least a passing acquaintance with two thirds of the signal figures in the history of business. Malcolm Forbes, who has already had two of them, doesn't merit a third biography, but he and his father can serve as useful if accidental guides to this attempt to learn how the great men were great and how the modern ones are not.

# CAPITALIST FOOLS

# ONE

---

# The Business
# of Booze
# and Schmooze

**F**OR MALCOLM FORBES it was not the perfect end of a perfect day. The most splendid of all his parties and entertainments had ended with a fusillade of old galoshes and rusty alarm clocks. The richly famous and the famously rich had come home from Tangier, where he had flown them for the affair, out of sorts and unhappy, while the press, his freeloading friends lo these many years, had turned on him.

Rarely had the happiest millionaire felt the sting of public derision. Years ago Stephen Birmingham had, in the *New York Times*,[1] of all painfully conspicuous places, called him "a compulsive spender, particularly on items that can be considered tax-deductible." Since that act of hostility, almost no one had had an unkind word for this likable man behind the owlish eyeglasses. Malcolm had stayed clear of controversy and, unlike the other two super-glamorous businessmen of his period, Lee Iacocca and Donald Trump, he had not become a public irri-

tant. Famous rich people are seldom popular rich people, but Malcolm was.

He had gotten famouser and famouser and richer and richer and everybody had thought it was wonderful until he had thrown himself a birthday party to mark his entrance into the seventh decade of life. The exact figures—six hundred guests or eight hundred guests at a cost of two million or three million dollars—have not been determined, but whatever the numbers, they were too much.

The invitations came from Malcolm's children, but the two plus million the affair is purported to have cost came from Papa Pasha since only death itself released Malcolm's grip on his wealth.[2]

For years the more Malcolm spent and the more he took joy over what he had spent, the more an approving public clapped and egged him on to the next purchase. When he bought Thomas Jefferson's bottle of wine, you'd have thought he was an Olympian doing his victory lap. That's the way the *Los Angeles Times* reported this minor milestone in conspicuous consumption, and no one knew better than Malcolm how to make consumption conspicuous: *"Forbes* magazine today paid a world record price of $157,500 for an 18th-Century bottle of red wine made for Thomas Jefferson, the third President of the United States. It was four times the previous record for a bottle of wine. The 1787 Chateau Lafite claret—inscribed with the wine's vintage and the initials 'Th.J.'—was bought by *Forbes* of New York at Christie's auction house in London. Applause broke out in the packed salesroom when the gavel came down."[3]

Malcolm was not of the print-anything-you-want-just-spell-my-name-right school of publicity houndage. He wanted to be loved, unfailingly loved, in public and private, and he had worked at being loved all his life, so, though warned a public relations problem was aborning, he was not braced for the Bronx cheers and catcalls which assailed him within hours of his return to America from his party in August 1989—the headlines which linked his name to "New Standards of Wretched Excess."[4]

But since when was excess wretched? The press had gushed over Malcolm's richly appointed private airplanes, gushed over his yachts, his French château, his this, his that, welcoming him

as the American epicurean, the happiest hedonist. If you ever won the lotto jackpot, the man who could tell you how to spend your money was Malcolm Forbes. He knew how to spend his, only suddenly he didn't.

By 1989, nice man that he was, Malcolm had entered the final phase of *megalomania extremens,* brought on by a diet of fifteen years of unremittingly favorable publicity, and therefore his antennae may have lost their acuity. Otherwise he should have sensed that the winds had turned adverse.

Without his knowing it, he had passed from amplitude to excess, and was being called an on-the-edge-of-the-law tax cheat. Accusing Malcolm of intending to make the party one big, multimillion-dollar tax deduction, columnist Leonard E. Larsen told the world that, "Publisher Malcolm Forbes, in an act that pushed arrogant self-indulgence out to new horizons, threw a birthday party for himself . . ."5 *The New Republic* jeered, ". . . Pressed on the point at his 70th anniversary blow-out in Tangier, Forbes conceded 'Some of it is a business expense.' . . . Maybe Forbes accountants can convince the IRS that 600 Moroccan belly dancers were not a substantial distraction, but what about the 200 Cavalry Guards? . . . Not exactly what the IRS is pleased to call 'a clear business setting.' "6 The gibe came with ill grace from a magazine owned by Martin Peretz, whose large and flashy parties make for impressive tax deduction material themselves. But this was an instance when he and other publishers, ordinarily careful of each others' feelings, allowed their editorial piranhas to take a few nips out of one of their own.

A confused Malcolm was heard to say, "Everything worked— I thought . . . until I started reading some of the commentary."7 Back in New York he would make everything work for sure by calling a press conference and surrendering to his critics. Not a farthing, not a centime of the party's cost would be charged to the taxpayers, the thoroughly defensive birthday boy told the running dogs of the capitalist press: "I would say 95 percent—it's business related . . . But the question is, are we using it as a business deduction? It was never intended to be, and not a penny of it is. But certainly a case can be made when 75 percent of your guests are your biggest customers."8

It must have pissed off Barbara Walters when the television

3

star read that. When she was still in Tangier, before Malcolm's frank avowal in New York of his uses and purposes, a fellow guest remembered, "Barbara Walters sat in the bar in this little Moroccan hotel that Malcolm had taken over, just saying, 'I feel used, I feel used, I'm supposed to traipse around here so that these people can pop their eyes out at me.' "[9] If she had any doubts about being one of the marquee attractions for the CEOs who put their ads in *Forbes* magazine, they ought to have been put to rest by the pre-party letter from Malcolm to the star-guests asking them not to rent cars, but to ride on the buses he had arranged to move the common garden variety CEOs from function to function. Malcolm wanted his stars to mingle with his customers. The lady was but a bait worm on the fish hook of commerce.

It was her own fault. She got on the airplane. Yet it is a demonstrable fact that highly placed Americans, members of Congress, news-entertainers and CEOs will accept a free airplane ride anywhere, regardless of how unpromising the destination. A party in Africa in August? No! Well, yes if it's away we go *gratis* in a Concorde.

People have lost their jobs or gone to jail for that free plane ride. It was the same in the nineteenth century with free railroad passes, which were used to bribe politicians and businessmen. The practice and its results were so notorious gratuitous travel was outlawed, but the desire to voyage to far places without buying a ticket remains as strong as ever.

So the CEO fish took the Barbara bait. When the shrewder of the stars, like Katharine Graham, controlling stockholder and Chairman of the Board of Directors of The Washington Post Company, had ignored their host's request and gone ahead and rented Mercedes for themselves, the simple up-country CEOs and their missuses bent over to look into the car windows and recognize the famous faces on the other side of the glass.

"Most of the notables were furious by the end of the weekend," said a non-notable sophisticate, but "What I found interesting flying back on one of the planes he'd chartered for this, walking up and down the aisle, just chatting with a number of the CEOs and their wives, anonymous people from all over the country running fairly sizeable companies, was that to a person they all had a simply spectacular time. They loved it. Having

4

Barbara Walters there and the Henry Kissingers did exactly what Malcolm expected it to do, it gave the CEOs a lot to go home and talk about.

"And they just thought it was great. The fact that there was no hot water, that it was too hot, that everything was late didn't bother them at all."[10]

It was no secret that Malcolm was mixing business with pleasure. A week before this squadron of fine-feathered persons took off for Africa, the gossip columnist Liz Smith was telling people, "Private parties are very rare these days . . . The Forbes party is a business party. He does do wonderful things, but they always have a raison d'être beyond personal enjoyment."[11]

Malcolm was the premier business host of his time, the Capitalist Tool in human form, the worldwide advocate and troubadour of American business. What makes Malcolm something besides just another rich guy with a big boat and ego to match is that he consecrated himself the archpriest of opulence, the hymnodist of wealth. God may or may not have been in His heaven, but our Malcolm was in the sky. This is a man who hung from a basket underneath a gold leaf gasbag in the American firmament for a generation, smiling down and shouting, "Look at me!" The nation, and indeed much of the world, did stare upward at this happy-faced, improbable hyperion. But to look at Malcolm is also to look at what Malcolm stood for—American business. He preferred the word capitalism, but capitalism is an abstraction. Business is capitalism, not as a theory but as it is lived; business is capitalism live on the hoof, in a particular country and culture.

Malcolm didn't know many of the major figures from the heroic period of American business. He may have met a few as a boy, but the most important men had gone to their graves by the time he was an adult. It was Malcolm's father, B. C. Forbes, who knew Andrew Carnegie, Pierre du Pont, Julius Rosenwald, Theodore Vail, Charlie Schwab, John Patterson, the men of the miraculous times of American business, men of the golden seventy-five years from 1850 to 1925, they who transformed the world. This was the short burst of American genius, comparable to those other brief eruptions of genius and invention which gave the world the civilization of Athens, the Renaissance in

Florence, seventeenth-century mathematics, French Impressionism, and so on. These are the solar flares of a nation, unpredicted and unpredictable, and, in the case of America, they gave us a cornucopia of business.

Business is different from things like the free market. They had the free market in the Middle Ages when you were lucky to live to thirty-five years of age and own an eighth of an interest in an ox. There was no General Motors, no General Electric when Frederick Barbarossa was marching his armies up and down Italy, and the minimum material comfort—let's not speak of shoes—did not exist. They had the free market in those times, but the great wealth-producing organizations, corporate America, if you will, are an invention of the golden seventy-five years.

Before the Civil War Americans had little or no choice as to price, quality and style in their purchases. Marooned on farms accessible only on ineffably terrible roads, they bought at the single country store or they didn't buy. We moderns have no conception of how narrow choice was, but the humor of the period gives an indication.

P. T. Barnum, who ranks high among business pioneers, summed up the widespread dislike of those cracker barrel monopolists, the country store owners, with his story about the owner who was also a church deacon. "John, have you watered the rum?" Barnum had him ask his clerk.

"Yes."

"Have you sanded the sugar?"

"Yes."

"And dusted the pepper?"

"Yes, sir."

"Well, then come up to prayers."[12]

This ditty, sung to the tune of "The Bonnie Blue Flag," expresses the opinion of farmers' wives in the cotton South on consumer satisfaction in the latter decades of the nineteenth century. Many had only one store to buy from, and were also forced to sell their produce to the same merchant.

> My husband came from town last night
> As sad as man could be,
> His wagon empty, cotton gone,

**6**

And not a dime had he.
Huzzah! Huzzah!
'Tis queer, I do declare!
We make the clothes for all the world,
But few we have to wear.[13]

Populists of the stripe of South Carolina's Governor and then Senator "Pitchfork" Ben Tillman openly campaigned against country store practices.[14] Aaron Montgomery Ward took note of the resentment at the high prices and poor choices early in the course of building his retail mail order business. He made common cause with the Patrons of Husbandry or the Grange, that vast quasi-secret fraternal order of farm families, whose local halls can still be seen in thousands of depopulated villages and hamlets. The twenty-two-page 1874 Montgomery Ward price list or catalogue proclaimed the company was "The Original Grange Supply House." The storekeepers fought back. In 1873, the *Chicago Tribune* carried a piece headlined, "Grangers Beware! Don't Patronize 'Montgomery Ward & Co.'—they are Dead-Beats. Another attempt at swindling has come to light."[15] Newspapers, everywhere under thumb and thrall of local merchants, refused Montgomery Ward and Sears, Roebuck advertising.

But Richard Sears, ever the more strident and enterprising merchant though he came along a couple of years after Ward, was more explicit in exploiting discontent over the lack of choice and competition. His 1895 catalogue proclaimed "War to the Knife—We are Waging War against Combinations, Associations, Trusts and High Prices." Eugene Talmadge, four times elected governor of Georgia in the 1930s and '40s, understood how completely the wool hat farmers of his state depended on the retail competition supplied by the mail order houses. On the stump, he used to tell them, don't trust anybody but "God Almighty, Sears, Roebuck and Eugene Talmadge."

Local merchants spread the word that Richard Sears and Alvah Roebuck were of African-American descent; anti-Semitic canards were circulated about Julius Rosenwald when he took the helm at Sears. In small towns storekeepers paid children as much as a dime for every catalogue they brought to the bonfires ignited in the public squares to destroy them. In other places

kids bearing catalogues were admitted free to the movies, and in Warsaw, Iowa, a candidate for mayor promised that, if elected, he would fire any city employee caught buying merchandise from a mail order house.[16]

Business converted the stodgy free market of a mercantile culture into the competitive free market which was able to deliver so much so cheaply it transformed what had been a grand array of rare luxuries for the aristocracy into everyday objects for the masses. After the mail order houses had achieved success, chain stores and discount houses had to contend with price fixing and blue laws as various interests continued to limit competition. In our own time Wal-Mart, the latest evolution in low-cost merchandise distribution, is being attacked for much the same reasons Sears, Roebuck was over a century ago.

Malcolm happened along in the beginning of the post-Augustan age of American business. Richard Sears was dead by the time Malcolm was born and the explosion of business energy, business improvisation, business trail blazing was dying down. The time of leveling off had begun and now we are in the time of decline. In his most famous years, the last fifteen or twenty of his life, the rate of decline was accelerating, although this was not apparent to him. He continued as ever, always active, always optimistic, the sign and symbol of past accomplishment, not present attainment.

But Malcolm Forbes, an outstanding space salesman in the magazine industry, a man celebrated as the national bon vivant, was also the custodian of the idea of wealth, a minister by self-ordination in a religion of green and gold, two colors which he surrounded himself with for years. We have had business preachers before Malcolm, men like Andrew Carnegie and Bruce Barton, who talked about getting rich, about how to succeed, but Malcolm was different. Yes, he gave lip service to those things, but it was wealth per se which Malcolm studied and Malcolm glorified. As a man, albeit a competent one, who inherited his business, a career like Andrew Carnegie's couldn't be much of an example, or role model to use the psychobabble term, because Carnegie had started with nothing, had begun with a broom in his hand, founded his own company and, in the process, been one of the few who kicked open the door to modernity. That could never be Malcolm, who, like many an-

8

other heir, was prone to conserve and build up, not commit money to business projects which sound men, prudent men would not approve of.

Malcolm, who forged himself into being *the* capitalist tool," never bought, it appears, a single share of stock in a publicly owned company or corporation. Nor does it seem that Malcolm ever borrowed a dime or a dollar, save once immediately after graduating from college when he got money from his father's friends to buy a couple of weekly newspapers in Ohio.[17] Donald Trump bought his yachts on credit, Malcolm paid cash. Cash, specie, coin, hard currency, wealth, not paper, funny money or IOUs is what Malcolm Forbes wanted in his Scottish sporran.

His dedication to wealth made him deviant. America is a culture which fastens on income. How much do you make? How much does she make? The lists are of the five hundred highest-paid CEOs, movie stars, athletes, or of the average family income, or the income above the poverty line. Always, it's how much do you make, not how much do you own. In Washington, libraries of computer tapes contain information on income; there isn't one floppy disk full of data on wealth and who owns it. The statistics aren't kept, because we are a public which wants to know what Madonna made on her last album, not the dimension of the Dorrance family holdings.

Who are the Dorrances? Originally, they were Campbell Soup; they can buy and sell Madonna every day of the week, although no great public has heard of them. Madonna has income, they have wealth.

But Malcolm wanted to know about wealth. To Malcolm, brought up half Roman Catholic and half Presbyterian, being wealthy was being in a state of grace. That's the doctrine he preached, but it wasn't enough for him. He needed a lick or two more than the buzz he got from the dazzle off the gold monstrance. So Malcolm initiated the *Forbes 400*, the list of the four hundred wealthiest people in America, a list which is markedly different from the lists of the highest-income people in America. The highest paid are not the richest.

The 1982 introduction of the *Forbes 400* was an enormous publishing success. It took a magazine that few outside of a restricted world of executives and investors had heard of and made it a name among the masses. For, as it happened, people

were just as interested in wealth as they were in income. The publication every fall of the list is now an annual event, the highlights of which get almost—not quite but almost—as much attention as the Oscars. Malcolm's list is American capitalism's Academy Award.

The fact that prior to Malcolm so little information on wealth had been accumulated is not accidental. The rich do not want to be known, and, as the single most powerful group in the society, they usually get what they want. Motives for keeping mum on wealth abound. The first is a tax system based on income. Wealth is unenumerated and untaxed; stocks, bonds, old paintings, real estate, wealth in any form grows and it is still not taxed. The rich have every reason in the world to discourage the collection of information on wealth and to encourage the concentration of publicity and attention on income.

More than fifty years ago Ferdinand Lundberg made the same observation: "The inability to produce precise figures on fortunes, rather than approximations, result, then, from no fault in plan or method, but rather from the extreme secrecy with which statistics on fortunes are guarded and from the very nature of fortunes."[18] Nothing has changed since the mid-1930s when he wrote those words.

This is not conspiracy theory. Would that the country was run by a conspiracy! Then we would know whom to turn to and whom to blame. A conspiracy would be evidence that the anarchy of cross purposes which keeps us frozen is an illusion. Without positing conspiracies, however, there is a community of interest among the rich to hide as much information about themselves as possible. The *Forbes 400* list is a startling departure. The information in it, gathered at Malcolm Forbes' instructions, represents the largest body of such information on wealth in the United States.

Though Malcolm wasn't a traitor to his income group or his wealth percentile, if he could make money doing something his peers didn't want done, he'd do it anyway. So Forbes studied the American rich. We have studies of African-American welfare ladies, we have studies of inner-city youth, but the subjects of these inquiries cut little ice, their preferences, opinions, decisions, life patterns are of less moment than those of the power-

ful. The people who count are the people who are never studied—the rich.

The meaning of Malcolm's life revolves around business,
around wealth and its uses. Otherwise Malcolm is a grinning
idiot, a simpy guy with a lot of money and a big smile. As an
idiot under a yacht cap, one foot up on the railing, one arm
around the movie star's waist, Malcolm is dismissable, but as the
apologist for the engine of enterprise in his time, as the emblem
of wealth and wealth well spent, as American capitalism's Number One Joy Boy, he merits closer inspection.

He gathered a great deal of information on wealth, who owns
it, what forms wealth takes, but past that Malcolm did not venture. He stayed away from questions about the distribution of
wealth, content to list the names of those who had it without
wondering overly much about those who don't. What he did
was to make a specialty of demonstrating how wealth was con-
sumed, of publicizing how to spend it, however you got it. He
became the presiding chief of the great potlatch as he made it
appear all his time was leisure time, but it wasn't. As Liz Smith
said, more often than not, there was a business angle to his
yachts, his parties, his noisy incursions into distant places.

Malcolm boasted[19] that the CEOs of 350 corporations had
been lured to Africa to consume 100 lambs and 830 chickens
prepared by 150 cooks in barely two days of gut-busting feasts
and brain-numbing imbibition.[20] It may not have been a lost
weekend, but these people drank enough so that their host
started running out of liquor.[21]

They must have been chugalugging a lot of hootch. By early
Saturday evening, the key ingredient for vodka and tonic was
already exhausted. The gin too was gone.[22] Even the most important of the guest stars or the star-guests couldn't get a drink.
Jim Hoge, then publisher of the *New York Daily News*, recalled,
"The night of the banquet itself, the lines to get into this place
took about an hour, an hour and a half. Malcolm had factotums
running up and down picking out important people, and
bringing them up front and getting them in, but they missed
Kay Graham.

"She had to go through the whole thing. By the time she got
up to this place where you were given, or you picked a color

**11**

card which told you which tent to go to, she was as mad as I've ever seen anybody—shaking with rage.

"I happened to come up to her and said, 'Hi Kay!' She said, 'Goddamnit, get me a drink!' I sensed the importance of the mission and fought my way through to one of the bars, which was manned by locals who didn't have the faintest idea of the difference between ginger ale and vodka. So they were screwing up left, right and center. I got there just as they ran out of vodka, which is what she wanted. I couldn't find anything else except scotch. So I just said, 'Look, fill it up with scotch,' and I brought it over to Kay and said, 'This is the only thing I could find, it's scotch.'

"She said, 'I never drink it, thank you!' took it and drank it."

It must have taken some of these guys two or three days to recover. Given that these men, most of whom were in late middle age, had flown from all over America to Tangier, of all godforsaken places, on a Friday, had eaten and drunk for two solid days, crawled back on the plane Sunday late for the second trans-Atlantic flight in forty-eight hours, been dumped out on the tarmac at Kennedy near dawn, what kind of shape were they in when they hit the office Monday morning?

But these CEOs are the Napoleons of business, men who can go days without sleep, winners, guys who have it under control, masters of the universe, lords of the multinationals. Why, if they want to tie one on, they deserve it.

Well, yes and no. Take the two Smiths. Take Frederick W. Smith, chairman, CEO and founding spirit of Federal Express —this man's needle is way over on the plus side of the success-o-meter. If he wants to take a weekend or a week or a month off, he gets to do it with no critical comments. The other Smith is Roger B. Smith, then Chairman of the Board and Chief Executive Officer or CEO of General Motors, as well as the laughingstock of corporate America. Both were at the party.[23]

If there is a single executive whose name had come, by the late 1980s, to symbolize dunderheaded incompetence in high places it was Roger B. Smith's. After release of the movie about him, *Roger and Me,* he had won for himself a national reputation as the prototypical auto-crat who has wrecked the American automobile industry. It didn't help that the man looks as though he needs to be followed around by a butler with a salver

**1 2**

and a damask napkin wiping spittle off his chin. Viewed from one perspective Malcolm may have been doing a favor for the nation, which depends on this once great corporation, by keeping the boy away from the office. In any event, while GM's chairman was gawking at Liz Taylor and the camels in Morocco, his company was losing market share back home.

There were other excursions, ballooning at Forbes' estate in France, joining Malcolm aboard the *Good Ship Lollipop* for a cruise to Bangkok, as Roger, the captain of the corporate Leviathan, let General Motors, which had once been the premier industrial organization, not just of the United States, but of the world, slowly founder. He had other poop decks to pound.

As Smith partied the consequences of his failures were to be felt by stockholders, suppliers, dealers and employees. Not long after one of these cruises on the *Highlander,* laid-off lower management people, suffering cutbacks in their health insurance benefits from the company, picketed the Great Recreator with signs declaring "Benefits before bonuses," and "Roger gets the gold mine, retirees get the shaft."[24] The reference to precious metals has to do with the pourboire flung at Roger of Rueful Memory by his Board of Directors prior to his retirement. CEOs of Roger Smith's incontestable stature, of course, never retire. To this day Mr. Smith marches on dispensing his peculiar brand of expertise to a needy business world. At last report he was receiving over two hundred thousand dollars a year for sitting on the boards of Citicorp, International Paper and Johnson & Johnson.[25]

If you compare Roger, who crab-crawled his way to the top of the GM bureaucracy, with the Federal Express's Smith, you can see why Frederick Smith deserved a weekend off in Tangier with the glittery people. Fred Smith was a throwback, a man who had started not only a company, but an industry. Before him, America had been reduced to dependence on the United States Postal Service and a premonition that soon there would be no way that the written word could be sent by one person to another. This is pre-fax, of course. Smith invented the fast-delivery business, figured out how to organize it, computerize it, finance it and, as important as anything else, how to run it. The measure of what he had accomplished in providing this service

is the number of competitors who have fought their way into the industry Frederick Smith had given birth to.[26]

There were, at the party,[27] men from other companies that were doing well, thank you, men like Masaaki Morita, the executive vice president of Sony USA. Brother Akio is the head of Sony the world over and an outspoken man who doesn't buy into the polite inscrutability stereotype hung on the Japanese, for he has delivered himself of some unflattering opinions about the quality of the work done by the men who direct some of America's most important business enterprises. A bootlegged, unpublished translation of a small book co-authored by Morita on this subject has been hopping and skipping through the modem of one computer to the next for the last several years. The gist of what Mr. Morita has to say to American business big shots is that they should work harder and cut out the frou-frou.[28]

This was a homily lost on a number of Malcolm's other guests. It doesn't appear to have been a text closely studied by Jimmy Three Sticks, as the guys around the water cooler at American Express refer to their CEO and leader, James D. Robinson III. Mr. Three Sticks flew to Tangier with Ron Perelman, another meteor in the cosmos of American business, whose imminent flame-out is a matter of perpetual gossipy speculation on the lower end of Manhattan Island. Their attendance at the party was described by one close observer thus: "Then there's the Jimmy Robinson/Ron Perelman act. Well, they flew over together with their wives, in either Jimmy's plane or Ron's—I can't remember which—they arrived, got the sense of the scene, that it was not politique to stay, it wasn't the high level thing they thought it was. [Too many ordinary CEO canaille.] But you do have to be recorded. So they had the plane wait while they went through the line, signed the guest book, and immediately turned around and went right back to the airport. They were already in the air flying home as the banquet was beginning. As far as I know, they landed stateside at about the time we were all getting through this arduous dinner."[29]

Who paid for that trip? The nation's taxpayers, or somebody's stockholders, or perhaps he paid out of his own pocket, but again, that's the least of it. Was Robinson or his company in

such good shape he ought to have flown ten thousand miles to get his social ticket punched? Malcolm wasn't his customer, he was Malcolm's. What kind of a lightweight behaves like that?

Robinson may not have put American Express as far down the toilet as Roger the Wretched had succeeded in stuffing General Motors, but he had taken a nonpareil cash cow and sliced at least one of the golden bovine's udders off. Billions were lost during Robinson's administration, which has been characterized by surprise announcements of losses of such gigantic dimension that the unthinkable occurred and American Express lost its once unassailable triple AAA credit rating.[30] The company confessed to its guilt in a smarmy scandal to defame a competitor, an affair which *The Wall Street Journal*, in a lengthy investigative piece, dropped on Robinson personally.[31] The shame was augmented by the end of a string of thirty-five years of profit increases and the news that the American Express card was being surpassed by such rivals as Visa and MasterCard. Robinson is an especially noteworthy personage because, in Wall Street's estimation, he has been one of business's glamour pusses. Jimmy Robinson has been repeatedly held up as a CEO role model for young and tender American businessmen to imitate. They might have imitated themselves straight into Chapter 11 bankruptcy, but Robinson will never get the blame. Even when people were in the streets of Pittsburgh cutting up their American Express cards because Amex was putting up the money for a foreign company to buy the locally owned Koppers Co.[32] the mess got blamed on one of his subordinates while Robinson lived up to his sobriquet of "The Teflon Executive."[33]

So how does a man in a position of such trust, importance and responsibility spend his time? Judging from the gossip columns, you'd think the guy was an early retiree. As far back as 1984 Robinson is reported in France, this time at Malcolm's château at Balleroy, again up in the air, but on this occasion waving down from his own American Express balloon. Gossip columnist Suzy reported that "all the American Express biggies" were wafting about, news that ought to have brought joy to Amex shareholders.[34] Somebody with a well-aimed arrow might have saved these investors a lot of money.

Another giant of American enterprise on the list to cut didoes in the African night was Willard Butcher, Chase Manhattan's

CEO and a living example that in American business nothing succeeds like failure. Only the year before *The Wall Street Journal* had noted that Willard the Wonder had been paid more than a million dollars while his bank racked up losses of close to nine hundred million.[35]

When people worship money they bow down so low they put their foreheads on the ground and are, therefore, unable to see the object of their veneration. Uninspected and hence invisible, the bank and the Rockefellers, whose name has been associated with it for so long, have been endowed with an intelligent omnipotence one can only wish they possessed. In actuality, Chase Manhattan is American high finance's Operation Oz. Behind the high tower, the old money and the legends, there are these funny, little, confused guys running around. The midget wizards. Here is a quote from Wizard Willard, and if these are not the words of a thoroughly mixed-up man, there is no bank and there are no Rockefellers: "When I joined the (banking) system in 1947, banks had almost 70% of the nation's financial resources. Today, we've got about 30%. It isn't a question of whether banking will occur; it will. It's a question of whether banking will be done by banks. And I have never had it proved to me why banks are such bad bankers and everyone else is such a good banker."[36]

Is he saying he's a bad banker, that he's going into another line of work and chance his luck? Is he saying Chase is going to sit there making the same mistakes until the banks control none of the nation's financial resources, which might not be a bad idea, considering what this particular Wizard of Wall Street did to the share of them under his control?

There are many explanations for dropping billions in bad foreign loans and lousy domestic real estate. One of them may be the way they made their decisions. There was a period in the late 1970s when David Rockefeller was Chairman of the Board and Butcher the bank's president, when they did their thinking on an electronic toy called the "consensor," which might be described as Nintendo for bankers. The top brass sit around a table, each with a computer keyboard which enables them to express agreement or disagreement by punching in any integer from 0 to 10, with zero representing, "I think the idea is a crock." At a four-day meeting in Woodstock, the officers of the

Chase Manhattan Corporation punched in their reactions to the proposition "God exists." The consensor lit up with a 5.5, meaning that in the opinion of these worthies there is a tad better than a 50-50 chance God is up there in the big boardroom or perhaps, it's Sunday in heaven and he's out on the golf course thinking of the Rockefellers.[37]

By the end of Butcher's reign at Chase, the disappointed manager of a fund which owned a chunk of the bank's stock told a reporter, "Chase seems to be a company in search of an identity. Over the last ten years, Chase has had a difficult time determining what its focus—its mission—should be. They restructure every couple of years. So they keep spinning the wheels without ever setting off. I do not think that the company has made very clear what its franchise is—perhaps they do not know."[38]

Malcolm's birthday party fell in the middle of a period when the bank, judged by the profit goals it had set for itself, had failed.[39] In the coming months Butcher's bank would cut the dividend it paid on its stock, have to cover hundreds and hundreds of billions of bum loans (or "nonperforming assets" in banker talk),[40] confess to enormous losses[41] and see the price of its shares on the New York Stock Exchange fall off a cliff. Thousands of employees would be let go.[42] Which leads up to the question that could be asked of so many of the CEOs drinking Malcolm's booze and eating Malcolm's food: Why had he accepted the invitation?[43] He had to know the condition of his business, he had to know that everybody in the bank would hear about the biggest, best-publicized social event in years. A man who can rely on a consensor to make decisions probably doesn't have to work weekends, but what kind of an impression does such flibbertigibbeting give the staff? Shouldn't the highly publicized tripping of the light fantastic be an activity associated only with the heads of corporations which are not distressed?

Year in and year out, Malcolm was in the newspapers, a dedicated business entertainer. He had a taste for the remorseless and relentless glad-handing of the flesh-presser politician and the super-salesperson, both of which he was. In 1986 an impressed *Los Angeles Times* reported that, "Two nights a week his staff runs his 126-foot yacht, for advertisers, complete with lobster, drinks and bagpipes. And the weekend guest list for the

*Highlander* for September through November includes no fewer than 428 chief executives whom Forbes is taking to Army football games or around the Eastern coastline."[44] Malcolm did his seaborne salesmanship for years. Back in 1966 it was reported that he had entertained no less than thirteen hundred people on the *Highlander*.[45]

The pleasures of schmooze and booze have long been offered to businessmen and one can argue that the successful ones may have earned a claim to their sweets and treats. A hundred years ago, J. P. Morgan, the elder, regularly took his customers on sails up the Hudson on his *Corsair*, so named because J.P. had the idea he was a descendent of Captain Henry Morgan, the seventeenth-century pirate.[46] Morgan's *Corsair*, which made *Highlander* look like a floating slum, was painted an ominous black. The gossip had it that once on the high seas, J.P. pulled down the stars and stripes and ran up the skull and crossbones.[47]

Morgan was reputed to have his chorus girls and his bacchanals on *Corsair*. Nothing of that sort has been imputed to Malcolm. The yacht, the houses in New York, London and Africa, were owned by the magazine, not by Forbes himself, as if to underscore their commercial nature, and Forbes had been using his establishment in Tangier to soften up his customers long before the birthday party. Back in 1976 he had had his gold-painted DC-9 ferry German advertisers to his African playground for a commercial frolic.

Perhaps the most sustained effort in softening up the CEOs went into the luncheons. These were held in the town house attached to *Forbes* magazine's office on New York City's Fifth Avenue just north of Washington Square. Virtually everybody walked away from these gastronomic sessions flimflammed by Malcolm's legendary good living. Enveloped by expensive knickknackeries, cozened and cosseted, given souvenirs—Malcolm was a great one for little gifts from Tiffany's—the guest-customer was rendered defenseless by the time Malcolm got out pen and contract.[48]

A loopy, but by all accounts accurate, version of the town house sales technique was supplied by a longtime magazine staffer, Wayne Welch: "He'd have captains of industry in there, and we editorial people would be present as, what Jim Michaels

[the magazine's editor] said, were 'the dancing girls.' The conversation would go something like, 'Well, gee whiz, what do you think about the economy, Mr. Zilch?'

" 'Well, if you get the goddamned government off our backs and the damned unions, we'd be in good shape.'

" 'Oh, that's really interesting.'

"And then, afterwards, the editorial people would go back to their typewriters, and Malcolm would take these guys to the living room and put the arm on them. A few times I saw him do that on his yacht too."[49]

This is work, not fun. Many small, laborious attentions to people went with Operation Schmooze and Booze. Norman Pearlstine, who left Malcolm's employ to become managing editor of *The Wall Street Journal,* remarked that, "He sent invitations to the boat with a note saying he would be crushed if you can't come. You knew it wasn't true but you were still touched."[50] Malcolm was always sending people little notes, usually scribbled in red pencil. Countless people remember them and still feel good that he took the trouble.

As the owner and CEO Malcolm had stolen a march on the competition when it came to selling advertising space. He could sit down, CEO to CEO, to make the sale, while the competition, at Time Warner or Dow Jones or McGraw-Hill, used men of lower rank to pitch the advantages of advertising in *Fortune* or *Business Week.*

"The interesting thing about Malcolm was his relationship with the CEOs," said Pearlstine, a man who's seen these guys for years. "CEOs are the closest thing to uncrowned kings that we have in this country with their retinues and their airplanes but they're still not owners and Malcolm was. . . . Malcolm was their fantasy figure, their Walter Mitty . . . He was the man who owned the castles in Spain, the hunting lodges in Georgia, the things just beyond their grasp."[51]

A writer on the magazine, a fellow *Forbes* staffer remembered, was obtuse enough to do a piece on corporations which used the Super Bowl to promote business. Malcolm, who had made a tradition of taking a boatload of CEOs up the Hudson to watch football games at West Point, wasn't going to let such an article in his magazine. "The story cut too close to home," said Jim Michaels, the editor of *Forbes.* "One of the ways *Forbes* makes its

mark is by entertaining people. It would have been bad grace for us to run an article like that."[52]

This form of commercial bribery is sanctioned by the American government, which makes subornation via entertainment a tax deductible business expense. Malcolm didn't invent the system, and there is no reason to believe he used it any more than others. Deluxe baksheesh is endemic in American business where every inducement—seashore vacations in the corporate time-share, golf vacations, fishing vacations, hunting lodge vacations, vacation vacations, "seminars" on cruise ships in the Aegean Sea and in Rocky Mountain resort hotels, gifts, sex, drugs, cash, anything—is offered in hopes of making a sale.

Commercial bribery didn't arise out of the greedy 1980s; it was already being used to get business in the greedy 1880s, and after a century it has been cemented into business institutions in many different forms. In the recording industry large corporations use people connected with organized crime to pay radio station employees to play their products on the air. It's cheaper than paying the radio station for an ad to plug a record. This way of doing business first came to light with the payola scandals of the 1950s. But despite that exposure, both the greed and the payola way of doing business persist to the present hour. The doings in the record industry have been documented, of course, because millions pay attention to music and broadcasting.[53] Similar shenanigans in the hardware industry go unreported.

The company represented by the officer taking the bribe is defrauded by payola whether it's illegal, under the table payoffs, or the legal kind which Malcolm practiced, influencing people with lavish entertainments. In business, as in government, the deal should go to the best bid. Anything else is cheating the stockholders. Whether it's taking the customers to the Super Bowl in the company jet or having them feted and petted at your North Africa birthday party, it's commercial bribery when you give a purchasing agent, or in this case, the purchasing agent's boss, something of considerable value in return for a sale. That's bribery and that's what Malcolm called a press conference to insist that he was doing.

(Properly conducted corporations make sure their people maintain an arm's length relationship with those they do busi-

ness with. John Hancock Insurance, for example, has a written policy which states that, "No officer or employee may receive or give any gift or other favor from or to any one with whom the company has or is likely to have any business dealings." For employees with questions, there is a compliance office; for exceptional cases a waiver must be obtained from the company's general counsel. No officer from a company governed by the conflict of interest rules obtaining at John Hancock could have licitly accepted the invitation to "Ali Dada's 70th," as the press kit called Malcolm's gathering on the African side of the Pillars of Hercules.)

Long before Malcolm was born, salesmen were bribing the businessman in order to get the business, often entertaining their customers into a defenseless stupor. One nineteenth-century businessman, Diamond Jim Brady, became a national celebrity through his lavish use of the expense account as a weapon in the trade wars of his times. Bribery in Brady's hands was a means to introduce a succession of technical improvements to a stodgy railroad industry.

Brady made Rector's restaurant on Broadway between Forty-third and Forty-fourth Streets *his* town house where he served customers lobster Newburg and White Seal champagne in his effort to sell them railroad equipment.[54] The credit or the blame for using celebrities as a sales tool may also go to Diamond Jim, who paid John L. Sullivan and William F. Cody to hobnob with his star-struck customers at Brady's socials, at which more than one sale was closed on the strength of Buffalo Bill's stories about frontier combats with the Native Americans. At some of these soirees, the colonel's associate, Ms. Annie Oakley, would toss down one snootful too many, pull out a gun and shoot the lights out.

Unlike Malcolm, James Buchanan Brady came from a poor family, did not go to an Ivy League college or any college at all, but, as a teenager, went to work for Commodore Vanderbilt's New York Central Railroad. After having learned about the railroad industry, he switched over to selling equipment to it, and, using his expense account in a thoroughly modern way, Brady was responsible for introducing new equipment, or technology as we would say today, which enabled the railroads to lay track quicker and to run freight cars with heavier loads faster than

before. Greater productivity. Part of the credit for development of the safer, all-steel passenger car goes to this flamboyant man who also played a part in setting up the manufacture of high-quality, special purpose steels.

"Get to know the important men in every line, find out which ones are doing the buying and if you can, find out which ones will be doing the buying a few years from now," Brady's boss told him when he first set out with his sample bag. "Make them your friends, make them understand that you are the man who will serve them in the years to come. Make them trust you, make them respect you, and most important of all, make them like you!"[55] The salesman's eye view of the world. Malcolm would have concurred.

Big shots or little, every kind of person was cultivated by Diamond Jim in his time and by Malcolm in his. Malcolm gave people vacations at the house in London, at the one in Tangier or France or Fiji or Colorado. Off you would go in his golden airplane, traveling friction-free without having to face officious customs people or snappish airline personnel to a beautiful place where all was comfort and loveliness. He did that for people of all ranks and callings who touched his life.

Diamond Jim gave people pleasures, as well. He had zinc-lined ice chests built, in which he shipped the produce of his farm. Cream, butter, eggs, vegetables, all the fruits of a farm in which every art and artifice of agriculture were used. Beginning at Christmas 1896 and for the rest of his life, Diamond Jim sent the makings of complete dinners in all directions across America to everyone in railroading whom he had come into contact with in the course of the year, firemen, flagmen, conductors, clerks, secretaries.

Every year he bought one hundred dozen ties at Budd's, a haberdasher of distinction, and had them placed in specially made boxes with an engraved card which read on one side, "Christmas Greetings—From Mr. James Buchanan Brady," and, on the other, "If you don't like these ties—take them back and exchange them for some that you do."

Like Malcolm, Diamond Jim made sure his customers were entertained, although Brady's soirees were not like the magazine owner's. Diamond Jim was a bachelor, and at his parties no wives were invited; Malcolm always invited them, and, in the

years before his divorce, if his own wife had to be absent, his children were there to help the guests. *Forbes* was a family business. It had been so in Malcolm's father's time and he kept it so.

Brady's was not and no one gave parties like Diamond Jim, some of which were designed and arranged by the architect Stanford White. White, a glamorous and successful man about town, was one of New York's better known sex fiends. Eventually he was caught with a chorus girl and shot dead by her maddened husband, but as the *magister ludi* of Diamond Jim's games, White was ideal for contriving Mauve Decade Roman orgies. At one banquet, Brady's guest-customers lay on couches while naked women swung on ropes above, feeding the recreating businessmen grapes. By the testimony of a contemporary, Diamond Jim sold carloads "of goods to the visiting gentlemen when they sobered up the next afternoon. He merely asked if they had enjoyed themselves the night before."

Flo Ziegfeld, he of *The Ziegfeld Follies* and the preeminent impresario of the period's show girl musicals, supplied dainty demoiselles to Diamond Jim in return for stock tips. Brady would meet the girls in the hotel lobby, slip them a hundred-dollar bill, many times that amount expressed in 1992 money and give them instructions such as "kid 'em along and hold their hand once in a while," or "Go as far as you like, girls,— and you won't make me mad!"[56]

From Brady's time to Malcolm's the use of sex has been— choose your own expression—institutionalized, made traditional, sanctioned, used in American business. It has been more than a minor element in the savings and loan, banking and insurance disasters the nation is suffering through now. The infamous Texas outfit Vernon Savings & Loan hired hookers to entertain the customers and bribe the bank examiners. At the sentencing of the institution's president, a lawyer argued that the accused shouldn't be punished for offering a bribe because the bank examiner in question hadn't actually accepted it. Though he had gone off with the woman, he couldn't get it up.[57]

Michael Milken, following in Diamond Jim's footsteps, used sex to get his customers to buy his worthless securities. By the most authoritative account thus far written[58] of the criminal confederacy which was Drexel Burnham Lambert, Milken had

a man named Donald Engel performing the same services for him as Flo Ziegfeld did for Brady. Engel may be credited with a remark as revelatory of certain aspects of business as William H. Vanderbilt's, "The public be damned,"[59] or Richard B. Mellon's, "You couldn't run a coal mine without machine guns."[60] What will be chiseled in marble on some commemorative wall above Mr. Engel's name is, "I understand CEOs, CEOs don't care about money, power or fame. They have all that. What they want is pussy. And I'm going to make sure they get it."[61] Engel made good at his calling. One of their colleagues observed that, "Mike always respected Don's usefulness . . . Don could make sure the clients got laid—and Mike didn't have to dirty himself."

But there are differences too, in the way business uses bribery. Malcolm entertained to sell advertising, a service with a proper and necessary place in the world; Diamond Jim, though he used sex to help him do it, increased railroad productivity and therefore increased the wealth of the nation. Milken's confederacy of whores, whoremasters and leveraged buy-out artists, indicted and unindicted alike, decreased the wealth of the nation.

Like political corruption, commercial bribery adds to the price the final purchaser must pay and steals profits, which belong to the stockholders of the company whose officials are being bribed. Every dollar of bribery is tax on retail customers, the ultimate consumers who must pay more money without getting greater value.

Nobody knows how much executives overpay for a host/salesman's product or service after a thorough wining and dining. Doubtless the cost is great, but no greater than the damage done by stealing the time, the attention and the energy executives should be applying to their work.

Malcolm never meant to do it, but when he put the spotlight on himself, the national embodiment of the word capitalism, and then showed the world a man who was partying, playing and gold-plated goofing off, he encouraged the notion that business wasn't about work. He sabotaged the work ethic. There are few pictures extant of the great banker of yesteryear, J. P. Morgan, on his yacht. In his time businessmen had their pictures taken at their places of duty, at their desks, staring

square-eyed into the camera. That is not to say that Morgan did not have his vices. He careened around two continents in private railroad cars accompanied by chorus girl acquaintances, so that it was said of him that, "He collected old masters and old mistresses." Nevertheless he conducted his florid sex life so that he didn't demoralize the business organizations he was connected with. The old photographs of the businessmen of yore convey images of men of affairs, of responsibility, steadfastness, men of dull virtues which yield great rewards. Look through the old picture files, and where is Malcolm? At one party after another, up in his balloon, off on his motorcycle, out on his yacht. The pictures of him at his office usually show him next to his jeweled eggs, his toy boats, his toy soldiers, his toy airplanes. As the business cliché goes, America's Capitalist Tool was sending the wrong message.

# TWO

# Clear Cutting
# the Mind

I N THE SPRING of 1988 Malcolm brought his father back
to his childhood home of New Deer, Scotland. Bertie
Charles For-bes (as the family name was pronounced in Scotland) had died in 1954 and for thirty-four years his Scottish-Presbyterian remains had lain in a hostile Roman Catholic cemetery.

Though he had lived in the United States for fifty years
Forbes had never lost his burr or his plain ways. Malcolm said
of him that, "My father was straight off the boat, so to speak; he
liked corned beef and cabbage on Friday night, roast beef on
Sunday and corned beef and hash."[1]

Born in 1880, the sixth of ten children, B.C. had grown up
poor. Jack Webster, whose family came from the same village,
was there when B.C.'s body was returned to New Deer. "My
grandmother was the same age as Bertie," he told a reporter,
"and my [great] aunt, Mary Jane, a haughty lass, refused Ber-

tie's attentions because he had patches on his clothes and was known as Patchy Forbes. She turned him down, not knowing what his future would bring."

Webster said that B.C. was the first millionaire to come from that part of Scotland, but at the time B.C. was a long shot for finishing in the money.[2] One of the reasons he beat the odds was that Mary Jane's father did better by him in the classroom than his daughter did outside of it. "Considering that it was a country school," Webster said, "he gave the students a good fundamental education in Latin, Greek and music, going beyond the three Rs in his cultural thrust. The only schooling Bertie had was from the age of 5 to 14."[3]

A school today which teaches twelve-year-olds Latin and Greek would be picketed by parents, teachers and the swarm of aggressive special agenda organizations whose goals are peculiar inculcations, sensitivity training and empowering the inner, creative you. But in the mid 1890s, particularly in Highland Scotland, where the fruits of industrial abundance had yet to fall from the skies, school was a place where one mastered the tools of work and learning, without which poverty was certain. This was poor poverty, not color TV poverty or food stamp poverty. When B.C. was a lad people remembered how, only fifty years before, near famine conditions had prevailed in Scotland and a million of the Highland Scots' brother Celts had died of starvation in Ireland. There were no discussions about poverty lines, safety nets and falling through the cracks. For millions the cracks were volcanic craters.

The contemporary sense that survival is automatic or should be, that whatever it is, it will be taken care of, was not B.C.'s life view. Not only was he a Calvinist—the word is not used here metaphorically but literally—but life had taught him what it doesn't teach many moderns, and that is nothing gets done unless somebody does it. It was a fixed conviction with B.C. that only baby birdies can sit in the nest, beaks open, with realistic expectations. "The young lions roar after their prey, and seek their meat from God," it said in B.C.'s King James Bible, which he had read through almost four times before he died,[4] but, "Man goes forth unto his work and to his labor until the evening."[5]

The phrase work ethic had not come into vogue in the early

decades of *Forbes* magazine but it was the foundation of B.C.'s world view. Call him a work ethnic. For decades the pages of the magazine reminded its readers that, "In the sweat of thy face shalt thou eat bread, until thou return unto the ground."[6] That was the gist of the endlessly repeated adjurations to get on with the job. The magazine was peppered with pieces of pithy exhortation and heartily felt doggerel like this not unrepresentative sample:

> However humble be thy work,
> No obligation slight or shirk,
> But meet it with unshaken will
> And ev'ry word of promise fill.
>
> . . . . . . . . . . . . . . . . . . . . . . . . . .
>
> Let this impress the languid youth,
> That honor waits on toil and truth—
> The things that beautify the earth
> And glorify the souls of worth![7]

"My father, a country storekeeper and tailor in Aberdeenshire, managed to get along somehow until the family multiplied much faster than his meager earnings did. Long before the tenth came along, the sledding was painfully hard,"[8] B.C. said. At fourteen years of age, apparently forced out of his parents' house by the family's poverty, he left home to make his way to Peterhead, a nearby town, with nothing more by way of credentials than a "merit certificate" from his grammar school. No diploma. The puffing up of minor accomplishments with major recognitions was much rarer in the time of B.C.'s growing up.

Not only was the society which young B.C. strode into different from our own, so also were the people in their training, life experience and character. Save for a minuscule number at the top, childhood was shorter and school a more serious undertaking for those who had the chance to attend. They had to learn much more, much more quickly, because there was no money for the long years of growing up which have become one of the hallmarks of the world they bequeathed to us. At fourteen years of age in 1894, B.C. may have had the equivalent or even a superior training to that of a twenty-two- or twenty-three-year-

old American college graduate one hundred years later. One of the reasons that post-collegiate schooling has become so common today may be the weakness of the schooling during the previous sixteen years. A number of our contemporary colleges and universities are known as "party schools" and "degree mills." To B.C.'s teacher, such expressions would have been a contradiction in terms. He would not have understood them, and once explained to him, their meaning probably would have offended him.

Only a rich society can afford the costs of running all those pedagogical institutions and the cost of keeping so many people out of the labor force for so long. B.C. started his working life at age fourteen; many today are double his age before they begin their first, full-time, grown-up job. The men and women of B.C.'s time had a new world to build. The men and women of this time have inherited that world, but whether they will be able to maintain it is uncertain.

At Peterhead, B.C.'s career in journalism commenced. "I had never been inside a newspaper office before; [and I was] entirely ignorant of the nature of the work," he wrote a few years later. "[I] Thought it probably something like clerical work." But a job was a job and so, "With great gladness in my heart, I signed an agreement to serve an apprenticeship of seven years, starting at 3 shillings (or perhaps forty cents) a week and advancing by a shilling each year. A rather stiff contract!" Moreover the innocent village boy had misconstrued the word compose in the job description. "An event worse than it seemed. For I discovered what I had agreed to become was not a reporter, but a compositor." It would not be articles he would be composing. "I soon discovered that what I had agreed to become meant that I was to stand in front of cases of type, day after day, month after month for seven years, doing nothing but pick up one metallic letter at a time, and place it in a 'stick,' the most mechanical of mechanical operations, calling for no originality, no creativity, no writing—I felt as if I had been sentenced to seven years penal servitude."[9] (For readers under forty, the compositor was a skilled worker in the printing craft. Every newspaper and printing house had its "composing room," now as obsolete as the Mergenthaler Lineotype machine, a specimen

**29**

of which is used as a statue in the foyer of the *Washington Post* building.)

An apprentice contract had the heaviest force of law behind it. A young man walked away from this obligation at his peril. So there was young Bertie, toiling away, living in a lodging house with a drunken landlady and a full cast of uncouth day laborers and fishermen. This would be enough to drive a modern to therapy, but B.C. found a way to enroll himself in a shorthand class, where he did so well he won a prize of one pound five shillings, and when a change in the ownership nullified his apprentice contract, he applied for a reporter's job on the *Dundee Courier*. There he was, by his own description, "a 16-year-old kid, about five feet nothing in height, wearing short trousers, and sporting a printer's apron," but there must have been something impressive about this young man because he was hired as an apprentice reporter and six months later was promoted to reporter first class. Next he taught himself to operate a type writer, as it was spelled and thought of in those days, after which, carried away by the excitement of the moment, he took a ship for South Africa and the Boer War. He got himself a reporter's job on the *Natal Mercury,* and seems to have done well for himself there, but his imagination was fired by the thought of America. Thus it was to New York that he made his way, joining a quarter of a million other Scots who also immigrated to America between 1900 and 1910.

It was thanks to his being Scottish that B.C. got his first job in American journalism. Hanging around a golf course, he was mistaken for a caddie by a fellow Scot, who took him up and introduced him to yet another countryman, John W. Doddsworth, editor of the *Journal of Commerce and Commercial Bulletin,* who had his reservations about this seemingly untried man. B.C. offered to prove himself by working for free, à la the modern business intern, and seven days later he had a fifteen-dollar-a-week job.

Through an accident of birth, you might say that B.C. was the beneficiary of an informal affirmative action program, conducted by Scots to help other Scots.[10] Mr. Doddsworth wasn't the program's sole practitioner. In this era affirmative action could get an ethnic group member a chance to show his stuff,

but if he had bad stuff, poor stuff or inferior stuff, a chance was all he got.

The place of ethnicity in Malcolm's life and in American business, in times past and present, can hardly be exaggerated. No strident black person asserting Afritude makes more of his origins than Malcolm Forbes did of his. Many of the hundreds of profiles and sketches of this man, broadcast and in print, made reference to his Scottish background, and this was not because of reportorial digging but because Malcolm was forever flourishing it.

Malcolm came by his Scots-o-mania honestly. B.C. put it in him, even carrying his love-of-old-country into the pages of his magazine. When the magazine was begun, *Forbes* carried short stories, one of which was "The Slender Thread" by Charles D. Orth, Jr.

The story is set in the home of millionaire David Metcalf, who is described as having footmen in powdered wigs and Corots on the walls. A grand collector, this chap, Metcalf, has an original King James Bible in his library and—more to the point—an author-inscribed volume of verse by Robert Louis Stevenson, which Abbott, Metcalf's secretary, is discovered reading while he waits for his employer. Metcalf enters and they fall to talking, with the boss denigrating reading in general, and dismissing poetry and philosophy with particular vehemence. He tells Abbott, "Do you know who molds thought and men? It's the man who controls the purse strings—that's who it is . . . Your poets and your philosophers can yawp and squeal all they want—but David Metcalf does more to men's lives than Shakespeare."

Next the abominable Metcalf targets Scottish national hero Robert Louis Stevenson: "Ha, Stevenson! I know him—the Scotsman, eh—the man whose idea of a useful life was to go off to some Pacific Island and make friends with a lot of niggers . . ." This last is too much for Abbott, who says, "You swine, you damnable swine! . . . You fat, rotten-souled hog." The slender thread breaks and Abbott puts his fingers around "the fleshy creases of [Metcalf's] throat . . . His gaze . . . fastened on Metcalf's bulging eyes." Abbot watches and Metcalf bulges, then the secretary reaches behind him, finds the letter opener on the desk and stabs his boss with it.

Obviously this was an instance of justifiable homicide in B.C.'s eyes, but he was, after all, running a business magazine and filling the pages with murders of CEOs whose crime was putting down Scottish writers might cause some of the readers to take an extra gulp or two. Lest this murder, not so foul, be misunderstood, B.C. put a box in the middle of the story reading: "THEY'RE PASSING. Editor's note.—This gripping story describes a type of multi-millionaire that, happily is passing. Not many of them have such an end; but under modern conditions, they are made to feel—bitterly—that they are out of place. A better type of millionaire is being bred."[11]

B. C. Forbes was not only Scottish but a true ethnic, one of the people who came over on the boat, an immigrant who did the hardscrabble dance, doing what he had to do to make a living, taking whatever job was there for him. The *Journal of Commerce* job was not to B.C.'s liking, but you may be sure he did it well. He left us this description of his days there: "I was sentenced to cover the dry-goods market as assistant to the dry-goods editor. Dry-goods! They were well named. I quickly discovered I hated the work, but I found that even dry-goods reporting could be made tolerable by striking out on a new track.

"For illustration: I had to write on raw silk. The custom had been for the newspaper to 'accept' current prices from importers. Importers always named prices well above the actual selling figures. They did this so that they could show customers quotations in the authoritative *Journal of Commerce,* and then tell the customer that, as a special favor, they would cut the rate substantially . . .

"I interviewed the leading buyers as well as the sellers, ferreted out the actual prices current, and printed them. This raised a storm. Importers abused me for not having published the figures they gave me, and some even refused to see me again. Protests were made over my head. However, both sellers and buyers began to take an interest such as they never had taken before in these reports; and by-and-by the gentlemen who had quarreled with me eagerly invited me to come to see them regularly, even showing me their books to convince me that they were no longer trying to induce me to publish incorrect quotations."[12]

B.C. was a contemporary of Clarence Barron, another man who was making a business journalism more suited to a financial and industrial universe expanding with speedy complexity, one which called for new kinds of information, presented with a celerity and sweep not to be read in business publications of the past.

The first business magazines appeared in the United States in the mid-1840s when only the smallest beginnings of modern business could be descried. Prior to that fledgling industrialists principally relied on English publications for technical information relating to such business as cotton spinning and weaving, then among the most advanced manufacturing activities.[13] In 1846 both the *Dry Goods Reporter* and *Commercial Glance* and the *Banker's Magazine* made their appearance. The *Railroad Journal,* voice of America's most important baby industry, saw the light of day in 1851.[14] Today these publications would be classified as trade magazines, because they were absolutely biased in favor of the industries they served, using their pages to help in every way possible. At one point the *Railroad Journal* was carrying detailed engineering articles on bridge and tunnel building, at another it became the industry spokesman against high tariffs on importing iron rails.

From the *Commercial Glance* have come tens of thousands of trade magazines and newsletters, all ineffably boring unless you are in one of the fields of work that they serve. Riff through the pages of any or all and what is apparent is the laborious care, the knowledge, the planning, the application and thought it takes to carry on even a relatively simple business enterprise halfway successfully. Modern packaging tries to make everything look easy, effortless, entertaining and user-friendly; it is so successful that most of us, even those in business, cannot appreciate that under every smooth cover, the machinery sits, quiet, complicated and kept in running order only by the sustained effort of people who know what the hell they are doing. Business magazines are primarily to help those people.

B.C. was recognizably out of the *Commercial Glance* tradition, but he gave a human twist to business news which fit into the kind of mass media that William Randolph Hearst and Joseph Pulitzer were perfecting. B.C. was groping toward a business journalism which was more for businessmen in general, not for

people in one or another industry. In personalizing and dramatizing, in making business a morality play, he would find a professional home in the Hearst organization.

B.C., ever the man to get on in the world, began moonlighting for the *Commercial and Financial Chronicle,* apparently using
the nom de plume of Broadanwall. Hearst or one of his talent
scouts discovered that the articles they had admired in two different publications had been written by the same man[15] and
B.C. was offered a job as a financial writer on the *New York
American* in 1911. It was the beginning of an association with
Hearst which was to last more than thirty years.

William Randolph Hearst was a gigantic figure, so big that
even today in this society in which the past is what they show
you at Disney World, his name is at least recognizable to the
corporal's guard who've had an American history class at college.

What they will have been told was the role Hearst and his
great rival, Joseph Pulitzer, the owner of the *New York World,*
played in dragging the United States into the Spanish-American War, a conflict whose most visible result was the arrival of a
large Puerto Rican population in New York and elsewhere in
the lower forty-eight. Hearst prided himself on hiring the best
talent, regardless of cost, which was why, in the months before
the outbreak of the war, Hearst had artist Frederic Remington
on his payroll in Cuba. Remington, bored out of his skull because nothing was going on, cabled Hearst he wanted to come
home. Hearst's reply made it into the history books: "Please
remain. You furnish the pictures and I'll furnish the war."

The hyper, around-the-clock, media thrill was coming up
over the horizon. Hearst and Pulitzer cranked out "extras," or
what we might call special editions, day and night, hawked on
every street and avenue by clouds of newsboys. The society was
going through the beginnings of media addiction, leading to a
future in which millions cannot live without their CNN/MTV
media fix. One shudders to think of the marvels Hearst would
have wrought had he had cable TV instead of the new high-
speed presses.

Assuming control of the *San Francisco Examiner* in 1887,
Hearst was one of the first to understand that thanks to changes
in printing and paper manufacture, newspapers could become

a mass circulation, entertainment medium. New high-speed presses and typesetting machines made it possible and inexpensive to print three or four hundred thousand copies of a daily newspaper in a few hours. At the price of two or three cents a copy three or four hundred thousand people couldn't afford to buy the paper, but the cost of newsprint, again thanks to new methods, had come down also. Hearst hit the streets with a penny paper.

One, two, three pennies may seem trivial because thanks to half a century of inflation the copper coin barely holds on as a unit of money. Today the cent sign cannot be found on the standard computer keyboard. A hundred ten years ago, when people said "Count your pennies," it meant something, and a drop in the price of a paper from two cents to one meant a vast class of people who couldn't afford to buy a newspaper suddenly could buy this wonderful form of entertainment and stay within the family budget.

The new technologies like electric motor presses gave birth to a cheap mass medium, but the profits from penny-a-copy papers came from advertising. In the twenty years before Hearst took over his first newspaper, Alexander Stewart in New York City was shaping the development of an institution dependent on mass newspaper advertising: the department store. What had been a two-way relationship between a journal and its readers now became a triangular one in which the editor had to serve two masters. In the passage of time the advertising master came to have the upper hand, as the bonds which connected reader and publication broke down, and those between editor and advertiser grew shorter and stouter.

Newspapers had been a serious place for serious white men. John Fenno's Federalist *Gazette of the United States*, published in the early 1800s, refused advertising because it was undignified. For years James Gordon Bennett, who loved a dollar as much as the next man, demanded that ads in the *New York Herald* be in agate type. No exceptions. Display advertising was not allowed; ads had to be confined to within the width of a column, and not spread across the page as they are now.

Instead of the news columns and features taking on the aroma and even the content of advertising as is routine today, advertising might mimic the forms of serious news to get the

readers' attention as with this from the *New York Times* for June 13, 1862: "It is currently reported that Beauregard's flight from Corinth was caused by panic. A reliable gentleman informs us that a Secession picket captured a Union man wearing one of Knox's elegant summer hats. The rebels, on comparing it with their own dilapidated tiles, became completely demoralized and fled. They are to be had at No. 212 Broadway, corner of Fulton-street."

The new relationship was perhaps twenty years old when the advertisers tried to take over in a ham-handed demand which would have left the newspaper owners without their self-esteem. Rowland H. Macy (yes, the original R. H. Macy of Macy's) put the blocks to James Gordon Bennett, Jr., to have the *Herald* support Nathan Straus, a fellow owner of the department store, in his campaign as the Tammany Hall nominee for mayor of New York City. To this Bennett answered that, "even if George Washington came to life the Herald could not support him if he were Tammany's standard bearer."[16] Pulitzer weighed in with an editorial backing the *Herald*'s stand, upon which the major department stores attempted an advertising boycott of the *World*.[17] This cost Pulitzer about six hundred thousand dollars in lost revenues, but Straus had to withdraw from the race.

Forty years later there was the "Malolo the Roller" incident. This was the nickname given to the Matson Line steamer in recognition of the unfortunate way the vessel sailed. At the cost of fifty thousand dollars' worth of advertising in the leanest part of the Great Depression a defiant *Fortune* magazine used the unhappy sobriquet.[18] Malcolm Forbes was occasionally accused by employees of going into the tank for an advertiser, but that goes contra *Forbes* magazine's reputation. The owners, publishers and top editors of most publications have their herds of sacred cows, and doubtless Malcolm had a few too. By and large, however, during the Malcolm years at *Forbes* magazine, if they were going to take a slug at you and your company, you got slugged regardless of how many cruises you had taken on *Highlander*.

Though few, if any, individual advertisers got special consideration, taken as a whole, the magazine was designed for advertising. It was made to be a place where a CEO wanted his corporation's name. In this it was in the tradition of mass

circulation publications of the era inaugurated by Hearst and Pulitzer in New York and men like Victor Lawson of the *Chicago Daily News*. These men would stand up to the Evil One, the spirit of filthy advertising lucre, on a particular article or editorial line, but what they did which was epoch making was they reshaped newspapers and magazines in their totality to become advertising mediums, acceptable vehicles for the new kind of merchandising.

The old-fashioned paper with a strong slant, social and political, repelled more readers than it attracted. A mass, across-the-board audience could not be wooed and won by what we today call narrow-casting. As Hearst and Pulitzer drove their respective circulations up, from three hundred, to four hundred to five hundred thousand and higher, a wider appeal was needed and that appeal was entertainment. Business had stumbled onto entertainment as the fertilizer of its prosperity.

The Spanish-American War, covered to cause gooseflesh on the arms of the readers, drove circulation to new record levels. Done right, war could be entertaining, as the great-grandchildren of that generation, who enjoyed watching the 1991 Persian Gulf War, know from their own experience. Before Hearst, once in a while newspapers had gone in for a little entertainment, some of it far wackier than anything we moderns have had set before us. It was, however, more for the delectation of the editor and the staff than for the reader.

In 1835 the *Sun* newspaper in New York reported that scientists had discovered people on the moon. A third of the way into the nineteenth century when everything was changing every minute, people bought the moon story, and when it turned out to be a hoax they laughed and didn't hold it against the paper. James Gordon Bennett, the Scottish owner of the *New York Herald*, took a swing at the *Sun*'s editor for publishing such lies,[19] but on November 9, 1874, the front page of his own paper was filled with a story headlined thus:

## AWFUL CALAMITY
### The Wild Animals Broken Loose from Central Park.
### Terrible Scenes of Mutilation.
### A Shocking Sabbath Carnival of Death.
### Savage Brutes at Large.
### Awful Combats Between the Beasts and the Citizens.
### The Killed and Wounded.
### General Duryee's Magnificent Police Tactics.
### Bravery and Panic.
### How the Catastrophe Was Brought About—Affrighting Incidents.
### Proclamation by the Mayor.
### Governor Dix Shoots the Bengal Tiger in the Streets.[20]

Such excursions had been the exception; the coming of Hearst made them the rule. His new approach marked the beginnings of the all-entertainment mass media environment. The twenty-four-hour-a-day entertainment culture of the late twentieth century was in the process of being invented and put into place by businessmen like Hearst. The invasive entertainment culture, commercial in origin, narcotic in effect, begins in that time, and can be seen, if but faintly, in B.C.'s own work as he goes about "humanizing" and making business news entertaining.[21] Evidently it was B.C.'s intent to make his topic colorful, his application of ragtime journalism to business, which recommended him to Hearst.

Hearstian journalism was the boss's personal journalism and B.C. gave his magazine the same kind of unique voice that Hearst imposed on his empire. *Forbes* magazine had its owner/editor's crotchets and passions. His stamp on his publication was even greater than Hearst's because in many issues B.C. would write three or four of the articles.

In Hearst's heyday newspapers, though often immensely profitable, were only half run as a business. They were the personal creations of the proprietor/editors who dominated the industry when B.C. went to work for Hearst in 1911. They had a whacked-out genius which irretrievably separates them from the mewky moderns in the communication industry. The wild stunts put on by these publications weren't thought up by press agents. Hearst, Pulitzer, Bennett and the rest of these owners

came up with the ideas themselves. One wonders how much of Malcolm's inspiration for publicizing his magazine came from listening to his father talk about the way Hearst went about keeping his newspapers firmly in the public view. Hearst himself said, "Putting out a newspaper without promotion is like winking at a girl in the dark—well-intentioned but ineffective."[22]

Did Malcolm get his idea for his Capital Tools motorcycle gang, each biker clad in the Forbes' cycle club uniform, from Hearst's *Journal-Examiner* Transcontinental Yellow Fellow Bicycle Relay? Hearst had his boys in yellow jerseys, an up-yours gesture to the purists complaining about yellow journalism, going coast-to-coast at the perfervid height of one of America's recurring bicycle fads. Did Malcolm remember B.C. telling him how Hearst had a balloon floating over San Francisco with the *Examiner*'s name on it while a daredevil minister married a daredevil couple in the basket underneath it?

It was the era for that sort of thing. Pulitzer dispatched Nellie Bly to see if she could hotfoot it around the world in under eighty days, but the all-time newspaper promotion stunt was the work of another son of a rich and famous man, James Gordon Bennett, Jr.,[23] heir to the *New York Herald*, the very one who said to Henry M. Stanley, "Do what you think best, BUT FIND LIVINGSTONE!"[24]

The formula of sex, science and murder, which Hearst and Pulitzer explored together in their antic competition, has dominated journalism, print and broadcast, ever since. The debauchery of public taste, never elevated and always vulnerable, for commercial motives was underway. It was a clear cutting of the mind like the clear cutting of the forests of the upper Midwest, which happened to be going on at the same time. Different sets of businessmen, each equally heedless of long-term consequences, directed the harvests and profited from them. They were heedless, not in the sense that they knew and disregarded what they knew, but heedless in that in their pell mell chase after their private objectives, they didn't have public concerns. Those who objected to the wreckage they caused seemed to have the odor of snobbism (called elitism now) on their clothes; there was about those who complained of the vulgarity and mindlessness of such new introductions as the comic strip an

aroma of fuddy-duddyism, if not an irritation that the lower orders were having pleasures made available to them which might spoil them and make them less pliant. The musky smell of aristocracy clung to these killjoys, and, indeed, there was more than a trace of it about them. Henry Adams may have been right in many of his sarcastic condemnations, but he was an aristocrat of lemonish disposition. The contemporary equivalent are the people with their Volvos parked in front of their houses who rail about there being too many cars and too much pollution. Or, people who having gotten their house in the country want to pull up the drawbridge and impose ecological zoning.

But ragtime wasn't all plinking banjos and quaking upright pianos. In the first decade of the century, there were so many homeless people no one called them a problem; it seemed the natural way of things. This was an era when there were thousands of child hobos riding the rails and having things happen to them that would make a thousand and one TV miniseries. It was a time when they were building orphan asylums as fast as we build jails.

The new world of plenty was only just aborning when Hearst made his appearance on the national stage. That the world of scarcity, of perpetual labor and exhaustion, was still regarded as inevitable and inescapable can be seen in these words, published in 1887, summing up how many people of that time thought: ". . . it was in the very nature of things impossible that the new hopes of the workingmen could be satisfied, simply because the world had not the wherewithal to satisfy them. It was only because the masses worked very hard and lived on short commons that the race did not starve outright, and no considerable improvement in their condition was possible while the world, as a whole, remained so poor. It was not the capitalists whom the laboring men were contending with . . . but the ironbound environment of humanity, and it was merely a question of the thickness of their skulls when they would discover the fact and make up their minds to endure what they could not cure."[25]

Hearst, with his penny papers, came along to change people's view of the world just as business was changing their lives.

# THREE

## "Rich Men Who Are O.K. and Others Who Are Not"

IN B.C.'S TIME, business was on its way to curing instead of enduring. In the first issue of his magazine he wrote that, "Business was originated to produce happiness, not pile up millions." Even for Americans who have seen communism declare its bankruptcy, who are told of places where there is no business to "produce happiness," the scale of business's accomplishment is not real, because the premodern business world and its hardscrabble existence have vanished. We cannot imagine a place or a time when intelligent, decent people believed that there was nothing to be done about slums, disease, beggary because there was—flat out and absolutely—not enough wealth.

The new style of Hearstian journalism was made possible by the coming age of plenty, but one of his first and greatest publishing successes showed the world we were leaving behind, a place of scarcity, where men and women pushed to rob and

fight each other and to labor until stupefaction for the smallest portion.

In January 1899 the *San Francisco Examiner*, the Monarch of the Dailies, as Hearst styled it, published "The Man with the Hoe," by Edwin Markham. For a few months turn-of-the-century America went ape over a poem written after Markham had seen Jean-François Millet's painting of a French serf, degraded by toil. In a matter of weeks the country was chanting:

> Bowed by the weight of centuries he leans
> Upon his hoe and gazes on the ground,
> The emptiness of ages on his face . . .
>
> A thing that grieves not and that never hopes,
> Stolid and stunned, a brother to the ox?

All of which and more that led up to the peroration which became the standard fare for two generations of high school elocution contests:

> O masters, lords and rulers in all lands,
> How will the Future reckon with this Man?
> How answer his brute question in that hour
> When whirlwinds and rebellion shake the world?
> How will it be with kingdoms and with kings—
> With those who shaped him to the thing he is—
> When this dumb Terror shall reply to God
> After the silence of the centuries?

Reprinted everywhere, in short order "The Man with the Hoe" was translated into forty languages and eventually earned its author millions of dollars expressed in modern money. The future reckoned with the Hoe Man in a way neither Markham nor many of his generation could have believed. Yet the poet, who died in 1940, lived to see his poor brute alleviated and made human with the five and a half day work week, healthy food, indoor plumbing and a shower of other material blessings. The businessmen whom B.C. revered were to calm the whirlwinds and quiet rebellion by pulling off a revolution of their own.[1]

A permanent change was taking place. It was in Hearst's time that the control and content of American culture shifted over

from clergymen and schoolmasters to businessmen, publishers, industrialists, merchandisers, advertisers and the like. In due course businessmen and business would purge the schools of religion, finish the job, already underway, of hauling down the doric pillars of Jeffersonian classicism, and substitute for the now demolished traditional relationships between people the new cash nexus. By the time this process was completed, even the bond between mother and child would be so altered a parent from the Federalist period, transported ahead in time, would think she or he had dropped in on a strange land concocted by Jonathan Swift or some other furious creator of grotesque utopias.

By 1916 when B.C. was planning his new publication, he was such a well-known business journalist that he was urged to name it after himself. To do so was not deemed egocentric since many magazines were named after their proprietors in that period, i.e., McClure's, Harper's, McCall's, Scribner's. B.C.'s idea was for a publication for younger men like himself, men ambitious to get ahead, and so the magazine was first tentatively called *Doers and Doings;* it would feature pieces on commercial dirty dealings and insider trading.* Stories which actually looked at what was going on inside a company, instead of offering the reader a rosy view, became a *Forbes* magazine trademark from the start, and the magazine still prints articles which help people who own stocks make up their minds on which to buy or sell.

But with all that, the business press is the helpmate of business, and even when it does burst out to expose, criticize or attack, as B.C. did when he went after Henry Ford, who had revealed himself to be an anti-Semitic horror, the purpose of the publication is to help business. Objectivity, that self-delu-

---

* This is a term for people who have secret information about a company which they use to make a profit buying or selling its stock. Thus if you knew that a drug company had secretly perfected a cancer cure, you could make a lot of money buying the company's stock since it would be sure to go up in price once the new cure was made public. You could then sell the stock at a profit.

Insider trading was legal in 1916; it is illegal today, but like gun control, it's one thing to pass a law against it and another to get people to obey it. Now and again business people are sent to jail for doing it, but the practice is probably as widespread as it ever was.

sionary word used by general circulation newspapers, has no place in most business journalism.

Booster or not, a persistent pattern of reprehensible behavior would drive B.C. to setting matters straight, even if some people thought he should only boost and never knock: "The attitude of those who have condemned what I have written about Henry Ford is that it is perfectly proper to employ oceans of printers ink to extol Henry Ford but that it is most condemnable to tell the truth if that truth is not wholly flattering to Ford. The truthfulness of our statements is not denied; what is denied is the right of anyone to do other than fawn on Ford and all his henchmen and all his and their doings. That some people— many people—should think Henry Ford is a god and everything he does is strictly angelic is not, perhaps, altogether astonishing, for the newspapers, with few exceptions, have never ceased to laud him and all his works."[2]

To start his business magazine B.C. needed money, and for it he went to one of the most ferocious men ever to take a leading role in American business. He went to the frightening and frightful Henry C. Frick, whose name is associated with some of the most bloody passages in the history of business violence.

Not that such violence began with Frick. Business violence begins with the beginnings of business. On June 13, 1840, Isaac Newton, a partner of Cornelius Vanderbilt, fired up his steamship, *De Witt Clinton,* and coming stealthily out of his berth, tried to ram *Napoleon,* a competing steamer. *Napoleon*'s captain and owner, Joseph W. Hancox, his passengers cowering in terror, fired his revolver into the steering house of his nautical attacker, causing the pilot to hit the deck and *De Witt Clinton* to strike only a glancing blow. Wounded but unsunk *Napoleon* proceeded to Albany, its destination, where the competition's political power was able to arrange Hancox's arrest, presumably for some high crime like resisting assault or ram avoidance.[3] Thirty years later small armies of men paid by Cornelius Vanderbilt and his competitors battled for control of strategic railroad properties.

When the free market failed or rules for conducting the market were in dispute, recourse was had to more direct means. Neither the mafia nor the drug rings were the first to introduce commercial violence into American society.

Even so, Frick was what we call a piece o' work and great-great-grandmother called a horror. A man with an eye for the main chance, when still relatively young he had come to control Pennsylvania's high-grade, metallurgical-coal fields, and by the 1880s he had earned himself the title of "Coke King." His generation of Americans knew that coke was not an effervescent drink or something you put up your nose; they knew coke, extracted from coal, was an indispensable ingredient for making steel. Andrew Carnegie bought Frick out and in the process Frick became the operational head of Carnegie's steel company. He was soon leading his side in a war with the labor unions. The struggle was continuous but from time to time it would break out in paroxysms of violence as when seven were killed in the Connellsville district of Pennsylvania in the spring of 1891 during the company's attempt to replace strikers with non-union workers. That was but a prelude to the shootout at the Homestead works the following summer when Frick sent two armored barges loaded with rent-a-cops up the Monongahela River to reinforce the plant. They were to secure it so that non-union labor could be brought in the next day. On the river-banks, armed and ready for them, were the strikers, their families and allies. Suffice it to say a sickening battle ensued and wasn't ended until ten were dead, sixty or more wounded and the Pennsylvania National Guard marched in. Frick, whose theme song seems to have been it's a dirty job but somebody's got to do it, wrote Carnegie that, "We had to teach our employees a lesson, and we have taught them one that they will never forget." Shortly thereafter a madcap anarchist with a cheap pistol broke into Frick's office and shot him. The inferior gun failed to carry off the captain of industry so the would-be assassin got out a knife and tried again, planting the tip of the weapon in the great capitalist's fanny.[4]

Industrial America was midwived by violence. The circumstances of the birth have conditioned many a business organization since to harsh attitudes, unilateral actions, abrasive secretiveness and a truculent, even proud indifference to the commonweal. Perhaps given the times, the technology and the society, the means used by Carnegie and Frick were the only means to build a great steel business. We can't know that, but it may be taken as a certainty that it was business practice and

45

policy, its private armies and its tight-lipped arrogance which called forth the bomb throwers and the wild-eyed radicals.

God knows what would have happened if the opposing forces in those battles had the firepower of a modern Los Angeles street gang, but in America's history, it was businessmen, as much as frontier gunslingers and road agents, who helped establish a lasting place for violence and coercion in the daily life of the nation.

In so many ways American culture is the culture business made. Too many people for too few jobs, the competition for places among members of different ethnic groups mixed a human rancor with the soot and smoke of the new industrial cities, excited the intergroup animosities which make it seem to this day that some mornings you can wake up in the United States and everyone has ten taut fingers around everyone else's windpipe.

The supremacy of business managers was established first by scarcity of jobs and the threat of firing but, failing that, by gunplay and force; there was to be a boss and sub-bosses and there were to be workers who were to do what they were told. A different, cooperative relationship was seldom considered and virtually never put into effect. Competition for jobs, competition for all things, would be used to keep people in line, and, moreover, be the nap and texture of living. It would influence the very character of the national culture.

At the same time that Carnegie and Frick were treating their employees as Al Capone and our own contemporary cocaine distributors treat their competition, these men were making wealth on a scale unparalleled. In the one decade between 1870 and 1880 steel production grew something like three thousand percent.[5] The jumps in the production figures for everything in this period are unreal. Yes, Carnegie got rich, probably richer than anybody except John D. Rockefeller had ever been, but new material wealth was flowing to the millions, not to African-Americans who were trapped in the quasi-slavery of post-Reconstruction Jim Crow to be sure, but to millions of others, who were getting the new cookstoves, the new non-smelly, nickel-plated kerosene lamps, sewing machines and living room furniture, not to mention living rooms to put them in.

This was real wealth, and the numbers describing it trans-

lated into real things, needed and wanted by millions. Those numbers aren't like the damn government numbers they release every month, hell, every week and every day now, announcing new increases while every year life is a little tighter. The happy numbers dance out of radio speakers and off the business pages while there is a little less for the modern millions as the great grinding down, the slow losing out, continues. Granted terrifying amounts of wealth are stolen and destroyed by the bureaucratic apparatchiks of American democracy, but they had their parasites then, and even with them life got better. No wonder Andrew Carnegie danced his jig and proclaimed, "The sixty-five million Americans of today could buy up the one hundred and forty millions of Russians, Austrians and Spaniards; or, after purchasing wealthy France, would have pocket money to acquire Denmark, Norway and Switzerland and Greece."[6]

The anarchist assassin who went after Henry Frick did not appreciate what such businessmen were made of; Henry Frick was so tough it is surprising to read that eventually Death gathered up its nerve and dared to carry the old heathen off. Nobody seemed to have been able to stand him. Charlie Schwab, the brilliant steel man, whom B.C. adored and whom Carnegie seemed to look on as the son he never had, couldn't take Frick: "He was to me a curious and puzzling man. No man on earth could get close to him or fathom him. He seemed more like a machine, without emotions or impulses. Absolutely cold-blooded. He had good foresight and was an excellent bargainer. He knew nothing about the technical side of steel, but he knew that with his coke supply tied up to Carnegie he was indispensable—or thought he was."[7]

B.C. called him "autocratic,"[8] and probably harbored yet more uncomplimentary thoughts, yet Frick was kind to him. The Coke King had two checking accounts, a serious one with serious-looking businessman-type checks written on it, and a second account for charity, the checks printed with the likeness of a dead daughter, still mourned.

B.C. went to the Fifth Avenue mansion, now a museum where El Greco's *St. Jerome*[9] greets the visitor, to try to get backing for his magazine venture. He did get Frick's support, but he said, "As soon as the butler closed the door behind me, I stood

on the steps and opened the check. It's hard to tell you how disappointed and chagrined I was to find the check bore a picture of his beloved child. For a moment—fleeting, I assure you —I was tempted to return it then and there. Later on I had a particular happiness in being able to repay the loan—with interest."[10] (Jacob Schiff, whose reputation as a man and a businessman was as good as Frick's was bad, also loaned B.C. money to help him get the magazine under way.[11])

B.C. may well have known Frick for what he was, but, grateful for the loan, refrained from writing about Frick's effect on American business. For B.C. throughout his career as an owner/ editor/reporter was sharply aware that there were businessmen who were bad for society and bad to other people, especially their employees. In an early "Fact & Comment" column, a sustaining feature which Malcolm continued after B.C.'s death until his own, the old man wrote, "RICH MEN WHO ARE O.K. AND OTHERS WHO ARE NOT—There are financiers who inspire Bolshevism; and there are financiers who inspire brotherhood. There are grasping, skin-flint misers like the late Russell Sage; and there are generous, large-hearted philanthropists like the late Jacob H. Schiff[12] . . ."[13] Three years before he started *Forbes*, B.C. published an article entitled "The Criminal Railroads" in which he went after them for keeping men working seven days a week.[14]

There are strivers today, men and women as ambitious as B.C., but they are solely creatures of the bottom line, people who have lied themselves into believing and proclaiming their private profit is the public's gain. With no wider goal than career and bank account, they are bereft of the merest notion of commonweal. Many do not know the word's definition, literally don't know what it means. They believe they are entitled to take, take away, take off and never replace, never give back, never restore. They are *rapax*, the Latin onomatopoeic word for grasping, greedy, snatching, ripping out and making off with.

B.C. was not rapax, nor, seemingly, were the men B.C. admired the most. In the era when B.C. came to America, some businessmen sought a way toward material progress and profit not based on fear, coercion or force. Malcolm inherited the business and the values his father put the greatest store on, but not his father's moral strivings, not the tireless zeal, not B.C.'s

incessant attempts in the magazine to point the way to making money, yes, but also making the world a better place. As long as B.C. was around, *Forbes* took no liquor advertising, although the old boy loved a snootful, too many snootfuls of the bonnie dew if his wife, Adelaide, was right and he did come home three sheets to the wind as often as she said he did. B.C. liked his Scottish whiskey, he enjoyed stogies, he loved to gamble— poker with the boys was his idea of a great night out—but he carried the weight of an informed conscience.

B.C. was always running contests in the magazine, once offering one thousand dollars' worth of prizes (no small potatoes in those days), to determine "Who Is the Best Employer in America." One can't imagine *Fortune* or *Business Week* running such a contest; in our era there is no business person who enjoys a national reputation, a reputation among the public at large, as someone who has broken new trails in dealing with employees or human relations in general. Let's hope there are such business people out there, trying, doing their bit, but their fellow executives who run the media corporations have done nothing to popularize them, to make them heroes. Such qualities have little appeal to the mass audience whose taste the same corporations have done so much to form.

In B.C.'s time, Golden Rule Jones was famous in the land. In 1895 he made himself an opportunity to practice a different managerial approach to his employees when he founded the Acme Sucker Rod Company. I don't need a sucker rod and you don't either, but the oil industry made much of this device with the double-entendre name. Jones' history was not so unusual for the successful men of his era. He left family and farm home at age fourteen to get a job in a sawmill in upstate New York. Next he was an engine wiper on a towboat working on a river connected to the Erie Canal, after which, hearing about the unheard of high wages being paid in Titusville, Pennsylvania, he lit out for the oil fields there, and then was on to Ohio where he struck oil and found himself a businessman. Moving on yet again, this time to Toledo, Ohio, he started Acme, which in due course began manufacturing other oil field equipment, including a superior natural-gas-powered engine and the "Only Ball Bearing Maypole, The Finest and Best Plaything Ever Invented. The Children All Want One. No Well-Regulated

School, Orphan's Home, Park, Summer Hotel or Private Family Should Be Without One."

Jones sold the ball bearing maypole to public institutions at cost, for Sam Jones was a different kind of businessman. He paid his workers a third more than the going rate, writing that, "As I learned that men were employed at common labor at one dollar a day and even less, the whole hideous wrong of the wage system began to reveal itself to me." He cut the ten-hour day back to eight, built a park for his employees next to the plant, instituted a company lunchroom where subsidized meals were served, began medical insurance and stock purchase programs, both paid for by his company. Given that such things were unheard of at the time, Jones' nickname explains itself, but that was not how it began. "It was the distress of mind occasioned by seeing a string of rules a yard long in another factory at the tail of every one of which was a threat of dismissal," he said, "that led me to say to my wife, 'I am going to have a rule for our shop; I am going to have the Golden Rule printed on a piece of tin and nail it up as the rule that governs the place.' "[15]

Golden Rule Jones, who went on to be elected mayor of Toledo and become a noteworthy figure in Progressive era politics, doesn't figure in *Forbes* magazine. One who did bulk large on the magazine's pages was John Patterson, the founder of the National Cash Register Company. He finished first to Henry Ford's second in the best boss contest.

Three years before the magazine was founded, on January 5, 1914, Ford had astonished America by announcing he would pay a minimum wage of five dollars per eight-hour day to his thirteen thousand unskilled assembly line workers. This was at least two and a half times above the going rate. It meant that an ordinary workingman would be able to support his family in a life with a modicum of dignity. The *New York Sun*, reacting like much of the rest of the nation, hyperventilated with an editorial saying, "It was a bolt out of the blue sky, flashing its way across the continent and far beyond, something unheard of in the history of business." For once the newspapers had it right. "The Ford idea" was welcomed, denounced and debated, while the man Ford, who previous to this had not been well enough known to be listed in Who's Who, was turned by the press into a

giant overnight. Ford said what he had done was "a plain act of social justice," but, beyond his motives, no other, single event so marks the changeover wrought by business from a society of scarcity to one of abundance.[16]

By the late 1920s B.C. was singing another tune about Henry Ford. By then a different man, the anti-Semite, the cruel employer, the jeering denigrator of intellectual accomplishment had replaced the Heroic Henry of ten years before. But the winner of the best boss contest, John Patterson, founder and presiding madman at the National Cash Register Company, never turned into a loser with B.C., or, even after his death, with Malcolm. As the years passed, and Patterson's name was repeatedly brought up in the pages of the magazine, the man's not inconspicuously satanic defects deserved more than the passing mention they got. Patterson and National Cash Register were big advertisers from the start, and that may explain the lopsided view of this strange, pioneering business executive, but there also seemed to have been a personal bond based on B.C.'s admiration of Patterson. Given the Ohio businessman's Napoleonic ego, the admiration probably was not reciprocated. It is hard to imagine that John Patterson admired anyone but himself.

At one point in the man's amazing career the *Dayton Daily News* reported that Patterson had a personal phrenologist on the payroll whose adverse reports on the bumps on the heads of several highly placed executives were used as a reason for their dismissal. Charles Palmer, the phrenologist, who had also been made a member of the company's Board of Directors, seemed to have played the wicked imp, thinking up new ways to devil and discipline the work force. Early morning horseback riding, during which one of the men was injured, was prescribed for all executives, as was yoga. Cigarettes, tea, cigars, salt, pepper, butter and eggs were forbidden at meals with customers. Patterson was also a Fletcherite,[17] a fad he shared with other prominent and powerful men who subscribed to Horace Fletcher's theory that the key to health and, more important, high profits and productivity, is to chew your food.[18]

When the *Daily News* first printed the stories about his court phrenologist, Patterson retaliated by filing a libel action against the newspaper. Then he decided to punish the whole commu-

nity. Failing to get the apologies and kowtowing he wanted, the CEO closed the company's plants, throwing two thousand people out of work. And out of work they stayed for six months. During the shutdown public meetings of obeisance and apology were held in Dayton to placate this powerful man who could turn the community's prosperity on or off according to the dictates of a happy mood or a savage whimsy.

Ultimately the *Daily News* backed down, but grudgingly. Its owner, James M. Cox, was a governor of Ohio, the 1920 Democratic party presidential nominee, a gifted man with no formal schooling, who was also the future owner of a string of newspapers, television and radio stations. Not without power himself, he was powerless in this situation, wondering editorially if there were no limits on the exercise of private power. The village mill owner, the proprietor of the foundry, the local banker, all of these types in the America that existed before the age of business were subject to the restraints of the community they were part of and dependent on. Before 1860 or 1870, there were practical limits to the power a man of affairs had or could exercise, but by 1911, with factories in Toronto and faraway Berlin, the Cash, as the company was called, was already a nascent multinational. Operating under the laws, regulations and commercial customs of the states of the union and foreign states as well, it was under the discipline of none. The old social controls and the old boundaries of behavior, effective because enterprises were small and local, were no more. John Patterson could tell anybody who objected to his putting two thousand families into penury that they could go blow it out the other end. If he wanted to shut down Dayton, Ohio, because of a lack of respect shown him, well, down Dayton went.

The import of the message Malcolm Forbes sent about money through his own much publicized forms of lavish living was that money is yachts and vacations and luxury. And so it is, but it's also power over other people, and of this he had no words for his public.

# FOUR

# Getting
# the Goods

T HE JOHN PATTERSON who brought such distress to
the people of his hometown is featured in B.C.'s book,
*Men Who Are Making America*. To B.C. he is the man who built
the nationally praised "Daylight Factory," the new glass and
steel company structures situated in what was once called
Slidertown, but then renamed South Park. Slidertown, where
people on the skids used to end up, had been replaced by this
new model industrial plant, which neither B.C. nor others
could say enough of.[1]

He told his readers how the air in the factory building was
changed every fifteen minutes, he wrote about the shower facilities for the workers. (Millions of turn-of-the-century families
had not yet attained indoor running water, bathtubs and showers, yet another fruit from the industrial cornucopia. As they
became commonplace for the first time in human history working people didn't smell like pigs.) B.C. wrote about the "hospi-

tal" with doctors and nurses, the free "electric massage treatment," about meals provided at cost with an orchestra playing
music, about Patterson's estate being open to the employees,
the picnic tables, a golf course, tennis courts, a baseball field for
them to use. He made special mention of the policy toward
women which permitted them to come in later and leave work a
half-hour sooner than the men. Women and the workplace was
an important topic for B.C.

In the fall of 1917, Patterson had B.C. come out to Dayton
where the company was located to talk to the "Convention of
the Wives of Salesmen of the National Cash Register Company," no less than five hundred of whom were present. His
speech contained a reminder of how women in other countries
were hardly more than slaves, an endorsement of women's
right to vote, coupled with an admonition that women must
"earn their laurels." He worried them about America's high
divorce rate, and thought one of the reasons for it was that
enthusiastic men came home from work wanting to "talk shop,"
with wives who didn't know enough to understand them, so the
men strayed.

B.C. reported that, "The whole plant of the Cash Register
Company is dotted with mottoes year-in, year-out. One giant
placard gave a list of things the wife of a salesman can do to
help her husband. They are not inapplicable to other wives!
Here are some of them: Serve simple food, Give him plenty of
fresh air, see that he gets plenty of sleep; study merchants'
needs and help with 'tips.' "[2]

That is par for the course with John Patterson, who must be
given the credit or the blame for developing organized, hyper-
thyroid, high-pressure salesmanship in the United States. This
is the original foot-in-the-door kid. The "commercial traveler,"
the traveling salesman catering to shopkeepers, small factories
and such, comes on the scene with the finishing of the national
railway system perhaps twenty years before Patterson began
National Cash Register in the mid-1880s. But Patterson wasn't
having any of the "101 Trombones" approach to salesmanship.
His motto was—and he only spoke in mottoes—"Don't chew
gum or tobacco. Don't tell funny stories." He had it all mapped
out. Good food was required eating, and calisthenics was a
mandatory exercise every morning for every person in the or-

ganization. Responsibility was individualized; hence the Cash became the first sales organization to assign exclusive territories. John Patterson wanted to know who was gold and who was a flub-up, a person to be reprocessed or trashed. Everything was planned. Before the salespeople moved in on the enemy— for business was war with John Patterson—the customer was softened up by direct mail bombardment. Direct mail as a sales tool begins with him, and he used it with ruthlessness. One of the enemy, groggy from mail attacks, returned one of the letters to Dayton with a plea scrawled on the envelope to "Let up. We never done you any harm."

War, war, war plain and simple. Patterson would face his sales force at meetings, screaming, "Kill them . . . Crush them!" He had been known in these meetings to stand in front of a blackboard, take up a red chalk, pulverize it in his hands, rub the powder on his face so that he was described as "looking like a tousled but well-tailored Comanche," as he screamed, "Dramatize, verbalize!" John Patterson was to do the thinking for everybody in the organization. His tool for getting his thoughts into other heads was repetition and sloganeering. His regimented, sloganized, frenzied onslaught was widely imitated. International Business Machines was designed on the National Cash Register model by Thomas Watson, who worked for Patterson for years before going off to found IBM.[3] For years every office in the globe-girdling Big Blue empire had the word THINK on every desk and every wall. It was pure Patterson.

The similarities between the Patterson business methods of the 1880s in Dayton, Ohio, and the Japanese business methods in the 1980s are striking. The same before-work calisthenics, the chanting and singing, the company as hovering mother and swinish tyrant, the incessant attention to detail, the never letting up, the constant checking up, never taking anything for granted, none of this was invented in Yokohama or Tokyo. Our media has represented the Japanese approach as a significant breakthrough in running business organizations. Perhaps it is, but the breakthrough occurred in places like Dayton, Ohio, and Pittsburgh, Pennsylvania, more than a century ago. The Japanese did not think up something new; the Americans forgot something old, something they thought up, which the Japanese may or may not have copied. Events in Japan are beyond the

scope of this book, but what happened in the United States is a letting down, a loss of institutional memory. American business forgot the perpetual attention, the ceaseless effort which Patterson, old devil that he was, understood was necessary for business success on a grand scale. Richard Sears, who gave his name to Sears, Roebuck, customarily worked a twelve-hour day and a seven-day week—including Christmas—year in and year out.[4] We still have more than a few business people who work hard, but they don't work smart. Long, dumb hours won't do it. An advertising, promotional and marketing genius, with lightning quick improvisation, Sears worked very, very smart.

You can't be on a civic committee, or at some pompous seminar, or zooming up and down in the company jet, or getting your picture taken for *People* magazine if you are going to run your company right. The failure of Lee Iacocca at Chrysler is a case in point. After a successful beginning, the ego left the earth's gravitational field, and he joined the cosmos. The company went to pieces. A number of important decisions weren't made or were incorrectly made at Chrysler and an outsider looking in has to conclude that one of the major reasons for the corporation's drift was that its CEO had become a glamour puss. You want to be a movie star, go to Hollywood, you want to be an automobile executive, stay in Detroit and keep your feet on the ground.

But what's the point of plotting, back-stabbing, campaigning, drudging to be a CEO if you don't have fun? The same might be said of playboy politicians. In both cases the job at the top is a grave responsibility which most of us should shirk because we lack the necessary dedication and the needed fanaticism. The boss must be the hardest-working person in the place, and because he or she is, few bosses can do the job right for more than ten or fifteen years. Men like Rockefeller and Carnegie and Richard Sears burned out and then sold out or retired relatively early. The day the new CEO takes over the old one is free to go play business statesperson or civic poobah. In fact, after leaving office they should. We need what they have to offer, but, as long as they are CEOs, they must let others enjoy star status. America must have its CEOs spending all their time and energy at work. Let's face it, we need the wealth these companies are supposed to generate.

The current CEO ethos permits the boss to play business celeb. We do have many diligent CEOs who get to the office, put in slave hours and do their work well. If they didn't exist, we'd be in rags, starving in the streets. We don't have enough of them. Those we have are not the famous CEOs, the dominant CEOs, the role model CEOs; they don't get the glamor, the attention, the adulation. It's the loudmouths, not the doers who get the spotlight. The CEO with the wide public reputation, a *People* magazine quality reputation, is either a loser or a criminal, or both. In the backseats of those limousines with mysterious black windows they are the vanguard of the downward inclining procession. Egotistical, abrasive and abrupt, surrounded by boardroom ticks and leeches, they are the corporate Bourbons, with swelled heads and swollen appetites, entrenched and useless.

John Patterson betook of some of these admirable traits but he was a founder, a beginner of the enterprise, and, despite his summary cruelties and malevolent toying with the happiness of many, his wicked hobbies didn't distract him. Indeed he remained so concentrated on his business that he crossed over from playing rough to criminal conspiracy.

Mere major market share wasn't enough for John Patterson. He broke into emotional hives at the thought that a single cash register of alien manufacture, new or used, might be sold any place, any time to anyone. The thought was an agony for the businessman. The thought was also father to a maniacal program of action. All competition would be obliterated. He would achieve one hundred percent market share in cash registers, new and old.

In his attempt to do so—he got to within five percent of his goal of one hundred percent market share—he escaped going to jail by the whiskers on his chinny-chin-chin. Thomas Watson was sent out across the country to set up stores under fictitious names to drive every secondhand dealer in cash registers to sell out or declare bankruptcy. Sometimes two of these dummy stores, one on either side of the secondhand dealer, would be opened for business, cutting prices, underselling, until the enemy owner belly-upped. Undercover businessmen/operatives turned competitors' employees into double agents spying on the enemy and sabotaging him. Patterson would also manufac-

ture exact copies of machines of enemy design and manufacture, except that they were pieces of junk which fell to pieces. If tricks like that didn't ruin the reputation of the enemy's product other schemes were devised to besmirch the competition's good name. For harassing fire on the flanks Patterson had a squad of lawyers filing nuisance suits for patent infringement or anything else he could think of to make the enemy bleed legal fees and keep him too distracted to do his work.

At length Patterson, Watson and other National Cash Register executives got into the Record Book of Dubious Firsts by becoming the first people tried and convicted under the criminal, not the civil, section of the Sherman Anti-Trust Act. In the end Patterson escaped jail on a legal technicality, and Watson, driven from the Cash by Patterson and his psychoses, went on to get into similar trouble at IBM because he too, having absorbed the Pattersonian view of the business universe, wanted no secondhand market in his machines which he didn't control. Hence for years IBM equipment couldn't be bought, but only rented. Ultimately the government came knocking on his door.

John Patterson can be made to exemplify the yin and yang of business's age of gold. He was guilty of any number of indefensible acts, some criminal, some merely despicable. Yet he left not only himself richer, but us richer too for his astonishing business career. In a world dominated by ineffectual bureaucrats, in both private and public organizations, it is temptingly romantic to insist that only cutthroat swine can get anything done in this world, but, examined close up, no persuasive evidence exists that John Patterson had to be a moral imbecile and a gangster to get the job done. This goes to the American culture, just as the shockingly different murder rates between the United States and Canada go to a difference in culture. Nevertheless, Patterson did get the job done, and this is more than we can say about his epigone running too many businesses now, as slowly, year after year, there is just a little bit less to go around.

In Patterson's time, it was the reverse: every year there was a little bit more, and some years a lot more, to go around. The businessmen of the period stuffed themselves with profits, binged themselves with acts of luxurious insanity, and there was still enough left over so that, decade by decade, life got better for everybody.

Where once there was a little wooden shack with a half-moon cut in the door behind every American's house, there came the woosh of the flush. The changes, quick and vast, transformed everyday life. Even in the 1880s five out of six urbanites took baths in metal tubs into which heated water from the stove had to be poured. The more fortunate might have small, second-floor bathing rooms, with cold water supplied from a rainwater cistern in the attic. Hot water was lugged up from the kitchen in pails, and when the bath was done, the used water was bailed out of the tub and lugged back down again.[5] In a place like Muncie, Indiana, there was no running water before 1885; in 1890 there were less than twenty-four bathrooms in the entire city. Not long after, the Scott boys, Clarence and Edward, brought America toilet tissue on a roll, and Sears, Roebuck catalogues were displaying bathroom suites containing a flush toilet, sink and bathtub, ready to be hooked up to hot and cold running water and drainage systems.[6] By 1925 sixty percent or more of Muncie homes had full bathrooms.[7] It was a new world.

Nothing in our own time constitutes such a jump in the standard of living. Middle-aged Americans can remember, but only barely remember, the coming of the nuclear electric generation, the computer, jet aircraft and the long-playing record; people in their sixties recall life before antibiotics or television in every home. The most recent of the major changes was thirty years ago; a generation or more has passed in which no new major systems have been put in place, unless you want to count the personal computer or cable TV. And cable TV improvements, while pleasant and useful, do not begin to compare to the exponential jumps in the standard of living during the Age of Gold. Which is not to say that incremental improvements like the personal computer are to be sniffed at, but the pace of change for the better has slowed down, and where we have progress bounding forward the millions may not have the use of it. Everybody who wants one gets a Walkman, but not the best in medical treatment. We have no Wal-Mart to put that in reach of every home and family. With color TV and food, our poor live better than Charles Dickens' poor. Nevertheless things aren't getting better for them. In grandmother's time and great-grandmother's time, a popular saying in America

was, "My! What will they think of next!" The expression has fallen into disuse, because next is increasingly the same as last. People in the 1890s, the 1910s, '20s, the '50s, even, were made woozy adjusting to all the marvelous improvements. While we are made woozy by the impact of AIDS or crack on ourselves, they debated the impact of the radio, the automobile or the birth control pill. It is not true that the more it changes, the more it is the same; it is not true that these things are a pendulum, swinging sometimes too much one way, sometimes too much the other. It is not true social life is progressive and evolutionary, automatically getting better and better. Nothing is automatic, nothing improves naturally. All progress, all improvement is deliberately made by intelligent effort. Life is what we make it, and it was on Malcolm's watch, during the decades his generation of businessmen were running things, that the goose's golden eggs began to get smaller and she began to lay them at greater intervals. Somebody has not been taking care of the girl.

Patterson understood: no goose, no egg, so he took care of the lady. He was not an inventor of things but of business methods, and without them, we would not have the material bounty we do. So much emphasis is put on technology, to the point it has become a voodoo word, that we overlook that it means nothing unless a business organization can be put together to use it. The Russians have technology coming out of their ears, and if theirs is not the equal of ours, nevertheless, they are the only other nation in the world to put a man in space, but little good it has done them back on earth. They don't know how to deliver the bacon. Chicago's Gustavus Swift, who gave his name to the now vanished Swift & Company, was the man who literally figured out the system to deliver the bacon but there were many others, men like John Patterson, who worked out how to get the goodies to the masses.

Often the difference in what company prevailed and which fell by the wayside was not the quality of the product, but the ability to get it to people. The Remington typewriter and the McCormick reaper succeeded, when their competitors didn't, because they built effective sales and service organizations. The reaper, that glorious piece of labor-saving equipment which liberated so many hundreds of thousands from growing food to

producing other kinds of wealth, might never have appeared in the fields if McCormick had not introduced installment plan buying. The not-yet-mechanical American farmer of the 1870s couldn't use a piece of equipment he couldn't get repaired and wouldn't buy one. Cyrus McCormick was able to invent a kind of organization which had never existed before, an organization of mechanics and technicians working with customers spread out over thousands of miles.[8] So, metaphorically, the corn was grown to fatten the hogs which became the bacon the businessmen brought home to a nation, seemingly miraculous in new-made wealth.

Patterson and McCormick exemplify how manufacturers invented distribution systems to get their products to would-be customers. Retailers, too, were endlessly ingenious in devising ways to increase competition, hammer prices downward and make an ever-widening diversity of products conveniently available to a public previously confined to the contents of the country store's small inventory. By the turn of the century the Sears, Roebuck catalogue had grown to be a thousand pages long, and had become something more than a list of merchandise for sale. Under the frantic and disorganized genius of Richard Sears it had become a major artifact in American culture.

The Sears catalogue was the means by which the wider world of late nineteenth-century life was brought to the majority of Americans who still rusticated in crude isolation on farms and in agricultural hamlets. By 1899 the celebrities of the day, actors and politicians like Teddy Roosevelt, were appearing in the publication's pages. Farm families were made fashion conscious by the catalogue and introduced to the latest improvements in *everything,* literally from automobiles and gramophones to Paris, France, millinery and the latest in horsehair-stuffed furniture for the front parlor. Before the 1880s and the coming of Sears and Montgomery Ward, its smaller but still very large competitor, the quality of merchandise offered at retail to most Americans was so crude as to preclude any question of style or even comfort. Shoes, for instance, were manufactured on straight lasts, so that there was no difference in shape between those destined for the right foot and those for the left. Often they came tied together and left in bins for the customers to sort their way through.[9]

With ordering instructions printed in Swedish and German, the catalogue had its part in knitting the nation together through consumerism and commerce. Orders came in written in a dozen tongues for everything the imagination can contrive, including mail order wives and husbands. The catalogue was, as they used to say, the national "Wish Book," a source of mass entertainment before phonograph or silent pictures, and a reminder of home for Americans abroad. Julius Rosenwald, who had bought into the company and succeeded Sears after he'd flamed out, took packing crates of catalogues to France with the blessings of the War Department to cheer up the wounded doughboys in the military hospitals.

An industrialist such as John Patterson set up a sales force which created a national and international market for his products. Sears performed the same service for smaller manufacturers who could not develop national sales and distribution organizations and were, therefore, in the same vassalage to the middlemen, the wholesalers and jobbers, as were the country storekeepers. Richard Sears was the first retailer to go to hundreds of small manufacturers and provide them, in effect, with a national market by contracting to buy large percentages of their production. In many instances Sears put up the money for a manufacturer to expand or buy equipment needed to make certain products the great mail order house wanted.[10]

Patterson learned early about the pitfalls of poor quality control and had the income stream and ability to correct deficiencies. Sears, especially after Rosenwald took command, had to work with many of its thousands of suppliers to raise the quality of the merchandise. Setting standards wasn't an easy job. It had never been done before so that when Sears set up its product analysis and testing laboratories it was breaking a fresh trail. Sears technical people advanced tool design and consumer products like refrigerators, as the organization, decade after decade, found new ways to raise quality and lower prices. No single social organization, of whatever character, has made a larger contribution to the nation's material welfare. The company's magnificent past makes its lousy present so much more saddening. Its record in recent years qualifies Sears to be an example of the failures of American enterprise. Another company which had everything—capital, advantageous real estate,

a seasoned organization, thousands of supplies and millions of customers rooting for it, everything that is, but an able management. In the 1930s the company hired its former co-owner, Alvah C. Roebuck, who had sold out to Sears because working with this talented madman had damn near done him in, to be a touring purveyor of goodwill. After advertisements announcing his personal appearance had been placed in the local papers, people would come, sometimes from as far as a hundred miles away, to line up to shake the hand of *the* Mr. Roebuck. People might walk around the corner to shake a fist in the face of the present CEO, but shake his hand? A measure of Sears' ever-deepening drop is that in an era when the catalogue mail order business went crazy trying to find new markets and customers, Sears, Roebuck, of all places, couldn't find a way to make its catalogue division profitable. (To a limited extent, a very limited one, Kmart and Wal-Mart fill the place which Sears, Roebuck carved out for itself.)

Patterson's company, National Cash Register or NCR, continued on until it was gobbled up by IBM, a firm which appears to be describing the same downward azimuth as Sears. In the glory days Patterson's market wasn't the retail consumer. He was manufacturing and marketing a device which was a material aid in the creation of modern business. He bought the rights to a half-perfected idea—the cash register—and made it into a tool almost as common as the knife and fork. He was not an inventor, not a man who fooled around in the shop, but a man able to find people who could engineer and design the cash register idea to make it a useful tool. He was able to put together all the ingredients needed to manufacture it, and, lastly, sell the idea and sell the product. He had to demonstrate to every merchant in America, and eventually, half the world, that they needed this thing.

They did need his tool. Patterson lived in a time when innumerable new tools were being invented. His tool is important because it is a business tool, a tool for the businessman to help him do business. The cash register gives information and it gives control. In a time when the merchant could sit on his high stool and watch his two apprentices on their low stools, information and control were easy enough, but business was ceasing to be a place where the boss could stand at the door and take in

everything that was happening on the shop floor. How could you keep track of what was going on when you weren't there to see it? The cash register, whose tape kept track of what was sold, for how much and by whom, was part of the answer to that question. The machine was one of hundreds of tools, some material, some organizational, that had to be invented before business could be business.

The word business, meaning something one does to make a living, goes back to the 1400s; businessman or man of business dates from at least the 1600s. Then and now, the words are the same, but the meaning is different. If an American businessman of 1850 were time-warped back to the offices of a Milanese businessman of the late Middle Ages, he could step behind the counter and take over without missing a beat. Double entry bookkeeping, factoring and other procedures, and instruments like letters of credit, would be perfectly familiar to the American. For centuries business remained pretty much as it had been. But time-warp the same businessman forward fifty years to Anno Domini 1900, and he would be lost. He would not be able to step in and take over. Everything had changed, not just the cash registers. The way the books were kept, the way business was done, the terminology, the way the enterprise was organized, everything would have been different.

B. C. Forbes wasn't given to taking the historical view; he tended more toward a belief in the magic of giants. Single men doing extraordinary deeds was his way of looking at things. As a young reporter it was said that he went about his work with a picture of Andrew Carnegie pasted to the inside cover of his shorthand notebook.[11] He liked to print lists of great men of the age. The heartiness of his encomiums argues that there was more in this than a bid for advertising. The powers of accomplishment of B.C.'s "big men" were so great he treated them in the pages of his magazine as though they were masters of necromancy. B.C. was not alone, for this was the time all America knew Thomas A. Edison as the Wizard of Menlo Park. Tesla, the Wright Brothers, Marconi, Eastman, inventors particularly, were the idols of teenage boys, and of adults as well. As the celebrities of the 1990s, the rock stars, the actors and athletes, know there are certain prescribed poses for them to strike in public, the Wizard knew what was expected of him in his time,

as this passage describing Edison meeting the media shows: "While the reporter was being ushered in, the Old Man disguised himself to resemble the heroic image of 'The Great Inventor, Thomas A. Edison.' . . . Suddenly gone were his natural boyishness of manner, his happy hooliganism. His features froze into immobility, he became statuesque in the armchair, and his unblinking eyes assumed a faraway look like a circus lion thinking of the Nubian desert. He did not stir until the reporter tiptoed right up to him, then he slowly turned his head, as if reluctant to lose the vision of the Nubian desert."[12] Boys dreamed of growing up to be inventors, to get rich thereby, but also to be powerful and prestigious in knowledge and wisdom. Boys and girls of today have no such dreams. The inventor has evaporated; he does not exist in the popular culture.

We know the names of no living inventors, unless perhaps Dr. Jonas Salk is moved from the scientist category over to inventor, but even he is unknown compared to the fame that was Edison's. The solo inventor, then and now, continues to make major contributions, and they are often doubly important because they are based on hypotheses which the big corporate and university laboratories have rejected, have willfully ignored or don't know about. The corporate research facilities are adept enough at taking someone's idea and engineering products out of it, but their record for breakthrough invention is unimpressive. The solo genius in the twentieth century has been given credit for at least the following: air conditioning, automatic transmission for automobiles, power steering, the helicopter, catalytic cracking of petroleum, cellophane, the jet engine, Kodachrome film, magnetic recording, the Polaroid Land camera, quick-freezing, xerography, all-purpose digital electronic computer and the laser.[13] You'll notice that these achievements are not recent. The giants are coming fewer and farther between.

Igor Sikorsky,[14] the helicopter's inventor, and to a lesser extent, Edwin Land, inventor of instant photography and free-lance scientist of signal accomplishment, won a degree of public acclaim. In general, however, in the era of big institutions of overweening power, the stand-alone inventor/scientist is a geek and crackpot. Anonymous people working as part of a "team" is why "progress is our most important product" at General Elec-

tric. The thrust of corporate advertising and argument is to downplay individual accomplishment. Where heroes are manufactured, they are of the Chuck Yeager sort, daredevil, brass-balled types, who help with merchandising but hardly serve as an inspiration for a little girl, gifted in the sciences, to strike out on her own, not in a space suit, but at a laboratory bench. Yeager, the manufactured merchandising hero of the National Aeronautics and Space Administration and the immense corporate organizations entwined through it, has no corresponding brain hero. Little Yeager dolls dressed up in fly-jockey zoom-zoom suits can be sold separately or as part of a fast food promotion. In either case they also glamorize the laboratory teams, both corporate and governmental, which put him in his supersonic jet and NASA's space-suited glamor pusses in orbit.

Cast into oblivion is the non-team player without whom there would be no NASA, no rockets, no jets, no nothing. Robert Goddard was both the quintessential Yankee tinkerer/inventor and the prototypic non-team player. Goddard, who held an amazing 214 patents[15] covering every aspect of rocketry and jet propulsion, worked for years alone among the cacti of Roswell, New Mexico, inventing, engineering, experimenting and perfecting. He got there because at age seventeen, on October 19, 1899, he had what has been described as a mystical vision of space flight. For the rest of his life he referred to the date as his "Anniversary Day." This is no role model for anybody in the color-me-vanilla corpo-cratic culture fostered by modern business. God, if only genius didn't play loony tunes, but then even many of our greatest businessmen couldn't get a job in the businesses they themselves founded if they were to apply fifty years later.

Business has been sterilizing the seed stock of invention by discouraging inventors, suppressing the fruits of their labors or stealing them. Edwin Armstrong,[16] a solo practitioner in the classic mold, invented FM radio in the mid-1930s after the engineers in the major research institutions said FM held out no hope for static-free broadcasting.[17] Institutions with a financial or egotistical interest in a given way of doing things cannot make a break for the open sea of basic, new departures. Although the engineers had the evidence of their ears—Armstrong had played static-free radio via frequency modulation

transmission for them—they denied the evidence of their own senses and insisted it was not possible. RCA (Radio Corporation of America, now owned by General Electric) had also played a part in preventing the introduction of FM. It had too much invested in AM technology. Between egos and profits, to be had or to be lost, FM broadcasting was delayed for thirty or more years, and when it was introduced Armstrong's patent rights were violated, forcing him into a long, financially and spiritually exhausting legal battle, which he won, but it was too much for him. He committed suicide.

RCA and FM is not a unique example. The modern corporation, with the life span of a sea tortoise, finds nothing more difficult than change. Disposed to move its flippers in stately fashion and swim on forever, rather than embrace the new and the different, it will ignore it or thwart it even if by doing so it allows itself to perish. The people in the gaslight industry would not involve themselves with electricity as a source of illumination; many railroad companies, failing to read the large-lettered message which said they were in the transportation business, chose bankruptcy and extinction; the engineers and executives at Western Union, once one of the most important companies in the nation, did not understand that they were in the communications business, and that survival, if nothing else, ought to have impelled them to take up the telephone. In more recent times IBM's Thomas Watson, the younger, found out he could not get his company's research facilities to get to work on computers. Their whole tradition had been electro-mechanical devices like the company's electric typewriters, and past that technology, they wouldn't or they couldn't move. Watson was driven to set up an entirely new research facility to get his company into the computer business.[18]

Business has been destroying its future to fatten its present. As corporations have, by violent inadvertence, conducted their business so as to kill off the birds and the beasts, they have been destroying the habitat which brings forth genius. The wetlands of invention have been drained.

George Eastman, one of the men B.C. admired and put on his super-achiever lists,[19] arose out of a time conducive to a person, more accurately a man, realizing his genius scientifically and commercially. The wetlands were still ecologically

sound in his day. Eastman devised a substitute for the glass plates photographers such as Mathew Brady used to make a pictorial history of the Civil War. Paper film was rolled on spindles, another object which gets taken for granted after it's been around for a hundred years or so. An early model employer, again of the kind who won B.C.'s particular respect, George Eastman began profit sharing and such in the 1890s, after he had perfected the five-dollar camera, thereby moving photography from the classes to the masses.[20]

Eastman was recognizably of a certain type who flourished in the golden age of American business. Hatched in the wetlands culture, he was one of the hundreds, probably thousands, of Yankee tinkerer-businessmen, who first invented something, then often manufactured and marketed it. Though the wetlands have been drained and degraded, in recent years what's left of the alluvial soup has nurtured a few throwbacks like William H. Gates III, co-founder of Microsoft, whom *Forbes* magazine classifies as a multibillionaire. So the type still exists in the techno-nerd computer hackers fiddling, fadoodling and futzing their way toward invention in basements and garages. Their predecessors spent their youth in what used to be called "gasoline alley," modifying, repairing, hot-rodding cars.

Alfred Sloan, graduate engineer and businessman most responsible for General Motors' success, understood the sources of American industrial genius. "In those early days remarkable progress was accomplished by self-taught men," he wrote. "Ford was a mechanic. Maxwell was a mechanic . . . The Dodge brothers were mechanics. Chrysler . . . was a mechanic too. These were exceptional men . . . In those years the American mechanic was a restless wanderer. Once he had skimmed the cream of experience from a job, he moved on to another in another city. There was something in themselves which made them seek places where skill could grow and opportunity could be found. They were not merely searching for a living."[21]

Sloan's favorite example of the restless-wanderer cum genius was Fred Fisher, who, with his brothers, manufactured the bodies for General Motors cars during the years when GM led the world and the Japanese used to send their guys to Detroit with cameras slung around their necks to learn from us. "The Fisher

boys learned to handle tools almost as soon as they could toddle. Their father had a little repair shop in Norwalk, Ohio, and
did horseshoeing, carriage work or any other job in metal work
or wood that was needed in a small town," Sloan related. "He
(Fred) had his apprenticeship behind him and was a first-class
mechanic, a woodworker, when he was seventeen. To learn
more he left home; he hit the road. Thereafter he had jobs in
Bellefontaine, Ohio; Richmond, Indiana; Akron, Columbus
and many other places. When he had learned the technique of
a factory, he quit. In big cities he attended night schools. He
took correspondence courses because he needed mathematics
to supplement his other tools. He took jobs only where superior
work was being done. If you should ask him about certain
towns, he'll say, 'Never worked there. They were only making
trash.' "[22]

In the tens and twenties, other Fred Fishers were the ham
radio freaks, and, before that, they were fascinated by telegraph
technology. Often they were school dropouts, self-taught, self-
starters who chose putting their hands on the work directly and
immediately instead of whiling away the years as inmates of the
ever less effective education bureaucracy.

They derived from a self-separated world of tunnel-visioned
young men, absorbed with machines, invention and mechanical
improvisation, a world discernible in the 1850s and even further back. Robert Fulton, a figure of the early nineteenth century and an inventor of the steamboat, was urging such a complete immersion in the crafts of design and manipulation when
he said an inventor "should sit down among levers, screws,
wedges, wheels, etc. like a poet among the letters of the al-
phabet, considering them as the exhibition of his thoughts, in
which a new arrangement transmits a new Idea to the world."[23]
By then, in addition to the older apprentice system, after-work,
night schools in the mechanical and engineering arts spread.
There arrived a blooming of popular magazines on mechanics,
electricity and chemistry, catering to young men who spent
their leisure putting together, taking apart, trying something
different, making, devising, improvising. The life of hanging
out at the machine shop, the garage, the engine house had
begun.

The woods were full of these ad hoc engineers, inventors,

scientist-businessmen. We had too many to list, to categorize, even to find. They are forgotten people like Charles Billings, a Vermont man born in 1835, who at age seventeen apprenticed in the gun department of Robbins & Lawrence, moving on a few years later as a journeyman machinist to work for Samuel Colt where he became an expert in drop-forging, and then on to Remington where he developed a drop-forge process which saved time and labor in making guns for the Union army. After that he patented a new method for making sewing machine parts, then, starting his own business, he brought out a succession of inventions of tools and of methods to manufacture them, ending his career getting into electric dynamos and giving this new field the "Billings commutator-bar," the purpose of which is described in most dictionaries. For the incurious, take my word for it, the invention was a useful step forward, one of many, many by such men, which, taken together, formed the base of our comfort and luxury.

As the wetlands have been paved over for mall parking areas, the breeding grounds of invention have been drained as well. Where a Charles Billings was spending his leisure playing games in the machine shop, young people of his age and native ability are spending theirs playing Nintendo. The adolescent culture of work and learning has been replaced by one of inert amusement. Don't blame it on the kids. It is the businessmen who have, in effect, snatched them off to shape them into passive, acquisitively needy consumers. The games of Charles Billings' youth were with lathes and drop-forges, his playmates other young fanatics fascinated with machines. His great-great-grandchildren spend their growing up at the joy stick of a computer, the workings of which they cannot begin to guess. In a complicated, specialized world, that in itself is tolerable, but these youths don't know what goes on under the hood of anything, for they have been trained from infancy forward by a commercial universe to lean back, eat and take their places in their appropriate market segment.

The text of this ad, pitched to potential MTV advertisers, delineates the business-created environment in which youth lives: "Just when you think you're too old for rock-n-roll . . . you're surprised to find yourself glued to the screen . . . our teenage viewers practically *live* in front of it [ad's emphasis]

. . . it actually has a good effect on them, as far as a marketer is concerned, anyway. You see, when our viewers aren't spending time in front of the tube, they're spending money. On everything from candy bars to new cars."[24]

The apprentice-boy, Yankee-tinkerer culture, that do-for-yourself, make-it-yourself culture of invention is obliterated. A made-by-others, commercially shaped culture forms the character and molds the interests of people trained not to achieve, schooled not to excel. The folk wisdom of our society knows it, that's why the phrase couch potato was coined. We know couch-potatoism retards youth intellectually, degrades youth spiritually and harms youth physically, but nobody can stop the micro-waving of our best spuds, turning their brains into the consistency of fluffed starch. Legally, financially and politically, there's not a thing that can be done. Free of restraint, MTV intravenously drips new appetites into the youthful millions and they somnambulate over to the mall to satisfy them. "This has a good effect on them," says MTV, but even MTV can't swallow that as it tacks on the concessive remark, "As far as a marketer is concerned, anyway." Translate that into, "Yes, we have a sneaking suspicion that what we're doing is socially injurious and individually damaging, but not to worry if the spudlets' minds are french fried. Merchandize we must."

The Bill of Rights, the First Amendment, doesn't put any control on commercial speech and behavior, and the laws of the nation are used to strangle the same nation's future, as business replaces an active youth culture with a passive one. This is assuredly not an organized conspiracy, and business does bring great blessings, but it also destroys what it depends on for life. Business doesn't want to turn young people into blithering idiots, it doesn't want to devour the organism which sustains it, but it operates like some mindless virus, killing off the national future because business has got to do what business does.

# FIVE

# Loss Leaders

IN 1850, half a century or more after the invention of interchangeable parts and steam power, the only large factory in the United States was the Pepperell Mills in Biddeford, Maine, with eight hundred employees. Most cotton plantations had less than a hundred slaves. America was a nation of small enterprises, run by owners or their families. In the sense we use the word, management did not exist, and therefore business did not exist.

If Western civilization was started between the Tigris and Euphrates rivers, then American business began somewhere between the Erie and the Pennsylvania railroads. In the 1850s we first see, in these two companies, business in a recognizably modern form; we see management up and functioning for the first time. With the invention of business, technical and scientific achievements could be used for mass production and distribution, something not possible before. Without business organi-

72

zation, technical know-how is sterile. The record shows that steam power, flange-railed technology—choo-choos—came before there were effective social organizations to use them. Technology without such social organizations is showpiece stuff of little consequence to the millions who get scant benefit from it. "Advanced" nations like China have the technology available but much good it does the populace, while other Chinese across the border in Hong Kong or down the Malaysian peninsula in Singapore have the social organization to use it.

Thus it was here in the beginning. The first railroads were small affairs run on the lines of the traditional, mercantile principles of a previous age. A little railroad of the 1840s avoided collisions by running its trains west on Monday, Wednesday and Friday, and east the other days of the week. These were short, short lines of fifty miles or so. Operating methods were informal and without a useful, internal communications system. The technology for one existed, the organization for one did not. The nicknames for them tell you what they were like. The Delaware, Lackawanna and Western Railroad, or D, L & W, was known as the Delay, Linger and Wait. The Newburgh, Dutchess and Connecticut, or N, D & C, was the Never Did and Couldn't.[1]

In Massachusetts the Old Colony Railroad stopped wherever business was to be had, which included a daily halt at Wheat Sheaf Lane to pick up eggs from an old lady. It is recorded that one day the train waited until the hen laid one more to make an even dozen.[2] It was a helluva way to run a railroad after the railroad had grown in size to hundreds of miles and to employ four thousand or more men.

Daniel McCallum is the man who told the engineer to skip Wheat Sheaf Lane and get on with the job. He is given credit for seeing management for the first time as a stand-alone necessity to be thought about in and of itself.

McCallum may also have had as much to do with winning the Civil War as Grant or Sherman. Appointed military director and superintendent of railroads in the United States, with one hundred thousand men at his command, he built and maintained two thousand miles of track upon which he operated hundreds of trains daily to keep the Union army supplied. While his unique services to the nation go all but unnoted in

most accounts of the Civil War, in the specialized annals of business history, the man is a giant.

In 1856 McCallum wrote a letter to the Erie's president, in which he laid out why profits weren't what they ought to have been, why there was chaos and what they should do about it.

"A Superintendent of a road fifty miles in length," he said, "can give its business his personal attention and may be constantly on the line engaged in the direction of its details; each person is personally known to him, and all questions in relation to its business are at once presented and acted upon; and any system however imperfect may under such circumstances prove comparatively successful.

"In the government of a road five hundred miles in length a very different state exists. Any system which might be applicable to the business and extent of a short road would be found entirely inadequate to the wants of a long one; and I am fully convinced that in the want of a system perfect in its details, properly adapted and vigilantly enforced, lies the true secret of their [the longer railroads'] failure; and that this disparity of cost per mile in operating long and short roads, is not produced by a difference in length, but is in proportion to the perfection of the system adopted."[3]

McCallum's "system perfect in its details" was a new order, the beginning of management, of the deliberate designing of systems for keeping track of and running an enterprise. His system had to make sure the trains didn't crash, which required that somebody in authority know where they were and what kind of shape they were in all the time. We moderns, even if we are not business persons, have at least a crude idea of the way a business is put together. You can't grow up in America without an organizational chart, something, by the by, McCallum invented. In short order McCallum's organizational chart was lithographed and sold for a dollar a copy. By 1858 the *Atlantic Monthly* published an article describing his organizational ideas in laudatory terms. These prophets were honored in their own time; it's their great-great-great-grandchildren who don't have a clue.

But McCallum had no model to use for organizing the running of what was then the most complex and far-flung of endeavors. Armies were organizations which had that kind of di-

mension and complexity, but armies of the era were sporadically in action and had simpler tasks to perform. Every day, all day and all night, a railroad carried out countless specialized functions, from repairing the engines' roundhouses to keeping track of thousands of pieces of freight. No human organization had faced such a variety of jobs on such a scale before. As one of Andrew Carnegie's biographers explained, "A passenger train conductor often made more collections in an hour than a textile mill did in a year. To ensure that this river of coin flowed into the company's treasury, not into the employees' pockets, required a system of numbered tickets and freight waybills, unique conductors' punches (no two alike and all registered), and station accounts, all supervised by a central office."[4] All this was new, all had to be invented *ab ovo*, taking what ideas McCallum and his contemporaries could from wherever they could discover them.

Hence was born the paper trail. By marrying steam technology with another technology, telegraphy, McCallum instituted a minutely regulated communications system which allowed the dispatcher at the division head to make traffic flow. Every telegrapher on the system had to fill out a form and send it to headquarters every time a train came or went, every time the clock moved to an appointed place on the dial. Nothing like this had existed before in America or in the world. Names had to be given to the new organization's parts—division, line and staff, semaphore. Borrowing where he could, McCallum lifted terminology and organizational ideas from the military. Much was new, however. Timetables, exact written instructions, McCallum's Book of Rules, fixed responsibility. Nothing had been run with such precision heretofore. "All that is required to render the efforts of railroad companies in every respect equal to that of individuals, is a rigid system of personal accountability through every grade of service," declared McCallum.

The social organization of work and technology had been put on a new plane. Men were supervising men whom they did not personally know in doing work according to written instructions from which no deviation was permitted. A glimpse of the developing new kind of organization, not to mention a whiff of the military influence, comes through Andrew Carnegie remembering an incident when he was a young manager on the

Pennsylvania Railroad: ". . . everything went well with the exception of one accident caused by the inexcusable negligence of a ballast train crew . . . That this accident should occur was gall and wormwood to me. Determined to fill all the duties of the station I held a court martial . . . dismissed peremptorily the chief offender, and suspended two others for their share in the catastrophe."[5]

The unbending manager-disciplinarian of American business, the person who takes neither guff nor suggestions from those lower down in the organization, stands in clear outline behind Carnegie's words. The obsequious, yes-man atmosphere of many a contemporary CEO's office finds its origins in the beginnings of business, in the first years of invention when unhesitating obedience was introduced into the nascent culture of business organization. The cigar-chomping boss of yesterday may have had his outward edges filed down, but the team-playing modern CEO is often the same guy under the skin. Health conscious and hep, he may chew cigars no more, but the old chomper is still biting down on people, although now he has a public relations department and takes lessons in media deportment, to hide his stainless steel teeth.

B. C. Forbes was upbeat about the younger executives who were taking over from the founding giants during the 1920s. "The newer men are, as a rule, essentially teamworkers; the older men were essentially individualists. Most of the old-time leaders were what might be called employers; most present-day giants are, rather, executives . . . Leaders in the passing generation very often were autocratic, whereas their successors mostly are democratic," he wrote.[6] What led him to his conclusion were men like Alfred Sloan at General Motors, who did indeed put in a committee system of management that was a marked departure from barking orders and telling subordinates to do what they were told and can the questions. Businessmen, as prone to new things as any fashion conscious teenager, started the management-by-committee fad but the CEO ethos can flourish as well under a committee system as with the lonely leader on the corporate quarterdeck. Slobbering subordinates around a committee table are especially unappealing and as uselessly ineffectual as those in a cleanly pyramidal structure.

Executive autarky is so common even some autocrats recognize it. "The worst disease that can afflict business executives in their work is not, as popularly supposed, alcoholism . . . It's egotism," wrote Harold S. Geneen, the former CEO of ITT, of a disease Mr. Geneen has occasionally been suspected of suffering from himself. Nevertheless there comes from the pen of a man hailed for a generation as one of the nation's best managers these words. He said of the egotism that "no one knows how to handle (it). The egotist may walk and talk and smile like everyone else. Still, he is impaired as much by his narcissism as the alcoholic is by his martinis . . . All those ego-feeding activities—the long hours in the limousine, the skylarking in the corporate jet, the collecting of press clippings, the unnecessary speeches . . . make a corporate problem out of what had been an otherwise perfectly competent, even brilliant executive . . . One situation in which a man's ego became caught in a large merger negotiation cost his company more than $100 million . . . if it were not for that malfunctioning, damaging executive egotism one might expect a 40 percent improvement across the board. The cost in lost performance is enormous."[7]

Geneen said these things almost ten years ago, after watching unchecked executive absolutism tearing up the pea patch of profitability for decades. The response? Basically, none. We have had a deluge of articles and books about how smart, even devilish smart the Japanese are, but most of the fear, dread or worship of the Japanese is nonsense. Without taking credit away from the many Japanese executives who do their work as it should be done, virtually all their business and organizational techniques were invented in the United States and copied in Japan. They have added their own wrinkles, some of which we might borrow from them as they once borrowed from us, but the American business problem isn't Japanese tricks, it's a question of character. It's a question of people in high places having the guts to do their jobs well, and that includes throwing egomaniacal bums out the door *sans* golden parachute.

In the 1990s some companies are so dominated by kowtowing orientalism that you will see men and women flatten themselves against corridor walls when the great man, trailed by his retinue of yea-sayers, flashes past. The underlings act as though

they thought they were too low, too vile to live in the grand personage's ambit.

America is suffering a managerial crisis. Large institutions, private and public, cost too much to run, are too slow to adapt to, or even recognize, changed circumstances and are delivering too few goods and services of too poor a quality. Business hasn't come up with an important new managerial idea in close to seventy years. The more fatuous, self-indulgent egotists we have clogging up corporate management at the top, the less likely we are to find better ways of conducting our affairs.

B.C. didn't get flimflammed by these displays of corporate orientalism put on for the honor and pleasure of the CEO pasha. His glamour boys were the doers and the makers, and of all the giants of his era, his love of Charlie Schwab was the greatest.* Charlie was a steel makin' man, perhaps the steel makin'est man there ever was. B.C. thought so. Among the headline phrases B.C. used to describe Charlie were: "The World's Greatest Steel-maker," "The Most Successful Salesman Ever Born," "The Million Dollar Salary Man," "The Originator of the Steel Trust," "The Boy President," "The Creator of America's Krupp." B.C. believed that Scotland would have fallen to Kaiser Bill and his Hunnish Hoards, and not even America could have saved it, had it not been for Charlie Schwab. Although Charlie did not win the Great War, as WWI was once called, single-handed, he did make signal contributions, most of which were apostrophized in the pages of *Forbes* magazine.

In one of the first issues of the magazine[8] B.C. told the story of the October 1914 secret message from the British admiralty to Charlie, then the principal stockholder and head of the Bethlehem Steel Corporation, asking him to make a secret trip to England. Taking passage on the *Olympic* after the Germans had warned the traveling public it would be sunk by submarines, Charlie was at the rail of the nearly deserted passenger liner when it came across H.M.S. *Audacious* shortly after it had hit an enemy mine. As *Olympic* rescued nine hundred sailors from the dying ship, Charlie stood on the deck taking pictures of the

---

* No connection with the modern stock jobber of the same name.

disaster, photographs which B.C. subsequently published in *Forbes*.

In London Charlie met with the Secretary of War, the First Sea Lord and Winston Churchill, the First Lord of the Admiralty, all three of whom placed a gigantic order for munitions of every kind. They asked Charlie to produce, among other things, fifty thousand artillery shells a day. They also wanted Charlie to build them fifty submarines. Charlie not only said he would, but he would cut construction time on them to six months, and offered to pay a five-thousand-dollar-a-day fine for every day he was late on delivery, if the Brits would pay him a ten-thousand-dollar-a-day bonus for every day he delivered them before the due date. Picture General Dynamics, McDonnell Douglas, any present-day defense contractor making such an offering and being prepared to live with it.

Well, Charlie lived with it and up to it, with the result that a single share of his company which could be bought at the bottom of the Panic of 1907 for seven bucks could be sold eight years later for six hundred. The same year the stock hit six hundred the German imperial ambassador to the United States, Count von Bernstorff, sent an agent to Charlie offering him one hundred million dollars in cash for a controlling interest in Bethlehem Steel. The sum in 1992 dollars is too large to calculate, but Charlie said he had promised the British he wouldn't relinquish control of his company until he got the job done.[9]

If his was an era of big men, Charlie was of Alpine proportions, but unlike Morgan or Rockefeller or the other stern and distant tycoons, Charlie was friendly, familiar and funny. He told jokes, sang songs and played the piano. Everybody loved Charles M. Schwab, except when it was strike time in the ghastly black caverns, in Vulcan's smoky caves, where the heat was so intense and the danger to the workmen so close. There is a particular brutality with which some men of the people govern their own. Charlie, whose grandfather came poor from Baden-Baden in 1830 to a German Catholic settlement in Pennsylvania where the family had gotten on, but not gotten rich, never conceded his ham-handed use of force, his scabs and his obdurate truculence. A man of his times, not a man ahead of them, Charlie told B.C., who printed his words, that, "One of

the deepest satisfactions of my life is that I have never had the slightest trouble with workmen—never a disagreement, never a strike, never any unpleasantness whatsoever."[10] It was all malarkey but in the end people forgot what he'd done or overlooked it.

In fairness to Charlie's memory he was no worse than many another industrialist and perhaps better than some in his industry, as this from B.C. on the topic suggests: "Judge Gary [who followed Schwab as head of U.S. Steel], before he died, underwent a change in his mental attitude, in his philosophy of life, a change many men experience but which they do not all acknowledge. Periodically for perhaps a decade I had heart-to-heart sessions with the veteran head of the United States Steel Corporation on his treatment of workers. I argued that the twelve-hour day and the seven day week should be abolished. The Judge contended that such a revolution was entirely unfeasible. . . . Why, oh why, do so many dynamic industrial and other leaders fail to get that kind of perspective until the eleventh hour and fifty-ninth minute."[11]

Charlie was always dancing in the pages of *Forbes* magazine because he and B.C. evidently got chummy enough to do some drinking together, and because he made such wonderful copy. There was, for example, the story of plain, hometown Charlie traveling to St. Petersburg in 1905 to get the steel contract to build the Trans-Siberian railroad, a contract which would come through obtaining the backing of the Czar's nephew, the Grand Duke Alexis Aleksandrovich. As Charlie told the story, he equipped himself at a cost of two hundred thousand dollars with "the most beautiful necklace I ever saw—of pearls, with a gorgeous diamond pendant." After having arrived in the capital city of the Czar of All the Russias, Charlie arranged to have a quiet dinner with the Grand Duke's mistress. It went well, and as he was taking his leave, he took the jewels out of his pocket, and putting them in her hands, told her, "Here is a small gift from your many admirers in America, among whom I count myself." He got the contract.[12] Today Charlie would be indicted for bribing a foreign official, a strange crime if you recall what scant success we have keeping bribes out of the hands of our own officials here at home.

If ever anybody fit the Horatio Alger legend it would seem to

be Charlie Schwab. He got into the steel business when he was hired by a Captain Bill Jones, the superintendent of Andrew Carnegie's works, who was taken by the younger man's charm, good humor and piano playing. Charlie later used the same skills with Carnegie, ingratiating himself by playing Scottish airs. Pleasant as music making was to these men, it was steel making which mattered, and here Charlie also excelled in the Horatio Alger way. With a skimpy high school education he taught himself enough engineering so he was able to design and build a railroad bridge. What's more he brought it in under cost. By getting a stack of books and making a lab for himself in his own living room, Charlie Schwab taught himself the chemistry of metallurgy.

If that were not enough Algerism, he vaulted over his rivals in the engineering department in the plant by winning a competition. Captain Bill, as Jones was known, had the chief draftsman inform the men under him that they would have to put in overtime without pay to work on a special project. The names of those who worked uncomplainingly and enthusiastically were to be sent to Jones for future preferment. Charlie's name alone was on the list.[13] No modern personnel department has devised a "motivational test" nearly as accurate in separating the human wheat from the human chaff. We are, however, speaking of an era when it was not assumed, and certainly not decreed by court or legislature, that all humans were wheat. You had to prove you weren't chaff.

Nevertheless Charlie was not a self-made man. He was a self-propelled man of huge ability, but he owed to others. In fact, as luck would have it, Charles M. Schwab was the heir and direct lineal descent of the short chain of men who invented business. Charlie went to work for Carnegie in 1879, about thirty years or so after it can be said that business came into existence.

Charlie and his contemporaries did leave more than they found, but they also got used to hearing themselves praised for their efforts. In the depths of the Depression, when questions were being raised about how business conducted itself, Charlie complained to B.C., "I really feel that I have contributed something to the development of this country's resources—Bethlehem gives employment to some 30,000 people. It hurts me—it hurts me very much—to be branded as nothing but a greedy,

selfish, self-seeking, mercenary, merciless fellow, callous towards workmen and towards everybody else."[14] A not unper-
suasive case can be made that Charlie was indeed greedy, selfish
and callous, but, after granting that and more, his claim to having made a contribution still stands. If Charlie took a lot, he
gave the society a lot in return. What sets blow-hard, horn-
tooting Charlie apart from the major figures in contemporary
business aren't his vices, but his virtues. In war and peace the
list of things Charlie did for America is an impressively long
one. What can we put down on the plus side of Henry Kravis'
ledger?

Criticism stings because it is something businessmen so rarely
hear. Charlie was one businessman who heard plenty of it because of his Trump-like personal life and the thick-handed
thwacks he let fly at the employees, especially the blue collar
men tending the mills and the furnaces. After his prodigious
contributions to the Allied victory in World War I, it turned
around for Charlie. The slave driver became the big back slap-
per, a national hero and every reporter's pal. Even in 1929, as
business was doing its biggest pratfall, *Time* honored no less
than sixteen businessmen, including the Forbes' neighbor,
Thomas W. Lamont, by putting them on the cover.[15] You cannot praise these people enough or in enough different ways.
The business genius, their taste, their wisdom, their humanity,
all must be highlighted, and the thirst for adulation will not be
slaked.

The appetite for flattery o'erflows the corporate boardroom
as every medium is set to the work of glorifying the midgets
who pass for modern captains of industry. This in *Newsweek*
about Henry Kravis, the Wall Street sharpie: "The 'High Voltage' Life of a New York Supercouple . . . Henry Kravis . . .
and his fashion designer wife, Carolyne Roehm . . . Almost
every night Henry and Carolyne race from boardroom to ball-
room, hosting dinners, attending charity functions and hob-
nobbing with the uppercrust layer of the upper crust . . . Today the pair personifies New York's new 'working rich.' While
Kravis puts in grueling hours doing deals, Roehm logs long
days perfecting her spring collection and new couture line."[16]
Kravis doesn't even advertise in the magazine. The *Newsweek*
prose proceeds from the prevailing group-think which accords

CEOs semiroyal status. The British royal family gets tougher media treatment than our ennobled American magnates.

At the office and on television they sail on, deferred to, their autocratic notions untested, unchallenged, unquestioned, their enlarged *amours propres* flattered and magnified. Malcolm's place in the firmament came in part from the worshipful authority accorded these white men. The hyperventilating obsequiousness of the "Lifestyles of the Rich and Famous" television program depends on a mass, willing suspension of the critical faculties in regard to business figures. Incidentally Malcolm appeared on the program with John Sculley of Apple Computer, Inc., a CEO who has played the corporate potentate role to the hilt. Mr. Sculley, a former soda pop salesman with a debatable record in the computer business, has published the *de rigueur* self-glorifying biz autobiography, an addition to English literature modestly entitled *Odyssey: Pepsi to Apple . . . A Journey of Adventure, Ideas and the Future*.[17]

Only when there is a business turndown is there a CEO putdown. For a few years in the 1930s there was a moderation in CEO adulation and, in 1991, after business had begun to sour, Alan M. Webber, the editorial director of the *Harvard Business Review*, experienced public twinges of doubt about the doctrine of CEO infallibility: "In the 1980s, much of American business worshipped at the altar of the CEO's ego. 'Leadership' replaced management as the defining task of the executive. And leadership, for the most part, came in one size only. It was on display on the cover of every issue of *Fortune* or *Business Week:* the handsome CEO, standing before his estate, clad in blue pants with green whales on them, swinging a golf club, his trophy wife by his side. The story inside was as prefabricated as the cover photo—an account of the Great Man's fitness regime and how he was applying the same aerobic thinking to reshape whatever company it happened to be this time: the corporate fat he was shedding, the muscular acquisitions he was adding, the balance sheet he was shaping up, the new organization that was emerging, strong and flexible."[18] Mr. Webber's indignation becomes him but it might have served more of a purpose had men in prestigious business pulpits made their criticisms a decade earlier.

The leader who is but a confection of his own public relations

department ought not be replaced by well-trained, managerial dweebs, twits and nerds, persons whose best claim to competence is high marks at Mr. Webber's Harvard Business School. It is not just business competence the nation needs, it is character. Any set of laws or regulations which would have effectively stopped Henry Kravis' capture of RJR Nabisco would hamstring or kill off dozens, perhaps thousands, of profitable and socially useful deals. The Kravis philosophy, as reflected in action over a long and hugely successful business career, is that if it looks good and it ain't illegal, do it. Men of a different character would have invented other, socially useful ways to make their millions instead of getting their plunder via the destructive leveraged buyout which almost invariably leaves the victim company half dead with debt.

Kravis' record is a reflection of his character, such as it is. A man of another character might feel ashamed or unfulfilled at scarfing up hundreds of millions and returning nothing of use to the community or nation. Character is not something one develops at graduate seminars in Cambridge, Massachusetts. Least of all at Cambridge, because Harvard University has been one of Kravis' partners, sharing the corporate carrion with the little Dough Boy.

We live in a time when university presidents are caught cheating on their expense accounts, when businessmen use the bankruptcy laws to break their unions and escape paying damages for the injuries their products have caused. Whether there is more dishonesty now or whether it seems as though there is because there are more people to be dishonest, no one can know. Yet some kind of shift in the moral self-definition of many a businessman apparently has taken place.

Two weeks before Mr. Webber made public his discovery that a hoard of softheaded jerks were at the helms of some major American enterprises, the doctors at *Business Week* made a similar discovery with a cover story about low characters in high places, entitled "CEO Disease." The syndrome was nicely described: "You know the symptoms. The boss doesn't seem to understand the business anymore. Decisions come slowly—only to be abruptly changed. Yes-men are everywhere. There seem to be so many distractions: a board meeting somewhere else or a power golf game at a remote resort—and the perks pile up

. . . Pampered, protected, and perked, the American CEO can know every indulgence. The executive who finally reached the top of a major corporation enters an exclusive fraternity . . . They take home 85 times what the average blue-collar worker makes, unlike their counterparts in Japan, where the ratio is closer to 10 to 1 . . ."[19]

The CEO disease has been around for a long time. Why was it not diagnosed until 1991? It may have been dredged up to explain the teleology of business going sour, or maybe it was the hot topic for a few weeks in the spring of the year. Like the June bug, or quirky teenage hairdos, biz fads may last a couple of years or a couple of weeks. Hot topics in the business press like hot topics in the rest of the mass media are like comets. They just come and they just go.

They go too fast to accomplish more than provide a grunt and a tickle. For a few weeks the tyrannical CEO, a figure long recognized and understood in American culture, gets a quick once-over lightly. Then on to the next thing, leaving the system which permits, even encourages, such abuse of office in place. The damage to the companies and to the country at large continues. Making positive changes in corporate policy to curb quixotic CEO tyranny demands returning to the subject time after time; it requires persistence over years, but the business press, as much subject to flighty, light-headed readers as the rest of the mass media, displays the attention span of a jittery chipmunk. To stay in business the content doesn't have to be good, only packaged to seem new.

The first several generations of business pioneers had to be tough cookies. They were pushing people to act and work in ways they weren't used to. Being on time every day, following instructions to the letter and the clock, working to closer and closer tolerances and learning the etiquette of hierarchical organization were foreign to country people. Stern bosses took these rural recruits and made them into soldiers of the new industrial armies. The drill sergeant-generalissimo CEOs of early days were a ham-handed lot but there was a need for it. The ham-handed authoritarian in a later era, when employees had come to know what was expected of them, was an invitation for purposeless corporate tyranny. Soon one has an organization in

which people think their job is to keep the boss happy, not to get the job done.

Little is known about Daniel McCallum's behavior, but Carnegie, after learning how to do business and organize it working for the Pennsy, was as autocratic as any contemporary CEO —with a difference, however. Carnegie surrounded himself with the best people at designing and running a steel business, and he listened to them.

Carnegie took the organizational forms and operating devices developed in the railroad industry and applied them to manufacturing, to making steel. In putting together the Edgar Thomson plant, named after his patron, the president of the Pennsylvania Railroad, Carnegie married technology, management and organization in a manner which blew the door open to a world of unimagined production. The Thomson works, its placement of storage areas, transportation, buildings and machines, enabled Carnegie to make steel at a volume theretofore unknown and sell it at prices no one else could touch. The flow of the iron ore, the coke, the limestone and other ingredients through a carefully juxtaposed series of processes until steel rails came out the other end presaged the moving assembly line Henry Ford would perfect forty years later. Thanks to the work of William Shinn, a railroad executive recruited to the new enterprise, the cost of every step, every sub-step and every sub-sub-step was known to Carnegie. This novel accounting machinery gave Carnegie a new means of management control of large, costly and complicated endeavors. Carnegie was a wild man about costs; he would spend huge sums on new equipment to get his costs per unit of production down a few pennies. His maxim was "Watch the costs and the profits will take care of themselves."[20]

The Scotsman would have been driven off his rocker at the way modern corporations waste money on showy skyscrapers, on antique-furnished offices, on deputy assistants and assistant deputies, on choirs of vice presidents, on millions of passenger-miles of travel and work years of profitless meetings. This is the man who asked Frank Doubleday, the book publisher, "How much money did you make last month, Frank?"

When the other man said he couldn't tell because in his industry the books were closed only once a year, an indignant

Carnegie exclaimed, "Do you know what I would do if I were in that kind of business?"

"No, what?"

"I would get out of it."[21]

His method of relentless concentration on the perfection of details came to be taken up by Japanese industrialists as his legacy was forgotten by the American managers to whom Carnegie and the others who invented the business of business bequeathed it. That's not the only thing American businessmen stopped doing which Japanese businessmen picked up on.

Even when opportunities were knocking on their shins, American businessmen were oblivious, as the history of the fax machine illustrates. This is an American invention and during the 1970s American companies made and sold them, but apparently executives of the companies which manufactured them began hanging out at conferences and seminars extolling the free market system or calling staff meetings in Acapulco. While they sat on their keisters, those people across the Pacific stole the American thunder. The Americans couldn't find a market for the fax machine; the Japanese asked themselves who might need and want such a machine and sold faxes to them by the cargo shipload, doing what John Patterson had done so long ago, when he introduced another business tool no one knew they wanted—the cash register—and then made a market for it. No fax machines are now made by an American company.[22]

The most famous and depressing of these stories about America missing the boat concerns the transistor, a device invented by three American scientists at the Bell Laboratories in 1948 for which they were awarded the Nobel Prize in Physics in 1956. We got the glory, the Japanese got the business, for it was they who understood that the little silicon chip could be used in making small, convenient versions of everyday things, starting with the radio. In the 1940s the United States was still feasting off scientist refugees from war and fascism as well as a generation of home-grown talent trained up domestically in the previous three decades.

It may have been that the entrepreneurial glint had already begun to dull in the eyes of that generation's hard chargers. Commercial laboratories had begun to substitute "the team" for hard-to-manage genius, changing the system of compensation

by cutting back on rewards and recognition for solo high fly-ers.[23] The dead weight of poorly designed and badly run large organizations may already have been snuffing out freedom of action for the sort of business-technical person able to imagine the million and one profitable applications for the little gizmo which allowed the Japanese to put an earpiece in every head in the world and make a profit off it.

It also is reasonable to suppose that by the early 1950s many of the nation's well-established businesses were getting a higher proportion of sludge-heads in high places. More people were getting ahead by virtue of pedigree than by virtue of perfor-mance. It was a subject that B.C. never ceased to rail about. In the first issue of the magazine, he ran a piece called "High-Placed Misfits. George Jay Gould, the Nicholas Romanoff of American Finance. The Tragic Story of How the Gould 'Em-pire,' the Greatest Patrimony Ever Left a Young American, Has Been Dissipated."[24] At the bottom of the Depression, B.C. was seeing good times ahead because, "The weak are being ruth-lessly weeded out; the fittest are forcing their way to the front. Favoritism is being abolished, nepotism eliminated."[25] And when it came to favoritism he named names, " 'Favoritism to one's own relations' is how the dictionary defines nepotism. One of the most flagrant instances of nepotism in the financial world was the electing of James A. Stillman as president of the largest national bank in America . . ."[26]

If B.C. were alive in the 1990s he might be writing that nepo-tism is affirmative action for white males with the right family connections. The ones who get the creamier internships and go on from there. A man as smart as B.C. would have seen that too many second- and third-raters were being dropped into the first-rate jobs. The brain cells of corporations are being clogged by well-connected idiots who jog, play tennis and are free of dandruff.

From the start, if business was to be run with near military discipline, it had to be a meritocracy. Daniel McCallum set up his system at the Erie so "that merit and training [were] the most potent of all influences in giving positions of every kind." These early inventors of the business organization, McCallum at the Erie and, at the Pennsylvania Railroad, J. Edgar Thomson and Tom Scott and, of course, Carnegie, were at great pains to

create record keeping systems which enabled them to judge who got the job done and who didn't. They were the first equal opportunity employers, yes, of white men only, but until that time hiring and preferment by merit were unknown. Not only business, but government, the military, the church, every organization was run on the basis of family ties, ethnic and tribal affiliation, nepotism, patronage, favoritism. Speaking of the installation of meritocracy on the Pennsylvania Railroad, where Carnegie first ingested these ideas, his biographer writes, "By 1864 it had been codified in the *Book of Rules:* 'Employees of every grade, will be considered in line of promotion, dependent . . . upon qualifications, and capacity for assuming increased responsibility.' Contemporary observers frequently cited the policy as a major reason for the Pennsylvania's success. *The Railroad Gazette,* for example, commented in 1882 on 'the resistance to outside influences which would place men in office on the ground of [considerations] other than proved merit.' "[27]

Without business the United States would not be the kind of egalitarian society it is. Andrew Jackson's America may have been democratic but it was a land of sharp social resentments and literally riotous encounters between the "aristocrats" and "the people," who, though they may have resented being assigned a certain station in life, found there was little they could do about it unless they went west to the frontier. Business changed that state of affairs by creating a practical, everyday type of democracy where men could reach any station in life they had the ability to fill. Base though a man's family background might have been, in the new businesses arising, the man who could do the job best got it. In the new world of business, an employee who had proven himself could get a loan to start his own business, though he had no family connections. It was his self-made business reputation which counted. The 1990s gives an anachronistic exegesis to the Declaration of Independence or Bill of Rights when it infers merit employment from these great documents. In the eighteenth century and the first half of the nineteenth, men of great ability did come to the fore, but it was against a background of selection and promotion based on blood and social connection. It was something new in thinking about social organization and social order when Carnegie, in answer to the suggestion that a certain employee

be promoted, said, "He may be just the man we need. Give him a trial. That's all we get ourselves and all we can give to anyone. If he can win the race, he is our race-horse. If not, he goes to the cart."[28]

Somebody like Jimmy Robinson at American Express would have been sent to the cart long since. He exemplifies the modern executive who loses huge amounts of money, gets himself involved in the most dubious situations and yet his job is safe. Amex is the antithesis of the Carnegie system of building individual accountability into the organization and then cutting, burning or blasting out failure. During Robinson's stay as the CEO at Amex the company has been involved in a series of debacles. In number and cost they ought to have disqualified him even from pulling Andrew Carnegie's cart. Boards of Directors being what they are, CEOs are safe at their desks, their benefits intact and growing larger, even as their companies go into the black hole of Chapter 11 bankruptcy. Carnegie, on the other hand, applied the policy of individual responsibility up the line and into the boardroom, where directors were required to give unequivocal advice, which was recorded and brought up later.

During Robinson's sway at Amex, Fireman's Fund, its insurance subsidiary, began mispricing its product and taking unwise risks with the result that a string of thirty-five consecutive years of growth came to an end and American Express, the mother company, pumped many millions into Fireman's to keep it going; after buying three large and expensive Wall Street stock brokerages, Shearson Loeb Rhoades, Lehman Brothers Kuhn Loeb and E. F. Hutton, and combining them, the merged entity racked up terrifying losses; an attempt to buy one of those glamorously private Swiss banks ended with more large losses and a smarmy scandal in which it came out that American Express, in connection with its failing administration of the bank, had tried to defame a European businessman. Robinson had to apologize publicly.

The American Express credit card came under severe competitive pressure from VISA and MasterCard, and a number of stores and restaurants, angry at their treatment at the hands of Amex, refused to accept it. Elsewhere in the corporate jungle Robinson covered himself with a substance which certainly was

not glory during the great hog squabble in which Henry Kravis and other sharp-tusked boars of Wall Street fought each other for control of RJR Nabisco.

Robinson's daddy was president of the First National Bank of Atlanta and his granddaddy was president of the First National Bank of Atlanta. In addition to having socially correct ancestors, Robinson attended socially correct Harvard Business School, then went on to the Morgan Bank, a socially correct business institution, if there ever was one. There he starred as special assistant to the Chairman. Next stop was American Express, reaching the pinnacle position of a great corporation by what appears to be pre-McCallum, pre-Carnegie channeling.[29] You may be sure everyone who had a hand in Robinson's getting where he is will say he did it on merit, but, add his background to his record in the job, and it sounds like affirmative action for a white, upper-class male.

Every afternoon these males tee off and complain to the other members of the foursome about the damn so-and-so's (fill in the name of your favorite minority) demanding jobs they're not qualified for. Why shouldn't some African-Americans and some Native Americans and some handicapped people clamor for jobs they're not qualified for? Andrew Carnegie may have believed the job should go to the best man; Charlie Schwab may have stayed up all night making sure he *was* the best, but what do people see when they look at our leaders today?

Having studied the record of the white men who've been running the twenty largest banks in the United States for the past twenty years, it would be easy to conclude you don't need a master's papers to run the tanker onto the rocks.

# SIX

## Ludwig's Castle

THE MEN OF THE 1850s made a sharp departure from the past when they adopted the principle that the job should go to the person who could do it best, and that principle is still applied, if spasmodically and fitfully, in business and in government. From the 1870s onward men of business background invoked the principle in their battles against the political patronage system, fighting for the establishment of a civil service, which in due course has itself come to be the enemy of promotion for merit and a crutch for time-serving sloth. It is easy to pay lip service to the doctrine of meritocracy, but painful to live by it. Be it a Jimmy Robinson or the newest group of oppressees putting forth a special claim that society lay merit aside, some advocate is forever on the ground to insist reasons more compelling than character and ability should give preferment to the less able.

In recent decades, ignoring the idea of a meritocracy and a

business planned and built around the best people has been made easier by the notion that business, left to its own devices, lives in a happy state of nature. Propaganda has it that business must be left undisturbed to develop "naturally" without "outside interference," etc. Left alone, business will grow, business will create the necessary number of jobs, and so forth, according to a metaphor vaguely drawn from biology. Without guidance, certainly without planning, the DNA of the free market system puts a chicken in every pot.

Neither America nor business came into existence by mindless adherence to human nature or by virtue of the laws of social zoology. With its written constitution, compared to Britain's unwritten, evolved constitution, America was an intentional, a planned country, replete with a planned capital city. The same with business. It was invented by a small group of men whose names we know as well as we know those who signed the Declaration of Independence. Business didn't just happen. It was made to happen. It was intended, designed, planned.

To make it happen the American character had to be reshaped and modified, American culture changed and redesigned. Time itself was remade to conform to operational needs of business. Until business standardized it for its own scheduling purposes, time was chosen by the people who lived it in a particular community. In the prebusiness era there were sometimes three, sometimes six clocks, each with their hands pointing to different places on the dial, in the same railroad station. On November 18, 1883, the great variety of local times in the United States was abolished and standard time became everybody's time. The *Indianapolis Sentinel,* ambivalently sniffing at the new civilization aborning, gave way with the complaint that, "People will have to marry by railroad time, and die by railroad time. Ministers will be required to preach by railroad time, banks will open and close by railroad time, in fact the Railroad Convention has taken charge of the time business, and the people may as well set about adjusting their affairs in accordance with its decree."[1] Not coincidentally, it was in the 1880s that Richard Sears started his business with Mr. Roebuck. Their first, and for a time, their only item of merchandise was watches, which they sold by the thousands. Also not coinciden-

tally, in that day before the government had instituted rural free delivery and parcel post, the Sears packages containing the watches were sent express to be picked up by their purchasers at the offices of the thousands of railroad freight agents in the whistle stops across America.

B.C.'s old friend Tom Watson, having been sacked by the eccentric Patterson from National Cash Register, came to head the company which made the machine which got people to the daily grindstone on time. His C-T-R Company* was the largest manufacturer of time clocks, but some people didn't always take easily to working by the clock. The efficiency experts who arrived on the scene in the 1890s sometimes touched off strikes by workers who refused to "go under the watch."[2]

But a nation, staggered by the accelerating rate of change for the better, accommodated itself. Today, we are brought up to be thankful for tiny, incremental improvements; we live in a time of modest hopes and crumbling expectations. We have begun to debate exactly how much poorer we're getting and how fast the process of impoverishment may be proceeding. If businessmen then often made themselves hideous by practices which brought on terrible strikes and inexcusable misery, they were forgiven for it because they were paving the streets with gold. Actually, they were beginning to pave the streets, as they manufactured so much wealth that the nation, which had spent titanic sums on building a railroad system which was the admiration of the world, now set about building a second transportation system, one based on the internal combustion engine.

In 1895 *The Scientific American* thought automobiles would be a long time in coming to the United States because there were so few usable roads to drive them on.[3] In the century's early years only seven percent of the nation's roads were paved, mostly in gravel. Probably not more than a couple of hundred miles of roads were suitable to drive a car on. *Good Roads Magazine*, the voice of the League of American Wheelmen (people who rode bicycles), tried to do something about the mud and ruts, but it was motor car builders and drivers, doing things like holding Good Roads Conventions, who began to get things changed. Nevertheless, the roads improved only because count-

* For Computing—Tabulating—Recording.

less individuals went out and improved them. In the early years of the century, for instance, the American Motor League gave its members the wherewithal to tack up danger signs on any available post. Other groups were out erecting directional signs along the nearly impassable country roads.[4] In the early teens people banded together to form the Lincoln Highway Association, the road which became transcontinental U.S. Route 30. To mark the highway of their dreams, people painted red, white and blue stripes on telephone poles, the sides of barns, trees or any other suitable upright object.

How they did what they did defies facile explanation but from 1904, when the car population of the United States was about eight thousand, people built a new universe. Sixteen years later, there were more than eight million cars puttering around. In the interim new forms of road surfacing were invented, plus the machines to use the materials, the automobile insurance industry was created, not to mention over thirteen thousand garages, each with at least one somewhat trained mechanic, and each stocked with spare parts or able to obtain them. Modern gasoline refining had to be invented and, as important, a distribution network to make it available universally also had to be called into existence.[5] No accomplishment of American business is more astonishing than the rapidity and thoroughness of the national distribution systems which make a commodity universally available across the great land mass which is the United States. The generation which lived through the changes and helped make them understood these things did not happen because some people chanted, "Hocus, pocus, free marketosis!" Free markets are necessary, but business and business organization, which are not the same, are more important.

Walk through the supermarket in any mall and wonder what prodigies of organization and coordination bring this richness to us every day of the year. The Russians have the same technology we do. They can and do make refrigerators, but they lack the social organizations, what we call businesses, to provide the necessities and the luxuries. They stand in line waiting, while we open the glass front of a freezer case and take out food which has been harvested weeks or months before, in fields a thousand miles away. We expect it, we assume it, we have only

the fuzziest idea of how it was done, and less interest in learning more because for us it is automatic.

During the 1920s what was called the "winter diet" disappeared. A Muncie, Indiana, housewife recalled the diet's contents: "Steaks, roasts, macaroni, Irish potatoes, sweet potatoes, turnips, cole slaw, fried apples, and stewed tomatoes, with Indian pudding, rice, cake, or pie for dessert. This was the winter repertoire of the average family . . . we swapped about from one combination to another, using pickles and chow-chow . . . We never thought of having fresh fruit or green vegetables and could not have got them if we had." People came down with "spring sickness," for which they took tonics and other medicaments to thin blood made thick by the heavy winter eating. The most prescribed remedy for the ravages of the winter diet was salad when at last greens became available.[6]

The transportation and distribution system of the 1890s wasn't up for bringing California greens to Muncie, but thirty years later the winter diet was memory, and *Forbes* magazine was carrying a piece about Clarence Birdseye, and the test marketing of his frozen foods in Springfield, Massachusetts.[7] We take it for granted in the 1990s, but a system by which food is kept frozen virtually from the field where it is picked to the microwave oven is exceedingly complicated to put together. Manufacture and sales of just one part of that chain, home refrigerators, jumped, leaped, zoomed or bounded[8]—one of those growth words—by hundreds of percents per year through the twenties and the Depression years so that it was not long before Mr. Birdseye's miraculous process for food preservation became commonplace among middle-level Americans. It was hard work, year by year improvements, not miracles which got frozen food in the home. An up-to-date 1922 wood refrigerator with the latest in water cooled-compressor and a brine tank, weighing three quarters of a ton, sold for close to a dollar a pound. Because the coolant in these machines was sulfur dioxide or something worse, they were often kept on the back porch lest a leak kill the whole family. They were too dangerous for hospital use, even on the back porch. By the end of the decade refrigerators were half the size, half the price and safe to put in the kitchen.[9] By dint of unceasing application, the way the Japanese of today are said to bring a product to market, this

one was made better and cheaper until almost everyone could have one.

The string of accomplishments which brought America from the winter diet to green veggies, frozen and fresh, the entire year is minimized by the very propaganda intended to glorify what has been done.

From the start, business's impact on individuals, families and community life was as great, if not greater, than the change caused by the switch-over from monarchy to democracy. The individualist, the independent-minded, had to be melted and recast as the obedient employee. The pioneer types had to be broken to the saddle of business organization, and it didn't come easy. Some of the first railroad strikes, the most serious of which occurred on McCallum's Erie, were called by men who didn't take kindly to being bossed around and told to the inch exactly how high to jump and to the second when to do the jumping.

McCallum's system had scarcely been devised when in 1855 the National Protective Association of the Locomotive Engineers of the United States was started to resist "the blind system requiring implicit obedience" instituted by the Erie's superintendent. The association's call to arms asked the aggrieved free spirits of the pioneer age, "Shall we longer submit to the tyrannical will of a few men who strive to aggrandize themselves and build themselves up the title of 'Napoleons' and 'Able Managers' by grinding down the pay and trying to suppress our rights as a free and independent class of men for the purpose of adding to their already enormous salaries for their 'Able Management'?"[10]

Some of the Locomotive Engineers' statement sounds like contemporary sentiment. The unhappiness about the lowness of their own salaries, the indignation at the highness of those of the top managers, that is still with us. The sneering about management's ability to do its job, however, is only occasionally heard outside of investment circles today. The modern manager's untested claims of competence are accepted by a wider public in the face of acts of the grossest idiocy. High-level foul-ups are passed over by pliant Boards of Directors while the supine business sections of the newspapers raise nary a question until the lawyers are on their way over to the courthouse to file

the bankruptcy papers.[11] On television all business executives are globe-bestriding giants, endowed with a wisdom and clairvoyance matched only by Emmy and Oscar award winners. Outside of the nation's President, and, of course, First Ladies and Gentlemen of Screen and Tube, i.e., senior stars about to get lifetime-achievement Oscars, the only other people who are customarily addressed as Mister on television are the presidents of large corporations when they appear on the monitor to give the check to the winner of a golf tournament. Everybody else is Frankie First Name.

No, umbrage is not taken at the deportment of our corporate Bonapartes. The CEO ethos concedes capricious, lascivious, spendthrift behavior to the company's supreme boss. Not all CEOs internalize the CEO ethos. There's many a man running an important corporation who's got his head screwed on straight and his values up and in proper running order; they're not all madmen, and not all the madmen are completely mad. Some of the CEOs who best exemplify the ethos at its most revulsive are excellent at their work, and if they steal the stockholders' money to lavish perks on themselves, they nevertheless make so much money, few complaints are heard about high living in the executive suite. Many of the powerful men of business history, Alfred Sloan of General Motors, Julius Rosenwald of Sears, Roebuck or John D. Rockefeller, once easily the most hated man in America, betook little or nothing of the CEO ethos.

It is a mixed picture, but according unquestioned power to men for long periods of time seldom ennobles them. It may corrupt some more than others, but on balance the CEO ethos is destructive to the health and wealth of a society which prospers by being a little dull and rigidly middle class. There is a reason the Swiss are so rich, and it isn't because they've struck oil in the Alps.

The CEO ethos goes to more than using the company to give bonbons to your mistress. It goes to the varied effects it can have on the organization which the top executive is charged with nurturing. This is a matter of utmost concern to the stockholders, the employees and the communities in which the company is based, but a CEO is also a trustee for the society. These organizations, these companies, these corporations and pro-

tected partnerships, they provide the nation with its wherewithal. They starve, we starve, they prosper, we prosper. Everyone has a stake in their well-being, which is why, in the end,
there is no such thing as private enterprise. It's all public.

The CEO ethos invites a company takeover by a corporate
reincarnation of Mad Ludwig of Bavaria.[12] The place becomes
suffused by capricious craziness. In its extreme manifestations
the craziness may take any form. In the 1960s C. Arnholt Smith,
presiding tyrant at the late U.S. National Bank in San Diego,
and for years that city's most powerful figure, had a thing for
beige. The bank, his car, his wife's hair, his clothes, everything
was done in beige.[13] In the end Mr. Smith went to the penitentiary and the bank to ruins.

CEO Armand Hammer, now seated in the big boardroom in
the sky, spent fifty million dollars of Occidental Petroleum's
money on a museum which he named after himself.[14] After
Peter Cohen was installed by Jimmy Three Sticks as the CEO of
American Express's Shearson stock brokerage subsidiary, the
Mad Ludwig distemper hit him and his wife. The usual jet airplanes were purchased, but the Ludwigian touch was having
one of the jets' interior wallpapered in Ultrasuede, which the
flight attendants were required to brush regularly to keep it
looking perky.† A different wrinkle was the twenty-five-million-
dollar conference center at Beaver Creek, Colorado. Mrs. Cohen, having learned how to play Queen Ludwiga, looked out
the conference center window one day and was disturbed to see
the Swiss chalets of other CEOs. To screen out the view of the
offending edifices she ordered up a small forest of fully grown
evergreens.[15] After Mad Bob Campeau of the Campeau Corporation, since gone into Chapter 11 bankruptcy, the land of the
living dead for insolvent companies, had one of his break-
downs, he put the boss head shrinker at the clinic where he was
treated on his Board of Directors.[16] Corporate Ludwigs put the

---

† Indeed it is often the smaller extravagances which betray the strength and breadth
of the craziness encouraged by the CEO ethos. This from the *New York Times* of September 7, 1990, is self-explanatory: "The Gannett Foundation, a non-profit organization
that supports journalism education, said yesterday that it used less than $40,000 of its
money to buy about 2,000 copies of an autobiography of its flamboyant chairman, Allen
H. Neuharth, the former chairman and chief executive of the Gannett Company communications conglomerate." Neuharth, who ran the foundation, pulled this trick, not
for the money, but for the ego satisfaction of seeing his book on the bestseller lists.

damnedest people on the boards as whim, ego and whatever else tickles their fancy.

The shrink, the mistress, the helicopter which takes the children to their piano lessons and their orthodontist, the vacation homes in the principal glamour cities of the world, it's on the expense account. In addition to the usual yacht, etc., the *New York Times*, September 25, 1989, reported that Thomson McKinnon, another Wall Street outfit long since gone ge-thunk, "paid school tuition for the 13 children of a former chairman, John J. Maloney Jr." The company pays for it, so eat your oysters and drink your champagne.

Malcolm cashed in for some publicity on the expense account joke when the newspapers said he set one of those "records" at auction by paying seventy thousand dollars for a document described as Paul Revere's 1774 "expense account," incurred in a journey to New York on behalf of the Sons of Liberty. Malcolm said that expressed in modern money, Midnight Paul took the revolution for about a two-hundred-thousand-dollar ride.[17] Everybody cheats, everybody does a little creative accounting on the old swindle sheet. The fuddy-duddy Founding Fathers were just like us CEOs, chiseling what didn't belong to them. All in good fun, boys, not really stealing.

The shape of American corporate enterprise had not been fully achieved when the CEO ethos was already up and running. Grasshopper executives were chewing up the greenery as early as the 1870s; locustlike behavior is not an aberration of the 1980s, but conduct built into the corporate culture at the basement level.

Ludwigism commences with the Erie Railroad, after Daniel McCallum left it. The railroad's comptroller, Jim Fisk, arranged to have the Erie buy Pike's Opera House at Twenty-third Street and Eighth Avenue in New York City as a corporate headquarters. Next came the Gilded Age expression of the Ultrasuede wallpaper spirit. By contemporary account, "It is unequalled in elegance by any building in the world used for a similar purpose. The doors are of massive, elegantly carved black walnut, all the offices are fitted up and furnished in black walnut and the most expensive glass . . . All the ceilings are richly frescoed, that in the main room being an elegant symbolic design having at the four sides of the world New York, San Francisco,

Chicago, St. Louis. On the floor above is a grand banqueting room (read executive dining room) fitted up in the same style splendor . . . Here, surrounded by all the luxury which his taste and wealth can devise he leads a much more lordly and imperial life than many a modern Prince, and in his sumptuous halls may well be called 'Prince Erie.' "[18]

Although Fisk had a wife in Boston, he set off the first corporate sex scandal by the number and visibility of the young women partying in the opera house offices of the railroad. Circulating the city were stories of sex orgies, at which the half-naked girls ate oysters and drank champagne sent over from Delmonico's, a restaurant where Fisk dared not appear with women lest he be shown the door and not let back into New York's premier eating establishment. In later decades any breach of morals committed by a CEO, regardless of how taste-less and offensive, came to be ignored but not in that era. Nevertheless the Prince of Erie set up his main squeeze, Josie Mansfield, in a fine house less than a block from corporate headquarters. There was no end to Fisk's ostentatious extrava-gances—the gold-lined coach, the stables where he had in-stalled canaries to sing to his fifteen prize carriage horses.

Given the absolutism already built into the management of business organizations, Fisk was establishing the principle that top officers can do whatever they have a mind to do. The stock-holders filed suit, and in their petition they stated objections which would be repeated again by other angry stockholders for a century and more into the future:

". . . it is injurious to the business of said corporation to have its offices in a building which in part is almost nightly occupied for operatic and dramatic performances; that the fre-quenting of said building and its approaches by the large num-ber of young clerks in the employment of said Company, and by opera and theater women at the same time, and the musical and dancing rehearsal by day, with the tread of ballet girls and the echoes of operas and song, and of all sorts of string and wind instruments resounding in said building, within hearing and almost within sight of numerous young clerks at their desks . . . are demoralizing to said young men, destructive of the interests of said Company, and without a parallel in rail-road history . . . [Such hijinks on the premises] caused to be so con-

fused and mingled in the thoughts and associations, especially of the New-York clerks . . . the ideas of 'Erie' and 'Grand Opera,' of work and amusement, of ballet girls and operatic spectacles, with trains, telegraphs and time tables, as to impair the sense of duty, and to injure the business efficiency of said clerks and employees, and in the good repute of said Company."[19]

Today Fisk's conduct would be called sending the wrong message—the wrong message to would-be investors, to customers and to employees who take their cues from their superiors. Hence the news that a present-day company, Time Warner, eleven billion dollars in debt at the time, had seven airplanes, and a disputed number of retreats in Acapulco and Aspen did something less than inspire confidence in the management. Nor did it help when *Business Week* accused CEO Steven J. Ross of getting almost eighty million dollars in compensation in one year,[20] an allegation which set off much clucking and pecking among Mr. Ross' defenders, who insisted that their leader was only guilty of being recompensed half as much. Pay packages for big shots like Ross are so fog shrouded in complication that people make their living being experts on "executive compensation." One such at Time Warner-owned *Fortune* magazine resigned his connection claiming the higher-ups were trying to hide the real dimensions of Ross' pay.[21]

From a distance Ross came across as the epitome of the willful, self-indulgent, deal-making CEO, nervously fearful of the world knowing what he was doing, but determined to continue his incontestably legal pillage. At each step he behaved like a man without a loincloth whose frontal, financial nudity had been caught by the celebrity-stalking paparazzi. He exuded a slinky shame, as he stood slightly crouched in the night, the light bulbs popping, clutching an attaché case containing fresh bundles of bank-wrapped money. He had nothing else with which to cover himself until his limousine came, and leaping bare-assed into the back, was taken off into the darkness.

Fisk made Donald Trump and Lee Iacocca look like a couple of shrinking violets with his loves, his battles in the countinghouse and his brawls on the streets. A simple visit to a friend was a showstopper when it was Big Jim Fisk who was doing the visiting, as this passage from George Templeton Strong's diary for January 10, 1871, tells us: "He made calls in a gorgeous

chariot drawn by four high-stepping horses, with four smart footmen in flamboyant liveries. When he stopped before any favored house, his mamelukes descended, unrolled a carpet, laid it before the carriage steps to the door, and stood on either side in an attitude of military salute, while their august master passed by."

The self-advertising businessman goes back to Phineas T. Barnum and must include Malcolm among its numbers. Usually such men make their megalomania work for them. The Donald Trump road show brought endless satisfaction to the show's impresario but it also convinced the bankers that Trump could, with his self-advertising charisma (a vogue word near the end of its run), increase the value of anything he touched by simply touching it. With Fisk, we'll never know when it was whim and carnality and when he was playing his deeper game. A self-made man who started off as a Vermont peddler, he hooked up with the textile manufacturer Jordan Marsh. With the help of yet another lady, a certain Lottie Hough, Fisk smuggled quantities of cotton through the Confederate battle lines to make Union coats and britches before he left Boston for New York. It may not have made this man, who loved to dress up in garish army and navy uniforms, a hero, but it muddies the picture a little. At the Erie Railroad his partner, and antithesis in deportment and personality, was Jay Gould, who comes down to us as Mr. Nineteenth Century Rapax personified. The prototypical robber baron, perhaps, but there was more to Gould's schemes than simple plunder, although, heaven knows, he did that with a verve and nerve which make the modern Milkens and the Kravises look like pedestrian cutpurses. In addition to enjoyment, Big Jim Fisk's wenching and carrying on in the limelight may also have been intended to distract while Gould's plots were set afoot in the dark.

We'll never know, because, if Fisk was playing a double game, so also was Josie Mansfield. She had another boyfriend, Edward Stokes, who came out from behind a pillar at the Grand Central Hotel and fired a revolver into the body of the flamboyant millionaire, who died the next day. The funeral was spectacular, including in the cortege a large representation from Tammany Hall, the 9th National Guard Regiment and a two-hundred-piece marching band. Fisk had been what no other American

businessman ever quite succeeded in becoming and that was a genuine popular hero. He managed—God knows how—to endow himself with a certain Jesse James-like quality. They sang songs in saloons about the man after his death:[22]

> I'll sing of a man who's now dead in his grave,
>   as good man as ever was born.
> Jim Fisk he was call'd, and his money he gave,
>   to the outcast, the poor and forlorn.
> We all know he lov'd both women and wine,
>   but his heart it was right I am sure.
> Though he lived like a prince in his palace
>   so fine,
> Yet he never went back on the poor.[23]

In doing so much to create the CEO ethos, Fisk set the precedent of including sex in the job description, should a man care to have it. A lot did. The rules for enjoying corporate *droit du seigneur* were easy enough. The CEO buys young flesh; most men buy young girl flesh; the minority buy young boy flesh.

In the modern era few lived out the CEO ethos as well as Robert Fomon, the top man at E. F. Hutton in the years before the Wall Street brokerage firm was engulfed in scandal and disappeared as an independent business entity. "Every older man likes young girls. I'm just honest enough to admit it," this business leader, who definitely could be put in the girl flesh category, told a magazine writer, and then the magazine's photographer shot pictures of Fomon holding a teddy bear as two highly female persons of the kind once routinely described as young things posed with him. Lest there be doubt about the scope of his interests, Fomon, who had once been married to Miss America 1956, explained that, "Basically, I'm very shallow when it comes to women . . . I don't want every dinner conversation to be about what people think of Muammar Qaddafi."

Whatever he may have wanted to hear about at dinner with his popsies, it was next to impossible to discuss anything with this casebook Mad Ludwig in his office because of the two Catalina macaws flying around the room on their three-foot-long wings, screaming "Shit, shit, shit!" at his visitors when his two feathered menaces weren't taking a bite out of their legs. The birds had room for aerial maneuvers in Fomon's two-story-high

office, one of only twelve taking up a whole twenty-eighth floor of the company's skyscraper headquarters. To give Fomon his due, some of the space on the floor was used for other purposes —for nine private dining rooms.

"I've never once seen the man sober," a banker on the Street remarked while another business acquaintance observed at the time if Fomon had "had as much interest in his company as he did in his libido or his own bank account, all three would be in better shape today." The CEO ethos being what it is, Mad Ludwig with his macaws kept his job for seventeen years. After the company was reduced to a smoking ruin, Fomon, babes, booze, birds and all, was eased out the door, and E. F. Hutton & Company was sold. To whom? To Jimmy Three Sticks and Peter Cohen. Who else? These organizations are passed around from one Ludwig to another.[24]

The billions pissed away in grandiose and useless corporate headquarters would go a long way toward paying for an entirely new and up-to-date American industrial plant. Thomson McKinnon, another Wall Street firm, spent six hundred sixty million dollars for offices it never occupied. That alone is two thirds of a billion bucks. Stories like it could be repeated *ad nauseam*. At the same time some want a special, low tax to encourage what they call "capital formation," that is getting people to invest money in companies to reequip themselves. With CEOs like Robert Fomon in charge, I leave it to your imagination—assuming you have a good one—to guess how that capital formation money will get spent.

Corporate America might think about initiating an annual award for outstanding CEO performances à la the Oscar or the Pulitzer. The statue could be called the Turkey or the Ludwig. The categories might include Year's Best Priapic Performance, Year's Most Off-the-Wall Act of Caprice, Year's Most Expensive Self-Indulgent Purchase, Most Indefensible Compensation Package, Largest Loss of Market Share, Twelve-Month Period, Most Preposterous Rationalization, and the reader is invited to join with his or her own suggestions. To such as these the jobs of millions and the prosperity of tens of millions are entrusted.

Some men use the casting couch in their executive suites, some don't. Malcolm didn't, and although he was not above putting the make on a handsome young man on the staff from

time to time, a refusal to comply with his desires wasn't a career-ending decision. If the topmost jobs at *Forbes* go to people by virtue of the accident of birth, in general promotions in the organization went, during Malcolm's sway and B.C.'s, to those who could cut the mustard on the job, not in the bed.[25]

Part of the CEO ethos is the protection afforded these men, which may or may not dampen the demoralization that knowledge of libertine behavior can cause an organization. In any event Malcolm came to a better end than another heir, Marshall Field II, who was murdered by a prostitute in 1906 in what was then possibly the fanciest, certainly the most famous whorehouse in America, Chicago's Everleigh Club. The murder of the son of the founder of the vast retail enterprise remained an unpublished fact for eighteen years until it was mentioned in the *Chicago Daily News* in 1924.[26] It is a rare CEO whose ethos is so badly cracked that news of his conduct gets out and it actually costs him.

Occasionally the partaking of the kingly latitude conferred on one by the CEO ethos will do a CEO in. During the course of running the Bendix Corporation into oblivion, its CEO, William Agee, got involved with a woman named Mary Cunningham, whom he ultimately married. As business columnist Allan Sloan wrote, "Little more than a year after hiring Cunningham, Agee had gotten a divorce, ending some twenty-two years of marriage, and had moved into an apartment across the hall from Mary Cunningham. He was spending a great deal of time with her; they went to lunch together on most days and often arrived at work together and left together. Executives began to complain that Mary Cunningham was blocking their access to Agee. And Agee promoted her twice—first to vice president of corporate and public relations, a position for which she had no apparent qualification, and later to vice president of strategic planning, a job for which she had only her Harvard Business School degree as qualification."[27] The mafia appoints a *consigliare* to sit by the don's side and whisper, "Hey, Don, you're actin' like a jerk." A Roman general riding in his chariot of gold while being accorded his triumph, the classical version of a ticker tape parade, had a slave perched behind him whispering in his ear, "Remember, you too will die." The CEO has nobody to rein him in, so that, with the aid of his vice president of

strategic planning, Agee put his own company in the ashcan in an attempt at a hostile takeover of another corporation. When it comes to bringing off a disaster, you can't beat a combination of pride, stupidity and willfulness. In the end Bendix was eaten alive by a shark with a slightly larger brain, but Agee made out just fine, walking away with the customary bundle.[28]

The combination of unbridled power and unrestrained self-indulgence has the same effect on a CEO as it does on a politician. Some CEOs have a direct power to help or harm which few elected officials have; politicians are under ceaseless pressure to make public what they do and explain it. The great CEOs seldom are. They are able to enjoy their power and their luxuries unquestioned, flattered and glorified. Like members of Congress, they can go forever, and the longer they're in, the more arrogant and irrational they become.

Something like that happened to J. P. Morgan, the elder, the single most important investment banker in the nation's history.‡ Lincoln Steffens, the muckraking journalist of the pre-World War I decade, called him simply "the boss of the United States." B.C. told this story by way of illustrating the orbit described by J. P. Morgan in the solar system of money and power: "I am reminded of a reply the late Charles S. Mellen, then president of the New Haven Railroad, gave Interstate Commerce Commission probers when he was asked if the late Mr. Morgan always sat at the head of the table at directors meetings. 'Where Macgregor sits is the head of the table,' flashed back Mellen, with a knowing twinkle of his eyes."[29]

J. P. Morgan, with his red, bulbous nose, his laser beam eyes, his silk plug hat and wing collar, the stately avoirdupois of his tummy swathed in a waistcoat and wrapped in a gold watch chain, was the model of the Money Trust cartoon figure. Dr. Dollar Sign, Mr. Evil Wall Street incarnate. There were times in J.P.'s long career when he earned his money and served his

‡ Investment banker is the vainglorious name for someone who raises money which is lent to others to buy businesses or improve the ones they already have. Sometimes this is done by straight loans, sometimes by selling bonds and sometimes, not by loans, but by selling shares in the business, that is selling stock. However the arrangement, the investment banker makes a fee off each transaction and, when doing the job with due diligence and a modicum of morals, makes a useful contribution. Putting together in one pot wads and wads of money needed to start a business or help it expand is the lord's work.

country, his clients and himself with profit and honor; however, like J. Edgar Hoover or Fidel Castro or half the members of Congress, the fierce old pirate hung on too long in the job.

As befitting the corsair he fancied himself descended from, Morgan was considered to be one of the great swordsmen of his day. The white-shoed financial and social world was full of stories of Morgan in Paris visiting the *bijouteries* with his chorus girl, lady friends, dropping handfuls of gems into their furry muffs. The talk of the town was that Morgan put up the land and the money to build New York Lying-In Hospital for the bastards he sired. At the same time, Morgan was a crazed Episcopalian who could be espied rocketing about the country going to ecclesiastic conferences in his private railroad car in the company of a nave of bishops.[30] It is something to imagine, Mr. Money Bags rattling along in luxury, everybody drinking champagne, the clergymen chanting their high church psalmodies at one end of the car and les girls singing whatever it might be they sung at the other.

If it came to pass that J. P. Morgan, aka Macgregor, reached a point when the laws of God and the customs of man no longer seemed to apply to him as they did to others, the cause was the indulgences his money, power and success brought him. In the end it affected his business judgment, bringing a plague down on New England by saddling the region of his birth with a decrepit, half-bankrupt and dangerously inadequate transportation system. In the 1890s Morgan, who had long played a large and positive part in railroading, got control of the New Haven line. It has been suspected this had less to do with business than that New Haven was his hometown and New England the region he had the greatest affection for. Whatever his reasons, using the New Haven line as his base, he went on a merger and acquisition kick of the kind we are familiar with, in order to achieve a regional transportation monopoly. His motive seems to have been a desire to provide the region with an up-to-date, efficient and profitable transportation system; what he succeeded in bringing forth was an antiquated, accident-prone, money loser. He paid too much for coastal steamship lines and interurban trolleys à la many a modern counting-house genius. Having assumed the office of executive vice president to the Episcopalian God, the only socially acceptable di-

vinity, Morgan acted as though his lowering look and mighty will could overcome the ineluctable truth contained in the books and balance sheets of these enterprises. On the occasion of the purchase of one useless Westchester County, New York, trolley line, which went from no place in White Plains to no place in the South Bronx, he apparently wouldn't look at the books and wouldn't listen to those who had. The property was bought at a ruinously high price, and the same thing happened to the railroad then which has happened to so many merger and acquisition victims in our time. It couldn't generate enough income to pay for such purchases. Christmas 1913, a few months after Morgan's death and after one hundred and thirty consecutive quarters of paying a dividend on its stock, the New York, New Haven and Hartford missed its one hundred and thirty-first.[31] The injury to New England prosperity owing to a struggling and inefficient transportation system cannot be calculated. Writing of the hundred million dollars in junk bonds issued by what B. C. Forbes called "the Morgan-Mellen regime that brought the road to disaster," Malcolm's father thought that, "It might be legal but it would not be ethical for J. P. Morgan & Company" to wiggle out of standing behind the company. Fat chance, with the old man dead and J.P., Jr., whom B.C. had said in print was decidedly not a chip off the old block, in charge of running things at the bank which bore the family name.[32]

A comparable instance of modern megalomania was the seizure of Trans World Airlines by Carl Icahn, an especially unappetizing Wall Street dude. A man said to be worth something in the neighborhood of two billions (as a reminder, one billion = one thousand million), his reputation as a stingy bastard is so well known stories about his miserliness make it between the covers of books: "When Icahn, carrying a briefcase, and his uncle, Schnall, carrying an umbrella, go to a restaurant together, Schnall takes Icahn's briefcase so that they don't have to leave more than one tip for the checkroom attendant."[33] This is the grand and good man who is said to have attempted an academic version of one of his greenmail* heists on Prince-

* Greenmail is money paid as a premium to somebody to sell his holdings in a company. It is paid to people regarded as too disruptive, destructive and threatening to safely own stock in the company. Men like Icahn whom other businessmen regard as

ton University when he told the school he would give it a chunk o' money if it would put him on the board. Evidently he confused the place with a copper mine or a Wall Street boiler shop, though perhaps Princeton deserves such treatment for an uncommon number of business brutes graduate from the place.

The university resisted being taken over by Mr. Icahn, an experience that others have likened to rape. After swooping down on the Dan River, Inc., textile company, and making a takeover swipe at it, a bruised resident of Danville, Virginia, where the company was based, declared, "Icahn has raped this community."[34] There are no support groups for those on whom the icon of financial rapine has forced himself. For confirmation check with the survivors at Ozark Airlines, swallowed up by Mr. Icahn, who abolished its pension plans, pocketed twenty-six million dollars and canceled the retired pilots' cost of living increase.[35]

Unlike J. P. Morgan, who kept his jaws clamped shut in public unless pried open by congressional subpoena, Icahn, who had never run so much as a hot dog stand, went about the nation telling all who would listen that he did what he did to purge companies of bad managers. He could sound like a Methodist street corner preacher when he got going on the cause of business's problems: ". . . bad management . . . The directors who chose these chief executives seem to study from a primer titled *In Search of Mediocrity*. All this makes a modern chief executive much like a feudal baron. He has a retinue, though the courtiers are more likely to be fawning MBAs than squires, and the symbols of power are jets and yachts instead of horses or castles . . . What to do? Layers of bureaucrats reporting to bureaucrats must end. Corporate staffers must deal directly with workers on the line. To accomplish this, senior management must be accountable to the true owners."[36] This cock of the walk doodle-dooed that ". . . if we can turn around a couple of these companies and make them more productive, that will make a statement about what I've been saying. Economic historians will see that I was proven correct."[37]

It remains to be seen if historians will say anything about him since he is a member of a class of alligators who so closely re-

---

being financially HIV positive made a lot of money out of the greenmail racket in the previous decade.

semble each other it is not worth the trouble to single one out for special attention, but by 1991 *The Wall Street Journal* was ready to pass judgment on his stewardship of Trans World Airlines. The newspaper concluded that he had all but wrecked the company, that the executives in charge of everything from airplane maintenance to finance had walked out on him to be replaced by his pals, who knew as much about running an airline as he did; the paper said that his cheapskate ways had left this once important and profitable part of the nation's transportation network with a fleet of wheezing, high-maintenance, antique airliners and a devastated organization to run them. Living up to his reputation as an abrasive business brute, the man, according to the newspaper, turned up at a dinner honoring outstanding airline employees and gave the crowd such a tongue lashing that some of the guests of honor left the dining room in tears.[38] Icahn, who had pulled hundreds of millions out of the airline and left it too heavy with debt to sustain flight, disputed *The Wall Street Journal*'s allegations, but within three months gave himself the lie when he announced he was working out plans to put TWA into bankruptcy. So much for the braggadocio of a Wall Street sharpie who thought you don't have to know your business to run your business. Like Morgan before him he nets out a big, fat minus.

# SEVEN

---

# The Great
# Begatsby

THE MEN WHO LED the merger and takeover charge in the past fifteen years, and then raised the money to pay for it by peddling bucket shop bonds to the innocent, claimed that they were goat glands for impotent old corporations. Out went stodgy and stolid management, they said, and in came new people to run the place, to use their lingo, lean and mean. Accurate enough. By the time men like Icahn had done with a company it was so lean it was down to the last bit of meat on the bones, and as for mean, the plundered pension funds, the canceled medical programs, the jobs lost, the production lost, the profits lost, the benefits, material and social, lost, that's mingy mean, nasty mean, bitter cold and freezing mean. Everywhere these men put their feet down, they left a mess.

A person with a Wall Street background doesn't have to make a mess, but the person must know that stock market cunning doesn't endow one with competence. E. H. Harriman, the little

social-climbing arriviste, whom the Great Morgan couldn't abide, got into the railroad business by taking over what would be the equivalent of a commuter airline today, a little New York State railroad, teetering near bankruptcy. Instead of stripping it of what few assets it had left, Harriman fixed it up and sold it at a profit. The quote by Harriman is a little stuffy, but it reveals something Icahn has yet to learn: "My experience with this railroad taught me a lesson with respect to the importance of the physical condition in a transportation property which I have never forgotten."[1] He went on gaining control of larger and larger lines until finally he had the Illinois Central and the Union Pacific. Each one he improved and perfected and made profitable, and if that did not make him a nice boy, and you could find a lot of people who didn't think he was, it made him valuable to the nation.

In some ways Icahn, though he cut wages and blew misery into the lives of his employees, was one of the classier takeover artists. He at least tried to run the company, although it turned out he wasn't as smart or knowledgeable as he thought. If he demonstrated anew it takes more than being an idiot savant with computer printouts to run an airline, he didn't put himself and all his relatives on the payroll at preposterous salaries, vote himself non-interest loans or use the company treasury to equip himself with the yacht and the jet. Icahn was restrained compared to Victor Posner, who got his hands on the Fischbach Corporation, made himself Chairman of the Board and walked in the company's office once in four years.[2]

The trail of companies disemboweled by Posner is too long for recitation here, but no good turn goes unrewarded. Posner, like Icahn, was a man not known for his generosity, so it was only fitting that when he was convicted of tax evasion it was for falsely overstating the value of property donated to a college. *Fortune* magazine, April 11, 1988, reported that Posner, sentenced to dishing out meals at a flophouse, was asked by one derelict passing through the line, "Can I shake your hand? I've never shaken the hand of a millionaire."

Even so, Icahn and Posner have certain things in common. Icahn is reputed to be a solid family man, and Posner, a convicted felon, famous in financial circles for his taste for teenage

**113**

girls, were both associates of Michael Milken, who later became a convicted felon. They both can wreck a company, although Icahn is less spectacular in that regard. Financial writer Allan Sloan once said that, "Letting Victor Posner take over a company is like unleashing Dracula in a blood bank."[3] But whether or not one's Giorgio Armani is splattered with bits of bone and brain, the damage to the nation is the same. Icahn was at the controls when Trans World Airlines crashed, and Posner damaged Fischbach nigh unto death, for its survival as a much diminished organization is still in doubt at this writing.[4] When Posner got his hands on it, with help from his criminal friends, Fischbach was the largest electrical and mechanical engineering company in the United States. Making money for its stockholders, providing jobs, it was also performing a richly needed service, unless one believes power plants and factories and office buildings, all of which Fischbach did the engineering for, will pop up by themselves if one sits under a New Age crystal long enough. You don't have to be a stockholder to be injured by men like Icahn and Posner, you only have to be an American.

Richard Whitney, a brother of one of the Morgan partners, went to the penitentiary in the 1930s for Boesky-Milken-type crimes. That was long after the old man's death. J. P. Morgan, the elder, was not the business associate of men who would be adjudged criminals; he was also openhandedly generous in his benefactions to cultural and educational institutions. Nevertheless, like Icahn, he had his TWAs; he had his failures, his New York, New Haven and Hartford, but he had his successes, his great years too, and while waxing randy and rich he performed a valuable and necessary service to the nation.

With J.P. in New York and his father, Junius, in London, the Morgan company arranged for the placement of hundreds of millions of dollars by British investors in America to pay for building the railroads. The same service was performed by Jacob Schiff of Kuhn, Loeb & Company for German and Swiss investors. (Schiff and J.P. were alike in bringing an ethical standard of some sort to their business transactions and in their philanthropies.) Doubtless the railroads would have been built without what these men did, but the work would have proceeded much more slowly.

From 1875 forward it seemed as though Morgan was in-

volved in every deal, if it was a big one. Some of the deals involved B.C.'s pal, Charlie Schwab. It was Charlie in a pinch-me-I'm-dreaming moment who made the speech which started the U.S. Steel Corporation. December 1, 1900, at the University Club, and Charlie was the guest of honor at a dinner which included a fair percentage of the biggest of the big-time capitalists. Morgan and Carnegie were there, of course, and guys like E. H. Harriman, H. H. Rogers of Rockefeller's Standard Oil, Jacob Schiff, and on and on. Now there was Charlie getting up to give a speech to these men.

The feeling of amazement never left Charlie and it may have been one of the reasons B.C. liked him so. Thirty years after that famous night, Charlie still couldn't believe what had happened to a kid from Loretto, Pennsylvania: "All I can do is wonder how it all happened. Here I am, a not over-good business man, a second-rate engineer. I can make poor mechanical drawings. I play the piano after a fashion. In fact, I am one of those proverbial jack-of-all-trades who are usually failures. Why I am not, I can't tell you."[5]

This son of the meritocracy told his audience that the time had come for the steel industry to stop killing itself with competition. They'd all go bankrupt if they didn't combine. As the low-cost producer in the industry, Carnegie would prosper regardless, but the rest were in trouble. "Cutthroat competition," to use the phrase of that era, was the frightened preoccupation of businesses in industries with huge start-up costs. Foremost among them were railroads and iron and steel. So many millions were tied up in such companies the men who ran them and owned stock in them were frantic to prevent the loss of the gigantic sums bankruptcy would bring. The business history of the period is awash with failed attempts by companies in the industries in question to rig prices and protect their profit margins. Successful price conspiracies depend on all parties believing they will benefit and sticking to their word, but, as we moderns have seen with OPEC (the Organization of Petroleum Exporting Countries) price agreements hold up fine when demand is high, but when oil users cut back, the oil producers start double-crossing each other and free market anarchy takes over. The Iraqi invasion of Kuwait was partly motivated by a

quarrel over who was cheating by selling more than the agreed-on amounts of oil and driving down the price.

If the late nineteenth-century American railroad and steel executives had been able to invade each other with armies to make their price agreements stick, they would have done so, but lacking armed force, they were always double-crossing each other. At one meeting called to forge yet another price-fixing agreement, A. B. Stickney of the Illinois Central Railroad, told his brethren, "You are all gentlemen here. In your private capacity as such I would trust any of you with my watch, and I would believe the word of any of you, but in your capacity as railroad presidents I would not believe one of you on oath, and I would not trust one of you with my watch."[6]

It was against this background that Charlie spoke, and Morgan and Carnegie listened, and because they listened there was born the humongous United States Steel Corporation, the biggest, vastest, largest company ever put together in America or anywhere else in the world up to that time. A titanic of a company in an age of business titans. We can't imagine what this great industrial agglomeration looked like to those alive at the hour of birthing. It owned industrial plants of a score of varieties, and fleets of ore boats and coal mines, and railroads, and mills and ore fields. In the childhoods of millions of people then living steel had been almost a semiprecious metal, a substance reserved only for swords and special objects, and now this Aetna of an organization had been reared up in the middle of America, to make steel by the millions of tons for everything from railroad cars to the skeletons of buildings. We have no company today in which we can take similar pride because the world has marched on and no behemoth organization could straddle the imagination the way the words of that famous name, U.S. Steel, once did.

At age thirty-nine Charlie was made the president of the new company. It was the first billion-dollar corporation, and judging from the editorial comment of the day, it was a gigantic conspiracy to extract monopoly prices from a defenseless nation. Looked at one way it was a plot, but it was a poorly executed one. Charlie struggled with it and with a Board of Directors composed of lawyers, Wall Street types and men who knew nothing about the steel business, and in the end Charlie lost the

fight. Far from being a conspiracy, U.S. Steel really wasn't a unified organization but a holding company, that is a headquarters company which owned a lot of subordinate companies, each of which more or less went its own way. U.S. Steel was an effort to reorganize a distressed industry, one subject to the most god-awful ups and downs, and regularize it by creating one unit so big and powerful it could flatten out the curves of the graphs and apportion a degree of prosperity to all. If one company had a large enough chunk of the market, the thinking went that it would be able to prevent prices from dropping to ruinous levels. The theory didn't test out very well, nevertheless the men who put what came to be called Big Steel together were trying to limit the damage wrought by swings in the business cycle. They were not powerful enough or perhaps smart enough or both to pull it off. In our time the full faith, power, credit and intelligence, such as it is, of federal government is employed to take care of that chore.

One of the contrasts between the famous Wall Street types of our day, a Warren Buffett, a Henry Kravis or a Carl Icahn, and those of the past like Morgan or Schiff, is that today's herd are mindless, grazing ruminants, sheep or cows with no other thought in mind but the instinctual urge to get on to the next piece of tender green. The great financiers, certainly Morgan and Schiff themselves, addressed the worst business problems of their time and tried to do something about them.

Today, investment banking has become like foreign aid. Millions and billions go into it and paltry thousands get to the intended targets. Or so it has seemed these past fifteen years when so many billions were raised to buy, sell and gamble with the corporate chips which provide the nation with its comforts and its necessities. Although the Milkens and the Kravises, the indicted and the unindicted, the convicted and the acquitted, made oodles and boodles, you didn't see that many new factories getting built. During those years the propaganda line pitched at us by the investment bankers and their stooges from academe was that the time of factories was over. Only chumps manufactured cars and bricks and sinks and beds and clothes and TV sets, scudzy Third World types. We are now the brain people selling services to make a living. Unhappily, we still have

a few brawn people in the population. What are they supposed to do?

The Morgans and Schiffs may or may not have had noble motives, but they understood you can't just take without putting back or the time comes when there is nothing more left to take. Grazing is one thing, overgrazing is another. If you extract the maximum buck, regardless of the damage done, sooner or later there is little left but twigs, stems and dead plant material munched down and destroyed at the root. The effort to put together Big Steel failed, but it was an ambition higher than the zigzag grazing for the next juicy leaf. Charlie wasn't allowed to run U.S. Steel as a unified, integrated organization. With no one firmly in control and with no well-researched and thought-out business plan, the new United States Steel Corporation was the man who jumped on his horse and galloped off in all directions.

Morgan miscalculated or didn't understand when it came to Charlie and U.S. Steel. He added up all the business all the companies which comprised U.S. Steel did and thought it would be sufficient for his intended ends. He came to his conclusion by looking at the numbers. He did not understand that without coordination, management, planning and cohesive organization, the sum was less than the parts. Thus it would not be at U.S. Steel that the puzzle of how to run the giant corporations of the new century, of the twentieth century, would be solved. It wasn't until the 1930s that U.S. Steel was organized into something approaching a unitary operation.[7] It would be left for another group of businessmen at Du Pont and General Motors to invent the ways a vast and varied enterprise could be effectively and profitably run.

Whether Charlie could have made the disparate parts called U.S. Steel a single organization can't be known, because his board never gave him a chance. Even before he found himself stymied, Charlie had availed himself of the perks and privileges of the CEO ethos—girlfriends and at least one illegitimate child —but when he was checked at the office, Charlie went amok à la Don Trump. He started running with Diamond Jim Brady's crowd and turned up at the gaming tables of Monte Carlo where his every throw of the dice was noted by the press with headlines such as *The New York Sun*'s SCHWAB BREAKS BANK. The

sternly puritanical and childless Carnegie, from whom Charlie had kept his vices hidden, reacted by all but breaking off their father-son relationship. "Of course he never could have fallen so low with us," he told the sinful Morgan, whom he apparently blamed for Charlie's fall. "His resignation would have been called for instanter had he done so." With the papers going happily hydrophobic about his doings in a manner any TV watcher can recognize, Charlie defended himself to Morgan by saying at least he hadn't been hypocritical and carried on behind closed doors. "That's what doors are for," the Lion of Wall Street shot back at him.[8]

Charlie left U.S. Steel an enormously rich man, but a restless one. Forsaking the green felt tables of Monte Carlo, he took his whole wad and wagered it on one, big gamble. He got control of a little steel company and discovered a new way of making a new structural form—what is today the ubiquitous I-beam—and borrowing from everybody in sight, including Carnegie who loved him too much not to forgive him, went into business for himself. His company was the Bethlehem Steel Corporation, and, given his technical knowledge, his ability with finance, his remarkable gifts as an organizer, administrator, recruiter and salesman, it left the stick-in-the-muds at U.S. Steel back in the road wondering what had thundered by them. (The I-beam remains Bethlehem's corporate logo to this day.)

When still president of U.S. Steel Schwab had offered the I-beam idea to his company but the board had turned it down. Like the lawyers and money men on boards in our time, they didn't know enough about steel, its manufacture and its uses, to appreciate what Schwab was telling them. When he decided to pursue the I-beam at Bethlehem, the Differdingen mill in Europe alone had invented a practical process for making the shape. Schwab, who had made trips to Europe for Carnegie to license German technology before, did it again.

Contrary to the impression one might get from many speeches and articles the last ten years, America was not living in business isolation until the 1980s. In the steel industry, for example, Americans did what the Japanese do so well now—they licensed foreign technology, particularly from Great Britain and Germany, and often put it to more productive use than its inventors. That is how the Bessemer, the open hearth, cer-

tain kinds of steel forging and, more recently, continuous casting technologies made it to these shores.

Like Donald Trump and other contemporary American businessmen, Schwab personally signed many of the notes on the money he borrowed to put up a mill to make the I-beams. Had he failed, he would have been wiped out. A comparison between what the two men staked their careers on gives a hint as to how the tone and content of American life, propelled by business, have changed in the intervening ninety years. No matter how profitable it may be or gloriously tasteless it may look, the Taj Mahal or any other gambling casino cannot command the respect of a great, grimy, high-stacked, steel mill. The one is doowop and the other is meat and potatoes. Moreover, unlike men such as Trump, Schwab knew what he was doing, knew that the beam would not only cut the cost of materials in every kind of large structure but also decrease the time and costs of construction because it was easier and quicker to use than the iron girders of the past.

Henry Grey, the I-beam's inventor, understood full well what part the steel executive had played in the acceptance of his work: "To Charles M. Schwab belongs the credit for introduction of this mill to the United States, as without his courage and backing the new structural mill and the new structural shapes would in all likelihood have been allowed to lie dormant for many years."[9]

Schwab, like Pierre du Pont and Alfred Sloan at General Motors, was of a class of executives who had mastered *all* the important elements of their business. They understood the technology, how to organize it in a factory situation, how to handle inventory, finance, sales. They knew how to get the job done, they knew their business.

Even after his triumph at Bethlehem, Charlie came under intermittent bombardment for the huge amounts of money he and his principal subordinates took home. Charlie was a CEO ethos kid, but he got the job done. If Charlie wanted to pig it up, the fruits of his labors were, and still are, visible across what used to be called the civilized world. What accomplishments can Jimmy Three Sticks or Steve Ross point to? The one has pissed away billions, the other has found a lawful means to swindle his

stockholders at Time Warner. Charlie's perks without Charlie's performance.

Malcolm grew up near where Charlie lived. Malcolm was in Englewood, New Jersey, a short ferry ride (before the completion of the George Washington Bridge) to Charlie's house overlooking the Hudson at Seventy-second Street in Manhattan. We don't know if B.C. took his boys to see his friend Charlie, but he must have talked about him—he wrote about Charlie enough—and if Malcolm "knew how to live," he may have picked up the kernel of the idea from Charlie.

"Riverside," to use the name Charlie gave to his house, has been called the most lavish mansion to be constructed in New York. It was a full city block square, with more than ninety bedrooms, swimming pool, gymnasium, bowling alley, six elevators, 115-foot tower, with a heating-cooling and electrical generation plant which demanded ten tons of coal a day. Charlie also had an estate in Pennsylvania, and if it wasn't competitive with William Randolph Hearst's San Simeon, an undertaking of the same era, it wasn't bad for a boy born with no advantages in life like those of the newspaper mogul's.

It is possible B.C. took his boys to visit Charlie's spread near Loretto where Malcolm would have gotten the idea it was permissible for rich, important men to collect toys and indulge themselves in expensive and showy puerilities. He might have seen Charlie's collection of automobiles, including a garish Packard with his initials in gold on the doors. Malcolm did much the same with motorcycles. Charlie's toy land dwarfs anything Malcolm, who never had anything like Charlie's money, did when he grew up but it would help explain where Malcolm got some of the inspiration for the way he spent the amplitude he did have. Charlie's biographer gives us this description: "His chickens were not kept in conventional coops; they were housed in replicas of French cottages (which today are motels). Schwab had once developed a liking for a village in Normandy, so, price being no object, he built a copy of it. He set aside sixty-six acres on which he had a small community built. The workshops, sheds, and cattle stalls in it resembled prosperous French farmhouses."[10]

If Malcolm didn't visit Charlie's private Pennsylvania Disneyland, there were other people in his boyhood to impress him.

B.C. had a gallant former German U-boat commander, Count Felix Luckner, who became a well-known figure of the interwar period, to dinner at the family home in Englewood. Some of the neighbors' children were invited for supper and then on to the high school where B.C. and the boys sat up on the stage to listen to Count Felix talk about his adventures and drum up paying passengers for sailing cruises on his boat, *Sea Eagle*. Malcolm said[11] that he remembered Dwight Morrow visiting them at home too.

Morrow was the top of the heap in Englewood, living in a great house with grounds and a gatekeeper. Nothing like the Forbes establishment. George Shultz, who went on to become a major businessman himself and a Secretary of State in the Reagan administration, has this evocative recollection of the Forbes' home and family: "I remember they had a big vacant lot or field next to their house, and there were all sort of interesting things to do there. They had a model T. It was a simple enough machine that boys could drive it, and even take it apart, and put it back together again. The Forbes family always had interesting things like that around that were a little unusual. Malcolm was undoubtedly part of that flavor of life . . . It was a large house and there were horse chestnut trees. The horse chestnuts were great things to get and polish and use at the end of strings to make a lariat that you could throw that would grip around trees and stuff like that."[12]

Comfy upper middle class, which was not the world that Dwight Morrow came from, so one wonders what this J. P. Morgan partner was doing over at Forbes'. Morrow, who became a United States senator and the American ambassador to Mexico, had a reputation as an alcoholic, so possibly B.C., who liked to toss down the usquebaugh with the best of them, was a drinking partner from time to time. There is no record of B.C. having the kind of deep and respectful admiration for Morrow which he had entertained for Charlie Schwab.

Everything about the Morrows worked to make them dominate the town in the years of Malcolm's growing up. Dwight's daughter married Charles Lindbergh, and then, of course, there was the kidnapping of the Lindbergh baby nearby, an event which Malcolm apparently was as struck by as the rest of the community. A man in Malcolm's World War II platoon re-

membered traveling with him through the state en route to embarkation for the battle to free Europe: "He was talking about that time when Hauptmann killed the Lindbergh child. And on the troop train as we went through this place where all that took place—it was around Hopewell—the railroad ran within several blocks of the Lindbergh home, and he showed me the window where the little boy was taken out, and dropped to the ground off of the ladder. He pinpointed it. The train was going pretty slow. So he took time to show me."[13]

Englewood was almost a Morgan suburb and quite Wall Street. It was first turned into a New York suburb in the 1880s and '90s, and, one longtime resident recalled. "People came to Englewood after World War I, the way they went to places like Wilton, Connecticut, after World War II . . . It was a Wall Street town then, now it's a doctor's town."[14] Two other, especially able, Morgan partners lived in Englewood during Malcolm's growing up, Thomas Lamont and Henry Davison. In those years the House of Morgan had two kinds of partners. The dumb, pedigreed, upper-class affirmative action beneficiaries—they lived on Long Island and played polo—and the smart young men, the go-getters without pedigree, the promising comers plucked from other companies—they lived in Englewood. The system prompted Carnegie to crow that, "Mr. Morgan buys his partners, I raise my own."[15] At Morgan, Stanley, one of the Morgan companies formed when new laws required splitting up the old empire, one fine young oaf was hired for the sole reason he had made varsity baseball at Princeton, where Malcolm would go to school.[16] In the early 1950s out of nineteen partners at the firm it was calculated that "five went to Princeton, three to Yale, two to Williams, and one each to Harvard, Columbia, Virginia Military Institute of Technology, and Cornell."[17] Benjamin Strong, the governor of the Federal Reserve Bank of New York, and a major business figure of the 1920s, was also an Englewoodian.[18]

No doubt about it, B.C. had been able to settle his family in the right community. It was heavily wooded with a pussy willow pond where the kids skated in the winter. The maids lived in small third-floor rooms in the homes where they worked and Mrs. Emma Florence, still wearing the long, flowing skirts of the Great War into the 1920s, taught the town's privileged boys

and girls to dance. Mrs. Dwight Morrow led a Shakespeare reading group in town and Thomas Lamont entertained literary figures like H. G. Wells, André Maurois and John Masefield. Englewood was not *Main Street,* not like the philistine community of bigots which Americans were reading about in Sinclair Lewis' novel. Movies and radio were changing leisure time, but children of this class were still primarily readers, and life was yet slow enough for them so that "lots of afternoons were completely free to kick a stick," a longtime resident recalled. "It was just like life in a New England village . . . Everybody went away for the summer, to Martha's Vineyard or Quoque on Long Island." She remembered that it took two days to get to Martha's Vineyard and can still see the automobiles, trunks strapped on to back and roof, leaving town as summer approached. The springs on those cars were terrible and the tires highly prone to puncture. The men would drive the families and it would take so long to get to the summer rentals they had to turn around and drive right back, but there was no thought in these pre-air-conditioned times of staying in Englewood, particularly because people were so afraid of polio. The town was struck by an epidemic during Malcolm's growing up and three children had died. "It was like a black cloud. There was nothing to be done if it hit you. This was like a ghost town in the summer except for the men."[19]

They may not have had a chauffeur like the Morrows, but the Forbes family lived well. They had a maid, there was a governess for the young children and during the 1920s more than enough money. A neighbor boy, who knew the Forbes family quite well, recalled Bruce, Malcolm's older brother, telling him that "his mother would sit there on a Christmas morning, and she'd start pulling on this string, and the old man had bills tied to the string and it went clear up to the attic, and she sat in there pulling twenty-dollar bills to the tune of about a thousand dollars. This was back in the Twenties, this was a helluva lot of money. You could buy an automobile with that. I can remember that incident very, very clearly."[20]

A Mr. Spencer was produced to teach the boys how to box down in the basement, and Bruce, though not Malcolm, apparently was quite good at it. The same neighbor boy had a clear recollection that the Forbeses were often given the best and

given it first: "Those Forbes kids, incidentally, were the first ones in town to have a Red Bug—A little four-wheeled jitney that was made of just slats, slats of varnished wood between four bicycle wheels. It had a place for two, and it ran on storage batteries. The Red Bug preceded the Smith Motor Wheel, which was a motor-assisted wheel which you attached to your bike." (Malcolm said the Red Bug arrived from F. A. O. Schwarz, Christmas 1929. The little bugger could get up to twelve miles per hour. The ultimate rich kid's toy.)

There were so many automobile accidents involving kids—Malcolm's brother, Duncan, was killed in one when still a teenager—that when oldest brother Bruce and the gang went to places like Ben Riley's Arrowhead Inn in Riverdale, B.C. hired a bus to take the kids there and get them back safely. Yet their father made the boys work down at the office.[21] They were not allowed to sit around, although the old man couldn't have been too hard on them. It was every other year to Scotland on the transatlantic steamship, with the Forbes boys being less than angelic. Arthur Jones writes that on the boat in 1926 they "started throwing everything, bedding, and linens, too, out of the portholes. Another vessel picked up the jetsam and imagined disaster ahead. When the truth came out, the Forbes boys really were punished."[22]

Occasionally the trip didn't come off. Roger von Rath, the neighborhood boy, said that, "I remember that Mr. and Mrs. Forbes were asked out to visit Hearst's San Simeon. She was a devout Catholic and she would have nothing to do with going out there with a—living in sin with William Randolph. She was a beautiful woman. She would go into a restaurant with the boys, and people would always ask, 'Is this your sister? She was a strikingly beautiful woman.'" For years Hearst, a married man with children, lived openly with a movie actress named Marion Davies. Concubine or no, turning down an invitation to San Simeon when over the years many another proper person had accepted must have bothered B.C. He knew Hearst was no man to be slighted or defied, which is perhaps why he referred to himself as one of Hearst's "trained seals."

The Forbes family didn't have to trot off to California to visit the proprietor of a media empire. There was one in Englewood, a boy's bike ride away from the Forbes' house, a pub-

lisher who was as well known in the America of the 1920s as William Randolph Hearst, and whose influence on mass culture may have been greater. Although no evidence of it comes to hand, he must have made some kind of impression on Malcolm. Bernarr Macfadden made an impression on everybody. George Shultz says the gang used to swim in the pool at his mansion, and that he took the boy George on his first airplane ride. George was in the co-pilot's seat, and for a brief instant, accidentally goofed up the controls, but, as a pilot or anything else, Macfadden was seldom fazed. His approach to aviation, like his approach to everything else, was just a little different. It was written of him that, "The managers of airports near New York commonly lock all their planes when they hear that Macfadden is coming out. His custom is to climb into the first unoccupied craft he sees and fly off, without consulting anybody."[23]

Macfadden lived from 1868 to 1955, a long and astonishing life. That he is not better known is owing to the fact that for the most part journalists and historians derive their prestige from those they write about and Bernarr Macfadden had scant prestige. He wasn't low status, he was no status. Nevertheless, he, more than any other individual, must be accorded the credit, or given the blame, for inventing the underlying form and thematic material which dominates American commercial mass culture. *People* magazine, the *National Enquirer* and television shows like "Inside Edition," "A Current Affair" and the raft of cop, fireperson, 911 programs which mix real people and actors owe their content, technique and inspiration to Bernarr, who thought it up first. The advertising industry owes him a debt so great they ought to rename Madison Avenue after him.

Macfadden is important for us because he is a major, early example of a businessman whose profits are directly tied into changing and/or damaging culture and society. A broad swath of Victorian era Americans favored sexual repression out of a wide variety of motives, some having to do with religious belief, some with standards of propriety, others for reasons of hygiene and social discipline. Without antibiotics, venereal disease was no joking matter, as modern Americans in the time of AIDS can understand.

The losing struggle against Macfadden waged primarily by church groups was one of the first attempts by the society to

defend itself against a business which posed a threat to the common well-being. The older, prebusiness-era enterprise of prostitution could be contained, but Macfadden was making money by sending the sexual message everywhere. It has transpired that the predictions uttered by Macfadden's blue-nosed enemies about the long-term consequences of allowing such a business to stay open have been borne out everywhere.

The voluptuary society they warned against has, in no small measure, come into existence, as all those who worry about what they discern as a slacking off everywhere and everyway, daily testify. While physical ecologists point out the disappearance of the ozone layer, social ecologists point to the disappearance of the work ethic. It remains to be seen if either or both have been exaggerated, but it is beyond dispute that beer and wine companies are free to do their damnedest to turn teenagers into alcoholics and the manufacturers of every product under the sun are free to sell their wares by keeping high-hormoned young people in a state of perpetual sexual arousal, despite the fact that AIDS permeates the land.

Many blame this state of affairs on psychology, permissiveness and liberalism, and though the liberals played their part they only provided the rationale after business had opened up these new veins of commerce. Thanks to them the watch and ward societies of the nineteenth century are laughable to us moderns; men like Plato who warned against the voluptuary society more than two thousand years ago may be shrugged off as grumpy old farts born too soon to get in on the fun, but doubt creeps in. Maybe some of these social thinkers weren't merely dyspeptic personalities. Those who were once laissez-faire businessmen or permissive absolutists are getting twinges to the effect that things may have been allowed to go too far. But how to bell the cat? Since Macfadden won his battles, business has been able to destroy any convention, violate any taboo, steal the minds of adults and children alike if it helps to merchandise the fall line. In the mid-1950s large corporations hung back from buying space in *Playboy* only until they were convinced it was a hit. A magazine executive recalled this corporate behavior by saying, "I had a closet full of ten-foot poles from advertisers who said they would never touch *Playboy* with a ten-foot pole."[24] Today the gleaming expanses of unclothed skin

which readers paid to see by getting a copy of *Playboy* are there for the eye's delectation in the TV beer commercials, so completely have Bernarr Macfadden's business ideas prevailed.

Born in poverty, Macfadden's formal education stopped with three years in grammar school. His path to fame and fortune began with his interest in body building and health. In common with many then and now, he nursed an antipathy toward doctors (who reciprocated) and invented his own methods of diet and exercise. He came along when America was going into its second great physical fitness craze, the first having taken place in the 1830s. It was the second craze which gave birth, among other things, to the breakfast food industry. Odd as it may seem to several generations reared to know that dry cereal is the epitome of mass-marketed, brand-name, nationally advertised, mainline merchandise, corn flakes, shredded wheat and grape nuts began life on the fringe as "health foods." Macfadden weighed in with a breakfast cereal of his own, something called Strengtho, but Strengtho turned rancid on the grocer's shelves before it could be sold.[25] The reason that Dr. Harvey Kellogg's[26] name is known to anyone who has walked into an American supermarket is that he invented a breakfast food flake with a long shelf life.

Macfadden's first, healthy commercial success dates from the 1890s when he opened an exercise salon in New York City for businessmen. Many years later *The New Yorker* magazine offered this description of the treatment accorded Bernarr's hapless customers, some of whom suffered from alopecia: "Macfadden stripped them down, made them exercise, forbade them alcohol, coffee, tea, and tobacco, and lectured them on the benefits of modest meals. As the money came in, he began to advertise in the newspapers. . . . he . . . turned the searchlight of his medical intuition on the case and came up with a remedy in the form of a hair calisthenic. This consisted of seizing his hair with both hands and wrenching at it fiercely. He passed his knowledge along to his clients, and it was not uncommon for a visitor to the salon to see a large collection of perspiring financiers doing self-conscious but orderly hair drills, counting, "One, two, yank, one, two, yank."[27]

Macfadden wasn't the first person to find that money was to be made out of health concerns, but he was among the first to

turn it into a business in the sense that the word business is used in this book. Part of his formula was to mix health and sex in a thoroughly modern way. In short order he had an encyclopedia out which informed the students thereof that, "Rape and murder may be due to constipation confused with sex passion."[28] But it was in his magazine, *Physical Culture,* that Macfadden first hit the jackpot.

The first issue began with a provocative cover displaying "Prof. B. Macfadden in Classical Poses." Before he died, it would have been all but impossible for an American not to have seen a picture of the short but well-developed Macfadden advertising his way to health and strength somewhere. For its day the first issue of *Physical Culture* was at least as daring as *Playboy* half a century later. When Macfadden started out the lid was on, and no kidding around. A photograph of a female ankle would cause more of an uproar than any repercussions on that minor milestone day when Hugh Hefner decided to drop the airbrush and go with pubic hair. In 1905 Anthony Comstock, the director of the New York Society for the Suppression of Vice, attacked Macfadden for having a picture of the *Venus de Milo* in his office. "So!" Comstock called out, as he led his raiders onto the premises, "You have pornography here, too . . . Tear all these pictures down, boys! . . . We'll take them in for evidence."[29]

The same year Macfadden was arrested in connection with his "Mammoth Physical Exhibition Show" at Madison Square Garden on account of poster photographs of women in the head-to-toe gym costumes of the day. Five thousand people had to be turned away from the Garden, so large was the demand for tickets for what the newspapers called "the beauty show." It was the beginning of Macfadden's campaign to put sex in the center of American pop culture, a campaign which would not end until naked, young flesh would be integrated into the mass merchandising of everything from soft drinks to automobiles.

Whether Macfadden can be given the credit for having invented the beauty contest is unclear, but he played an important role in taking it away from the arena of the stag party and the Friday night smoker, and making pulchritude a respectable mass-merchandised commodity. In 1912 Macfadden, who was born in the miasma of rural Missouri poverty, hied himself

overseas to stage a contest for "the most perfectly formed woman in England." With tape measure in hand he noted the dimensions of the finalists, selecting as the winner a swimming champion named Mary Williamson, whom he then married and by whom he had seven children. As if that weren't enough he adopted an eighth. Ms. Williamson reacted to this treatment by calling her husband "The Great Begatsby."

The authorities let Bernarr off for his transgressions with the posters advertising his show, but the next time around the dance floor with the antivice crusader was not so pleasant. Comstock had a place in the national life for which we have no modern equivalent. Neither Jerry Falwell nor Billy Graham can mobilize public sentiment and command official action as porn-suppressor Anthony Comstock could. This was a man with power to inflict injury, as historian William H. Taft (not the President) wrote: "Two years later it was a different story when *Physical Culture* Magazine carried a story by John R. Coryell, better known for his 'Nick Carter' stories, titled 'Wild Oats, or Growing to Manhood in Civilized (?) Society.' Comstock convinced the postal authorities that this effort to discuss the facts of life was nothing but an indecent account designed to improve the sale of the magazine. Fined $2,000, Macfadden was kept out of jail by President William H. Taft. Three decades later Macfadden received a full pardon, but he never recovered the fine."[30]

"Growing to Manhood" contained a clear description of how one could contract syphilis, and must have been of at least minimal help in raising the level of public health. Like the battles today over sex education and the distribution of condoms in high schools, there were two sides to the argument about what Macfadden had done. Some prestigious names rallied to Macfadden's defense. After Comstock stopped performance of *Mrs. Warren's Profession,* George Bernard Shaw struck up a friendship with Bernarr and published several pieces in *Physical Culture.* H. G. Wells was also a contributor and one of Jack London's books was published in the magazine as was Horace Fletcher, the far-famed slow-chewer.

Nonetheless "Comstockery," to use George Bernard Shaw's word for it, ruled the land. It ruled, that is, until it came up against Macfadden, a man whom Upton Sinclair described as a

"symbol of the vulgarity and cheapness of America." Nevertheless, Macfadden destroyed Comstockery, because he took sex
out of the cheap bordello and out of the hands of free-love
utopians and made it a big business. American conservatives
lecture that it was the permissives, the Freudians, the
psychobabblists, the left wing social engineers and the humanis-
tic relativists who dropped the sex bomb on America, but it ain't
so. These types may well have wanted to drop it, but the deed
was done by a new thing loose in the society called business.
Bernarr Macfadden, the exercise freak, vegetarian, health
quack, businessman, was the George Washington of the sexual
revolution. He did it somewhat for principle and belief, à la
Hugh Hefner, but he also did it for what business does everything for—money.

# EIGHT

---

# The Mumbling
# Millions

ANTHONY COMSTOCK was the pluperfect central
casting puritan. He did more to discredit his cause
than his opponents, yet it is a thoughtless person who would
insist that making sex a commodity in American culture has not
had broad and deep effects and a blind one who would not see,
even granting the health-giving benefits of escaping Victorian-
ism and sexual repression, that most of the effects range from
so-so to rotten. From sexual inhibitions to AIDS in a hundred
years may or may not be progress.

Certain passages in the Old Testament remind us that business did not invent lust, but it made a major contribution to
destroying the things which contained and segregated it. In a
society where millions of copies of a record with a woman singing "Hurt me, jerk me" are sold, there is no red light district,
no tenderloin, no way to contain and school the libido by geog-
raphy, religion or enforcing social values.

When one listens to a small and impotent band of parents complain to a congressional committee that they are helpless against multibillion-dollar, multinational corporations filling their children's heads with visions of candy and sex, a sensible person thinks that something is askew. Yet that is the plight of the fin de twentieth siècle mother and father when trying to protect a nine-year-old from having childhood prematurely curtailed thanks to the sales campaign requirements of Sony Records, whose home office is ten thousand miles away and unreachable in Tokyo. The ones headquartered in New York, Los Angeles and Nashville are as sociopathic but closer to hand, and therefore less illustrative of how impermeable they are to any influence short of plastique and dynamite. Nevertheless, cultural, familial, artistic, ethical, moral messages are now being framed by foreign-owned corporations who also own the most powerful means of inserting them into the heads of children and adults.

Matsushita, an electronics manufacturing corporation, owns MCA, which owns, among many other communications properties, Universal Studios. MGM/UA (that's Metro-Goldwyn-Mayer plus the old United Artists studio) is in the creel of Italian-owned Pathe Communications, Sony has got Columbia Pictures and Sony (nee CBS) Records, while News Ltd., another foreign-owned entity has ownership of Twentieth Century-Fox. The CEO of the conglomeration of movie studios, cable networks and publishing enterprises called Time Warner was, when last sighted, out cruising, not unlike a cheap whore, for foreign money.

A management structure less accountable and more remote cannot be invented, but such is the distant mechanism for decision making which determines what the children and the youth of the nation see, hear and think. Don't blame the foreigners. It was American businessmen who sold them the companies, and there are still companies in the hands of American executives who might as well be foreigners. Foreign control of American motion picture making is new and comes with many promises that Tokyo will keep hands off. Considering how American businessmen have filled the heads of American children with unalloyed garbage for decades, one is hard-pressed to see how the foreigners can do worse.

**133**

Talk of the downtrodden, is there any group in modern America more helplessly at sea on the ocean of commercial culture than a committee of concerned parents, headed by Tipper Gore, laying its petition on the table for some form of succor from the society at large in defense of hearth and home?

Their threats of boycott are laughable. In an era of big organizations, they have no power; in a time when money talks, they have laryngitis. They get their brief twenty seconds on the TV news looking like uncomfortable boobs and sounding like white-hooded, book-burning Klansmen, then on to the weather. A circular depression hangs over the mid-continent, smog in the West and acid rain everywhere.

In 1905 important organs of opinion like the *New York Times* sided with the Comstock faction of the society as this editorial suggests: "We are bound to say that Mr. Comstock appears to have the better of it . . . Let Mr. Macfadden . . . show his culling of the results of *Physical Culture* in private . . . but let him not project a money-making show of them, for the express attraction of the 'baser nature,' which will be its effect, if not its purpose."[1]

A hundred years later the power position has been reversed, because now sex is being aired, not by a cloud-nine hippy-dippy crank, but by a large, money schlurping business.

Harvey Green is one cultural historian who has traced Macfadden's pioneering mixture of sex and advertising and understood that it was Bernarr whom we have to thank for the tit cult: "The Olive Company of Clarinda, Iowa, defined . . . physical conditioning for women in 1924, with an advertising campaign for its 'New National' bust developer. Calling the twenties 'the age of beautiful women,' the company asserted that 'if you are not physically attractive, you lose half of life's joys.' 'Womanly beauty'—in this instance equated with a full bust—was obviously a sales pitch for a bust-developer manufacturer, but it corresponded with a more general cultural definition of and openness about female sexuality in the 1920s. Macfadden had defined an ample bosom as a mark of a healthy woman two decades before the Olive Company advertisement . . . he encountered similar legal difficulties after he published *The Power and Beauty of Superb Womanhood* in 1901 because the

book contained photographs of bare-breasted women exercising to improve their bust size."[2]

The invention of the breast in modern commercial form is but one of Macfadden's many contributions to contemporary culture. "How a woman can wear a support for her bust from childhood and then have the incomprehensible audacity to expect it to remain round, firm . . . until advanced age is more than this writer can understand," he wrote, and in due course "health corsets," much lighter than the whalebone and steel getup great-great-grandmother suffered, found their way onto the shelves of ladies' unmentionable departments in the stores.

"He kept *Physical Culture* in a continuing ferment of dispute," a 1950 *New Yorker* profile of Macfadden remarked. The profile was written at a time when many of his ideas were way out of favor and it seemed a mystery of the madness of crowds and popular delusions that this guy could have been taken seriously; today much that Macfadden preached in the area of health would be more favorably received, and less importance would have been given to the bizarre turns of his mind than *The New Yorker* accorded them: "Considerable space was given to a Persian physician who cured his patients by treading on them with his bare feet, and a lively article appeared on one Eusebio Santos, a grass eater, and was illustrated with a photograph of the ruminant, clad in an opera hat and cape, grazing with a herd of cattle."[3]

Though Bernarr was a dedicated grass eater, he and most of his ideas were not on the fringes of American life. *Physical Culture* grew like mad during the World War I period. It was a commercial success. Then in 1919 Macfadden hit the newsstands with a blockbuster publication, *True Story.*

On the cover of the first issue was a picture of a man and woman looking intense with a cut line declaring, "And their love turned to hatred." Inside the reader-voyeur got pieces entitled "A Wife Who Awoke in Time," "My Battle with John Barleycorn," "An Ex-Convict's Climb to Millions," plus interviews with such movie stars of the day as Douglas Fairbanks, Billie Burke, William Farnum and Dorothy Gish.

"Macfadden has the first new idea in the publishing field in the last fifty years," an executive with the American News Company, the magazine distributors, said as *True Story*'s circulation

took off, going over two million in a short time.[4] Advertising revenues went over four million, although many of Macfadden's publications derived so much revenue from newsstand sales, they didn't need advertising to show a profit. Macfadden's magazines didn't receive big account, national brand advertising. The manufacturing sector of business, the muscle corporations, were somewhat circumspect in their use of sex up through the 1930s and '40s. Pretty girls in tightish sweaters and blondes riding carefree in Cadillacs were permissible, but the corporate logo was kept out of magazines and off television shows which might bother a practicing Presbyterian. *Esquire,* the mainline men's magazine of those decades, contented itself with stylized drawings of anatomically fetching but impossible females. Even satyrs could read it holding a copy with both hands. Restraint collapsed forty years ago, however, as scores of up-market brand names bought their way into close association with pictures and text showing behavior which turned Sodom from Swinger City into a saline urban renewal project. Founded in the early 1950s, *Playboy,* with a circulation of a million by the sixth year of its life, was an irresistible advertising medium.[5]

One of Macfadden's new ideas was using actors to pose for photographs illustrating the true scenes of his true stories. It was a gimmick that would be widely copied, becoming in our own day a standard device of commercial television. Macfadden was also the first to know how to titillate with sex without offending, thereby not only reaching a mass market, but merchandising sexiness into the culture. "There was no pornography in *True Story,* but it had a yeasty undercurrent of sexual excitation," said *The New Yorker,*[6] which pointed out that the shrewd Macfadden, to protect himself against accusations of purveying immorality, had gotten up a board of "censors," the membership of which was a minister, a rabbi and a priest. Today, the same merchandising tactic would be used with the addition of a couple of psychologists and other "experts." It was not, however, any group from what we now call the helping professions who had the determining say over what went in and what stayed out of the publication. According to Macfadden's only academic biographer, "Bickering over the amount of flesh to show in illustrations never ceased. When an editor or ad manager cried 'too much,' Macfadden would order the flesh to

vanish. Sales would decline and a circulation manager would cry to the boss, showing him the impudent eroticism of a rival magazine while appealing for a little more flesh exposure."[7]

*True Story*'s success was so great Macfadden imitated himself, coming out with *True Romances,* which sold out its first issue, and *True Experiences* and *Dream World.* Dell tried to compete with *Modern Romance* and *My Story.* Fawcett weighed in with *True Confessions,* but Bernarr was ready with a barrage: *True Experiences, True Love Stories, Love and Romance, True Marriage Stories, True Love Stories, Secrets, Personal Romances, Intimate Stories* and *Revealing Romances.* After striking out in somewhat different directions with *True Detective Mysteries* and *Photoplay,* by the mid-1930s Macfadden was able to boast of a combined magazine circulation larger than that of any other publisher including Henry Luce (Time-Life), Crowell, Curtis and Hearst, the giants of the field. He had his failures. There was, for example, *Babies —Just Babies,* which he co-edited with Eleanor Roosevelt, and which died in the traces at the starting gate.[8]

In a business society, any taste, any predilection, any desire that can be catered to by mass production and distribution will be seized on and manipulated. Those doing it will prosper in the face of the angriest criticism, of which Bernarr Macfadden got a lot, although whether more than his share is debatable. The health magazine *Hygeia* expressed the opinions of many worried people when it wrote of Macfadden's publications that, "Every issue reeks with sex appeal . . . The usual cover design is that of a woman in as little clothing as the law allows, so disporting herself as to show a maximum amount of nudity with retention of second class mailing privileges. Within the cover one finds the same theme played up. Women in tights, women in bathing suits, women with little on but beads, all dished up to appeal to the pornographic tastes of the male. Nor is the female neglected. Macfadden himself in various stages of undress and various other supermen with little on but a surcingle doubtless attract many quarters from girls and women who feel the biologic urge."[9] But sex, when lashed to the penetrating power of the new forms of business organization, would become a sales tool no one could keep from crossing the threshold of the home, unless it were, perhaps, such remote people as the Pennsylvania Amish, isolated by a rural, religious refusal to

use the fruits of modern manufacture and by speaking a form of seventeenth-Century Rhineland German.

September 15, 1924, saw the appearance of Macfadden's contribution to the development of the infotainment industry with the arrival of the *New York Evening Graphic*. *The Pornographic*, as it was soon called, did elicit some praise from the literary critic Alexander Woollcott, who said, "It educated readers up to a point where they were able to understand the other tabloids."[10]

It is true that in this instance Macfadden wasn't the first in the picture tabloid business. The idea was imported from England in 1919 with the founding of the *New York Daily News*, but Bernarr may have been the most memorable practitioner. *The New Yorker* remarked that 1924, in recognition of the *Graphic*'s birth, was "a year that has more than once been referred to as the blackest in the history of American journalism."[11] It may also have been the most entertaining.[12] Macfadden jumped circulation thirty thousand in one day by ordering up a photograph of a man being electrocuted for the full front page except for the space needed for the headline: ROASTED ALIVE! Many of the *Graphic*'s headlines were doozies: HE BEAT ME—I LOVE HIM, BEAT TWO NAKED GIRLS IN REFORM SCHOOL; WEED PARTIES IN SOLDIERS' LOVE NEST; THOUSANDS APPLAUD WHILE WOMAN IS TORTURED FOR AMUSEMENT; RUDY ASKS $1,433,000 FOR KISSES; RICH RED DROPS FREE LOVE; TWO WOMEN IN FIGHT, ONE STRIPPED, OTHER EATS BAD CHECK. Anticipating the Second Coming of Elvis Presley, the *Graphic* scooped the world with "spirit letters" from movie star Rudolph Valentino, at whose wake in 1926 a riot broke out among thousands of women waiting to bid the great lover-boy of the period their more than fond adieux.

Central to carrying out Bernarr Macfadden's formula of sex, crime, health, celebrity and anguished love was the "composograph." Actors were posed for pictures of real, semireal or imaginary scenes of stories in the news. The composograph has become a staple with all media. Radio adopted the composograph technique in the 1930s with such news programs as "The March of Time" (magazine). The show had every well-known actor from Agnes Moorehead to Orson Welles impersonating everyone from Adolf Hitler to Franklin D. Roosevelt.[13] What is euphemistically called "computer-enhanced" pictures

are today routinely printed in the nation's newspapers and magazines.

Bernarr, in a piece of cant the equal of anything coming out of the mouth of a contemporary GE/NBC or Time Warner executive, declared, "You have to dramatize the news and features that you present in such a manner as will not only interest your readers but will have an uplifting influence mentally, morally and spiritually."[14]

The degradation of the culture is such that when similar things are said today, there is neither the pulpit nor the person to make the worthy reply. Seventy years ago, there was H. L. Mencken, whose vocabulary and syntax render him all but inaccessible to many a recent graduate, but who then had a public literate enough to understand when he told them:

"Macfadden himself sees the paper as a great moral agent. When a lady in Park Avenue, getting news that her confidential male friend has gone broke, heaves herself out of the eighteenth story window, he is not content to record the overt facts (with a composograph that shows her passing the tenth floor); there must also be a moral homily upon her two falls, and her old mother in Skaneateles must tell why she was not taught the facts of sex hygiene in infancy. And when Chief Justice Taft dies prematurely at seventy-two, it must be delicately pointed out that putting on too much fat is suicide. This scheme, to be sure, has not been carried out in every detail, but all the same the *Graphic* takes a predominantly moral line, and if it has accomplished nothing else it has at least made hundreds of thousands of New Yorkers privy to the crimes of the Medical Trust."

Henry Mencken knew what a pathfinder Macfadden was, how he would be widely imitated and then surpassed:

"In this endeavor, it seems to me, Macfadden has cramped himself by yielding too much to the literati that he is forced to hire. These gentlemen, despite his training, yet harbor prejudices in favor of fancy English, and so his paper is probably often unintelligible to its customers. Some day, if he doesn't watch out, some rival will blow him up with a tabloid that is really a tabloid, and not simply a smaller and better edition of the *Times*. In that perfect tabloid, as I envisage it, there will be no word of more than one syllable, and no word at all that might be a picture. The news of the day will be told precisely as

the gory fictions of the comic strips are now told—in a series of graphs, with an occasional balloon. And the vocabulary of the balloons will be restricted to such terms as even infants of three are hep to: blahh, bang, boom, shhh, wow, wooof, hell, damn, and so on."[15]

During the 1920s, the years of Macfadden's greatest success, other men were also deciding the shape and content of what would be going into people's heads. Theirs, too, was strictly a business decision, although the ramifications branched out to touch every person and every institution. The corporately controlled all-entertainment society did not unconsciously evolve into life any more than the business itself did. As Daniel McCallum sketched out the organizational forms of modern business, so other businessmen designed the shape and nature of the communications organizations which would come to have a pervasive dominance and controlling influence over the nation. During the 1920s, business, which had done so well by the nation, was entrusted with the power to change values, language, diet, sex and even alter the American character. No other nation saw fit to give such power to business amoralists, who, guided only by getting as much money as there was to get from the advertisers, would appear to serve old-fashioned beliefs, even as they destroyed them.

In 1922 David Sarnoff, beginning his remarkable career as the builder of the Radio Corporation of America (RCA), and the National Broadcasting System (NBC), made a proposal which, had it been accepted, might have moved the subsequent history of the nation in a significantly different direction. It doesn't do to exaggerate these might-have-beens, but it is a fact that Sarnoff wrote a memo to the controlling executives at General Electric, urging that radio set manufacturers, all of whom were patent licensees of GE, AT&T and Westinghouse under a pool agreement, be required to pay a two-dollar fee for every set they made. These moneys were to go to "a separate and distinct company, to be known as the Public Service Broadcasting Company," which would supply the growing number of stations and the nascent national system with programming. Seeing radio as an educational and informational medium, he didn't want radio to rely on advertising for its money. It would

"debase" radio, he thought, in much the same way that advertising would degrade a library or a museum.

Sarnoff was anything but a lonely eccentric in his opinions. Calling advertising "outrageous rubbish," Bruce Bliven in the June 1924 issue of *Century,* declared that, "The use of radio for advertising is wholly undesirable and should be prohibited by legislation, if necessary." At least one congressman announced he intended to do just that.

Sarnoff did not live to see institutions like the Metropolitan Museum of Art turned into adjuncts of high-fashion rag shops' merchandising and promotional programs, but he may have been tuned in on WEAF in New York City on August 28, 1922, at 5 P.M. to hear the first broadcast commercial, an advertisement for Hawthorne Courts, a Queens apartment house development in Jackson Heights. The Hawthorne Courts commercial was also the controlling precedent which dictated the shape and substance of the social organizations which would control television when it first came along less than twenty years later.

Hawthorne apartments was soon followed by Tidewater Oil and American Express, after which came the major department stores. Advertising in and of itself is not objectionable. It may not be the only way that a mass production business system can distribute its goodies, but it is the means American businessmen chose in Daniel McCallum's time, when in the middle of the last century the first advertising agencies opened their doors. Advertising has been entwined with the way business does business from the start. No good reasons exist why advertising shouldn't have used radio, but many good reasons exist why it should not have been allowed to control it. The question is who should have the power to control the medium.

Sarnoff's conduct in this struggle is a reminder that business people do not only think about squeezing the last possible nickel out of every situation. He was troubled by the consequences of commercializing and by the opportunities which would be lost if advertising turned radio into an exclusively entertainment medium. Taking his case to Herbert Hoover, then Secretary of Commerce, the two made common cause as the future president exclaimed, "If a speech by the President is to be used as the meat in a sandwich of two patent medicine advertisements, there will be no radio left."[16]

But the American Telephone & Telegraph Company, which owned WEAF, decided it would go for the sandwich. It began putting together the first radio network, each station being connected via long distance telephone lines, through which programming would flow. Its scheme depended upon there being relatively few radio stations, and those would have to be profit-making ventures which were cooperating with AT&T. The company was in a position to realize its plan by having the major manufacturer of radio station transmitters, its own Western Electric affiliate, discourage orders. There was more money to be made by repeat business from commercials than one-time only sales of transmitters. Thus when New York City, at the suggestion of some of its leading businessmen, wanted to buy a transmitter and start up its own station, AT&T turned down the sale, saying that, if New York had anything to say, it could buy time on WEAF to say it. At length the city bought a secondhand Western Electric transmitter which somebody found in Brazil.[17]

At this point the nation was at a major juncture. Broadcasting could be a service that much of the population supplied for itself, by the action of individuals or through locally controlled institutions, or, it could be a service supplied by commercial organizations. The latter course was taken and the nation was on the way to the living room to adopt the lifestyle of the one-celled animal, the modalities of the couch potato. The passive characteristics of the population, America, the land of the mumbling millions who don't go to public meetings, don't vote, don't take part, don't come out and can't get involved, were in train of creation. A once participatory population was killed off, and deliberately so, by King Commerce.

In the 1920s the foundation existed for a kind of broadcast mass media different from the one which business created. Regardless of AT&T, in the middle of the decade nearly a third of the nation's 571 stations were owned by educational institutions and churches, and perhaps as many more were owned by locally owned and operated companies like newspapers, department stores and radio shops and run on a non-commercial basis. WCFL, "the Voice of Labor" in Chicago, mixed "labor news flashes" with the "Irish Hour," the "Polish Hour," and "Earl Hoffman's Chez Pierre Orchestra."[18] To pay WCFL's (the call letters stood for Chicago Federation of Labor) expenses thou-

142

sands came out to the city's Soldier Field on Labor Day, 1927, for a money-raising benefit. In addition, the city had four or five ethnic and religious stations including WMBI, for the Moody Bible Institute.

To match this soup of community-based broadcasting, a radio Yankee-tinkerer universe had brought itself into existence as thousands of blue collar Chicagoans who couldn't afford manufactured radios built their own. Jerry-rigged antennae could be seen on the roofs of houses in all the city's working class communities. WCFL's *Radio Club Magazine* explained how to make a radio. Young men built them from kits and if they couldn't afford kits, they did as Joseph Provenzano did who built his set with a discarded oatmeal box, scavenged copper and a few parts which he did have to buy. In the pre-Walkman, precentralized precorporate era radio wasn't an experience (that overused word of a passive and pacified culture), but an activity with the families gathering to listen to the pre-loudspeaker crystal sets together. Another Chicagoan, recalling his radio days, remembered that he "monkeyed around with the crystal until it got real loud. Then we'd take the earphones and we'd put them in a pot . . . and the sound there, you know, would reverberate in the pot and then we'd all listen to it."[19]

RCA did its level best to make it impossible for the radio Yankee-tinkerers of the 1920s to get the parts that they needed to work in their shops. The company, which at that time was the sole source of vacuum tubes, warned distributors that they were only to be sold as replacements for radio sets of RCA licensed manufacture. At one point the company even went to the extreme of asking its parts dealers to send back a used tube for every new one they received.[20]

Although RCA was David Sarnoff's company, he continued to try to make broadcasting a non-commercially sponsored medium by creating a public service network backed by GE, Westinghouse and RCA. It too would have been linked by telephone lines save for AT&T refusing to lease them. A resourceful man, Sarnoff made one last attempt to bring a commercial-free radio service into existence by arranging to use Western Union and Postal Telegraph lines to carry his programs to his network affiliates. Unhappily, the telegraph wire was unsuited to carry sound, so that Sarnoff's only hope was to turn AT&T around,

something which proved impossible both because the great telephone monopoly smelled money and because of the odor of anti-Semitism in the executive offices of Walter S. Gifford, AT&T's honcho, or so concluded one of Sarnoff's biographers. Sarnoff had to capitulate, but his fight shows that there were businessmen—and he was not the only one—who understood that moral and social consequences adhered to their business decisions. They were willing to curtail their profit, perhaps out of striving for a higher level of civilization or perhaps out of a foreknowledge that a lower one would weaken the social base upon which everything, including business, has to stand, but there were too few Sarnoffs and too many Giffords.[21]

So the choice was not between government dictation and corporate rapacity. The kinds of social organizations which might have been entrusted with the responsibility of operating radio and television are as various as the imaginations of people like David Sarnoff to invent them. We get what we deliberately and purposefully make. There was nothing inevitable about the decision, nothing unavoidable; the outcome was not in accordance with the laws of nature or other theories of predestination. The question wasn't decided by God or by History. It was decided by people and it was a bum, shortsighted decision. Short-term gains over long-term losses. The consequences of the decision, the making of the mumbling millions, may have been unintended, but they were not unforeseeable. The decision has contributed to the lowering of literacy and taste, the shifting of values and ways of living, so that now, seventy years later, we have a queasy feeling when we walk the night streets of our jittery communities.

From the start, broadcasting was controlled by businessmen and large corporations. There were no wild men owner-proprietors. The broadcasting industry has no Horace Greeley, no Cissy Patterson, no James Gordon Bennett, no Hearst, no Pulitzer. None of the scores of impassioned, furious, stubborn, eccentric men and women who ran American newspaper and magazine publishing for so long are to be seen owning, controlling or running any significant part of the broadcasting industry. The variety in opinion, quality and scope, which characterized print communications when they were a mass medium, is altogether absent in the broadcasting mass media. Print com-

peted by price but also by content; broadcasting, begging for a tapioca audience of its own creation, doesn't. "Narrow casting" radio competes by offering different "sounds," but television competes by offering more of the same more intensely. Political sectarians, doing obscurantist textual analyses, claim to find that one network is more or less liberal or conservative than the other, but in actuality the structure of ownership and the nature of management have reduced all content to nearly identical formulas.

William Paley, the founder of CBS, and a gorgeously colorful and gifted entrepreneur, bears a certain resemblance to the mad men of the age of print in his art- and woman-collecting, and from his propagandizing about CBS being the "Tiffany network." In the end, though, Paley was a highly public specimen of the CEO ethos, with no message to impart beyond the happy news contained in his annual report.[22] Ted Turner, an equally able businessman who made cable television into the industry it is today, harbors the strongest views on political and economic questions, but you would never guess what they are from watching CNN or Turner's other properties. He never editorializes; the communications' barons of the precorporate age always did.

Newspaper and magazine publishing had always been a mixture of business and advocacy, a sense of mission and of profits rolled into one. For generations the proprietors ran their publishing enterprises as much to spout off in their own peculiar fashions as to make money. For them, the medium was not the message. The messages themselves varied from the antibusiness slant of an S. S. McClure, who published the greatest of the muckrakers in the magazine which bore his name, to Cyrus H. K. Curtis and his famous editor, George Horace Lorimer, at the *Saturday Evening Post*, who were dedicatedly pro-business. These men liked a dollar as well as the next, but there were limits to how far they would curb their tongues or what they would let into their publications. They had more than one bottom line. Thus at *The New Yorker*, editor Harold Ross had the power to kill ads which detracted from his vision of what the magazine ought to have been. Briton Hadden, co-founder with Henry Luce of *Time* magazine, took a certain pleasure in running copy which drove advertisers nuts. At one point he got the

145

Fisher Body Division of General Motors so crazy they killed fifty-two full pages of advertising.

Under the editorship of its founder, *Forbes* was a medium with a highly personal voice. B.C. was an enthusiast, a moralist, an optimist furioso, who pined to strum his lyre in praise of upbuilders and was as ready to use his publication—and it was *his* publication—to attack Henry Ford for his anti-Semitism and his hateful treatment of his employees. B.C.'s agony in the Depression years, his confusion and his refusal to give up on the high destiny he believed was business's mission and its future are palpable. The editorial advocacy of Malcolm, his son, was strikingly different. Malcolm was emotionally withdrawn. You got no sense, as you do reading his father, of Malcolm out there in the thick, battling for the right and for the Lord. Malcolm came across as a civilized, middle-of-the-pack Republican, who leaned starboard or larboard, depending on how the coxswain of the moment signaled. In the pages of the magazine Malcolm expressed his individuality by writing or having other people write about his consumption. He wrote endlessly about food and drink, about buying things and taking trips. Then he had other people write about him doing the above.

For B.C. the magazine was an instrument, and he fashioned it by working like a dog for years. There is many an issue in which he had three signed articles, but, beyond his own forbidding production, the whole magazine had a piquant individuality about it. The publication was crawling with insertions that must have been placed there by the owner-editor's instructions —poems, jokes, sayings, adjurations and admonitions. It's almost as though it were the *Farmer's Almanac* of business.

Much of the modern *Forbes* distinctiveness comes from approaches and even features which date back to B.C.'s times. But there is a change. Under Malcolm the presentation was smoother, easier, less personal, far less *engagée*. *Forbes*, under the ownership and control of the founder's son, began to sound as though it were published by a corporation. Many family or individually owned businesses have done the same thing, fleeing their own individuality to mimic the cautious tones of the publicly owned corporation.

In times past there were also amoralists in publishing who would have fit in at NBC or CBS or Time Warner. Frank Mun-

sey, a vastly successful publisher of newspapers and magazines eighty years ago, was one. When Munsey died in 1925, William Allen White, the owner-editor of the *Emporia (Kansas) Gazette*, and long regarded as the unofficial national sage, wrote[23] of his fellow newspaper proprietor, "Frank Munsey contributed to the journalism of his day the talent of a meat packer, the morals of a money changer and the manner of an undertaker. He and his kind have about succeeded in transforming a once-noble profession into an 8 per cent security. May he rest in trust."[24]

At no point was broadcasting controlled by anyone who had a desire to say anything. How could it be otherwise since it was dominated from the start, not by entrepreneurs endowed with some kind of editorial fury, but by the largest of corporations, which held the key patents. Westinghouse, General Electric and AT&T had wrapped themselves and radio in a series of interlocking agreements, which resulted in a theretofore unheard of situation. The three companies and their child, RCA, were involved in legal antitrust problems before the industry was an industry, before it had yet started, before it had turned a profit, before more than a handful of stations were up and operating across the country. This was a purely big-business-created industry, a corporate endeavor, and it showed it from the beginning.

The corporate executives had the medium, but they had no message. *Ab initio* the medium was for hire, the product of bizthink at its narrowest, and it was dominated by men who saw their properties as common carriers. Like owners of any other common carrier,* long haul or short, they were set to carry the freight of whoever paid. Whatever the cargo to whatever destination, it made no difference. They never peeked into the crates and packing cases to see if they were delivering brain rot, moral necrosis or social morbidity. The manifest said it was prepaid, FOB from Hollywood and Manhattan, to everywhere USA, and if you got a problem, lady, buy time and put on your own damn program.

Common carrier is not a farfetched metaphor, but a restatement of AT&T policy as it was agreed upon at an executive

---

* The expression is used as a metaphor. Lawyers for television networks have long opposed being designated common carriers by the government for profit, not editorial, reasons.

meeting held in early 1922. A memo summarizing the decision taken at the meeting lays out the future of American broadcasting: "We the telephone company were to provide no programs. The public was to come in. Anyone who had a message for the world or wished to entertain was to come in and pay their money as they would coming into a telephone booth, address the world, and go out."[25]

Thus advertiser control over program content begins when the industry begins. It knows no other tradition, and though it does have another history, only a few scholars know about it. For the rest, the sponsor system, as injurious as it has been to home life, education, culture and even health, seems natural, inevitable, somehow right and superior to a 1984ish government alternative. Sometimes advertiser control has been indirect, but often it has been total. Then blocks of time are sold to the advertiser during which it may program any way it wants. The practice dates from broadcasting's beginnings and continues to this day as evangelists and diet plan purveyors purchase large chunks of time for their gospel hours and "infomercials."

Communications executives respond to two stimuli, hope of gain and fear of loss. That being their nature, accusations of media bias are usually false. Executives will put anything on the tube or in their publications for which they think there is a demand. They would put Communist propaganda on the air if there were a market, if it were to goose their ratings upward. They would televise their own hanging for bigger audience share.

In the late 1960s and early 1970s, the nation's mass media, broadcasting, mass circulation magazines, record companies and movies, pushed recreational drug taking, because that's the way they thought the market was moving. From the Lovin' Spoonful to The Doors, drug songs, drug celebrities, drug jokes, captured audiences and moved merchandise. Every form of commercial mass media cashed in on the 1967 "Summer of Love," culminating in hundreds of thousands of young people going to San Francisco and drugging themselves into a stupor. In the 1980s and 1990s they were writhing with antidrug fulminations because that's the way they thought the market was moving. For good numbers in the next three quarters, broadcast managers would and have assisted in killing their own cus-

tomers, by giving airtime to drugs, alcohol, tobacco. They don't mean any harm by it, but when they meet with stock market analysts, the men and women who recommend which stocks to buy or to dump, they want good numbers.

Malcolm had opinions and he expressed them in his magazine in the tradition of the owner-proprietor. They were conventional, as has been said, however, and seemed to carry little weight in the world of business. One of his secretaries who watched him at work over the years concluded that the "Fact & Comment" feature, started by B.C. and carried on by Malcolm, elicited little mail. She said that the lightly regarded man was reduced to sending tear sheets to the people he praised in the column, then waiting and printing their acknowledgments as though they were unsolicited letters to the editor.[26]

Malcolm was to BizWorld as Herb Caen, the genial, home-town-proud, San Francisco columnist, is to his city. But often Malcolm could rise no higher than being pleasantly inane: "A number of very serious problems confront businessmen today. One in particular has long concerned me. Why, in restaurants, clubs, at home and everywhere else one eats, are slices of lemon provided when the dish calls for lemon juice?"[27]

Sometimes he was running a private circle jerk: "THAT SUPERWITTY BASTION OF WRITER'S BLOCK, FRAN LEBOWITZ wrote us recently asking for a contribution to a benefit reading on behalf of the Literacy Volunteers of New York City. In responding with a contribution, I wrote, 'Nobody should be deprived of reading Fran Lebowitz just because they don't know how to.' "[28]

On the cutting edge of this year's banalities, Malcolm moved neither too fast nor too slow. He himself described his method when he confessed that he had thought so little of Rachel Carson's *Silent Spring* when it first came out and was pressed into his hands by the seventy-six-year old James Rand of Remington Rand, that he wrote, "I thought he was nuts at the time, and later remarked to my wife that it was a shame to see senility erode the mind of such a brilliant man."[29] As environmentalism got fashionable, Malcolm got with it.

Such editorial forthrightness and a reputation for dropping a wee giftee now and then won Malcolm sixty, count'em, sixty honorary doctorates. We are contemplating a man who made

too few enemies. Ye gods! The places he went and the degrees they gave him! Risible titles like doctor of commercial science, doctor of international entrepreneurship, doctor of public service and business leadership and doctor of economic journalism. Honors not from Quack 'Em an' Fool 'Em U, not from take-their-tuition-and-run joints, not from *infra dig* degree mills with dusty quads, but impressive places of learning like Oklahoma Christian College, Armand Hammer United World College of the American West, and East Texas State University. Big time schools also played at this pompous swindle. The hood of shame was put over Malcolm's head at The Johns Hopkins and Carnegie Mellon universities, as well as at the cow-and-coed schools.[30]

Evidently Malcolm took his cues for editorial opinion from the conventional sources, particularly the *New York Times*.[31] Short of pith, spleen and brilliance, he cranked on, through the years, praising American capitalism in language too pedestrian to bear quotation. Compared to editorial offerings of his contemporary, Robert Bartley at *The Wall Street Journal*, Malcolm's writing was aqueously conformist. The strident conviction, the hotly held opinions expressed in *Journal* editorials, are closer in energy and force to B.C.'s writings than to his son's. But the *Journal* is deviant. As owner-proprietors gave way in publishing to the corporate ownership forms of the modern era, opinion has vanished. At *People* magazine, a Time Warner product, the subject of the cover is determined with the assistance of focus groups, those gatherings-up of just plain folks who tell the advertising agencies and the political tacticians how they feel about dentifrices, movies stars, laxatives and the Department of Agriculture. A comedown for a corporation started by Henry Luce, a man who used his great publishing enterprise to nominate presidential candidates and put Dwight Eisenhower in the White House, the man who coined the phrase "The American Century," and then made it the guiding star for a generation of national leaders. The last thing that would have occurred to Henry Luce was to gather up a collection of yokels off the streets and shopping malls to tell *him* who or what to put on the cover of his magazines. Unthinkable. An elitist, but agree with Henry or not, he had something to be elite about.

Malcolm had neither Luce's intelligence, passion nor vision.

If he and other media proprietors leave it to others to decide what to air or publish, it is doubtless just as well. The pioneering media people of our era, Ted Turner and Christopher Whittle, came to communications with no message, nothing to say. They both have had better business ideas. Luce had a better business idea in *Time* magazine, which was a real departure when it came on to the newsstands.

Time, Inc., is now Time Warner, and the boss man is Steve Ross, the Pinky Ring Kid, whose opinions are unknown. His career path isn't, however: this is another non-Horatio Alger story. Ross started out in the son-in-law business. His father-in-law was an undertaker, whose business got so good, he started renting funeral cortege limos when they weren't carrying the bereaved to the cemetery. Business got better, he got into car rentals, and one thing led to another. In due course the father-in-law was shucked off and Mr. Ross turned to pure gold.

To a somewhat wider, non-investor public Mr. Ross is best known for the unseemly dispute over how the press should calculate the amount of his salary. From time to time his picture flashes on the screen of life, and we briefly see this white-haired man getting out of his long black car looking like what? A mafia don, a down market CEO, a Las Vegas headliner, one of a type who wear their hair over their ears and give the impression they are swathed in iridescent clothing. Hollow man of the media wasteland, man of the hour on Wall Street.

# NINE

---

# The Music
# Never Stops

**M**ALCOLM'S grammar school years were the happy 1920s; prep school and college were the tight years of the 1930s. One may attribute to the Depression his caution as a businessman, his not buying into opportunities which made the men he palled around with far richer than he. Men like the dismal John Kluge or stock market player Warren Buffett or the real estate speculator-investor Laurence Tisch, who used his winnings to pry his way into the CEO-ship of CBS. That was his pessimistic, careful 1930s side; the side of Malcolm which knew how to spend a dollar was strictly 1920s, the years of B.C.'s greatest prosperity. Malcolm had this Jazz Age aspect to him.

Such was the bifurcated experience of Malcolm's generation, which was born in the sun and plunged into the shade. So abrupt was the switch that the 1920s have ever since been checked off as an aberrational interlude, one of those piggy

decades which come along every so often, an act-of-God decade of greed which nobody can explain. Be that as it may, the 1920s was also the decade in which the new business-built culture and social system were for the first time clearly to be seen in triumphant detail. The old America died in the 1920s and modern America arrived.

Its arrival was noted with mixed feelings by the writers and artists of the time. As the decade ended, one man, Aldous Huxley, saw what had happened with special clarity, and in 1932 published *Brave New World*, the anti-utopia in which he foresaw it would be possible to rule and control a population through sex, drugs and rock 'n' roll. *Brave New World*, written before the Nazis and Communists had reached their zeniths of horror, was blotted out by *1984*, an anti-utopia which explored the delights of totalitarianism. Now three generations later the Nazis are gone, the Communists are on their way to the dustbin of history and business's *Brave New World* is on the march everywhere. Huxley imagined a world in which science and technological accomplishment are used to keep the population in a sort of hedonized thralldom, in which vulgar entertainment, sex and drugs are available around the clock as a means of behavior control. The high culture, Socrates, Shakespeare and all those other double-domed thinkers, is locked up and denied the *Brave New World*'s youth.

The masters of Huxley's futuristic state build their tyranny of pleasure for political reasons. America's plush thralldom is an unintended side effect, brought into existence without plan or deliberation. If a sizable portion of the nation's population is, on any given day, under the influence of some kind of chemical, the reasons aren't to be found in political motivation, as in *Brave New World*, but in one form of business activity or another. (There may be political effects, however, in a democracy in which ten or twenty percent of the eligible voters are groggy, stoned and dazed half the time.) If you add up all the people who are, on that given day, under the influence of drugs sold to them by licit businessmen*, by businessmen in the wine, beer

* Licit and ethical are words with variable definitions in the field of marketing drugs of whatever kind. The cocaine and marijuana trades could not operate their vast nationwide distribution and retail sales networks without the assistance of banks, real estate brokers, automobile agencies, the aviation and maritime transportation indus-

**153**

and hard spirits industries, and under the influence of psychoactive drugs (tranquilizers and such) sold to them by the ethical pharmaceutical industry, the number runs into many millions.

In the let's pretend *Brave New World* imagined by Aldous Huxley, the small ruling group eschewed the sex, drugs and rock 'n' roll. Those pleasures were for the proles, the ordinary people, to control them without harsh measures. In the real *Brave New World* of contemporary America, the society from top to bottom is soaked in the taking of dangerous and debilitating pleasures. So common had drug taking become by the 1960s, an incumbent President was being regularly injected with feel-good chemicals by a licensed physician.[1]

The full scope of the business-built and business-controlled society showed itself to Huxley and other investigators in the 1920s, not as a nightmare to come, but one which had arrived. If they were too dismissive of the importance of the physical benefits which the new commercial order brought, they were the first to see how business values, business ideas, business necessities, business merchandising of fun and pleasure, had entered home and family, changing day to day life patterns, child rearing and even character or personality formation.

The 1920s was the payoff decade for what the invention of business in the previous century had wrought, the decade in which the building of heavy industry and the transportation systems seemed to pay off in a higher standard of living for average people. Thanks to sales devices like installment buying, business was making available to huge numbers of families an array of items which would shortly change the life of those who bought them.

Clocks and furniture were first sold on the installment plan, particularly in New England, in the early years of the nineteenth century, and Cyrus McCormick used installment selling for his reaper, but that was selling a tool, not a consumer item. It wasn't until the 1850s that time-payments were introduced on a mass, national scale for an item for the home. Edward

tries. What are called the "ethical pharmaceutical" companies have found ways to advertise and market an array of psychoactive drugs on such a vast scale to so many people that it is not possible to say where illegal sales end and legal ones begin or what percentage of drugs, legal and illegal, are sold just to make people feel good.

Clark, Isaac Singer's partner, came up with the idea of selling sewing machines for five dollars down and three to five a month.[2] The sewing machine could also be considered a tool, since many a family made its living sewing for clothing manufacturers, but primarily it was an item for home use and signaled the rise of installment marketing for pure consumer merchandise. Sears, Roebuck, which didn't relish the cost or the complexity of mail order installment sales, resisted the idea until around 1910, when too many other merchants were satisfying the appetites of the dawning consumer society for the company to hold out any longer.[3] The twenties saw the start of the General Motors Acceptance Corporation and wholesale use of the installment device to sell practically everything.[4] By the 1920s credit was the modern way of life. The only appurtenance that was lacking was VISA or MasterCard.

As late as the 1880s the majority of families still had little money to spend on anything but shelter, food and clothing,[5] but by the 1920s, enough people had a surplus to put the phrase, "keeping up with the Joneses," into common use.†

The years after the First World War hatched the idea that there was no stopping America. Every tomorrow was going to be better than every yesterday and good times would go on forever. The inconceivably rich East Texas oil fields were coming in; the factories were pouring out goods; the whole country was a gusher. The flow of goods and services out of the business-invented horn-of-plenty was vulcanic in its dimensions.

Wealth was being created on a scale which did more than simply better society, family and daily life. It changed it.

Those meticulous social researchers, Robert and Helen Lynd, tracked and described the changes.[6] Indoor running water, gas stoves and commercially baked bread made it easier for more women to work outside the home. It was an emancipation for millions, although millions of others were still forced to adhere to the tradition of Mondays for washing, Tuesdays for ironing, Wednesdays for baking, etc.

Nevertheless, the Lynds descried the leisure-entertainment

† This once ubiquitous locution was coined by comic strip artist Arthur R. ("Pop") Momand, who first used it in 1913 in the *New York Globe*. It doesn't seem to be employed as often as it was, but there is scant evidence that the practice is dying off even if the metaphor is.

society aborning. The film industry already dominated the dream life of people in the decade of flaming youth, banishing minister, schoolmaster, eminent lecturer and belle-lettrists. And behind the films were the people who were shaping the culture and morals of the country—the businessmen. The decline in the prestige and power of pulpit, schoolhouse and editorial office is palpable in the post-World War I era, when commercial organizations vied with teacher and clergyman as the arbiters of morals and taste. With the coming of radio the process of making entertainment ubiquitous and continuous was underway. Business was about to bring forth something utterly new in human history, a world in which the music never stops. The all-entertainment culture, brought to the society by businessmen incapable of knowing when enough was enough, would change the facts of daily life only somewhat less than the invention of fire.

Businessmen in the 1920s were already being accused of pandering to the lowest common denominator in the entertainment they sold, because the lowest denominator was the only commercially profitable denominator. The Lynds described one attempt by a Muncie businessman to offer educational movies prepared by Yale University to the public; he got a house full of empty seats for his pains. "Never again," they quote the exhibitor saying after his second attempt to get moviegoers to buy tickets to a movie with undisguised educational intent. Business did not invent the taste for vacuous pleasure, but it exploited the vacuity which it found. If it had found a nation of people who would have paid to listen to *The Brandenburg Concertos*, Bach, not Muzak, would play in America's elevators. Business took the worst which was already there and made it the norm, the national standard.

Businessmen did not intend to wreak havoc with high school learning in America. They did not intend to be the Evil Coachman seducing America's high school Pinocchios to sweet, pleasure land. They did it anyway, but only for the money, not for ideology, not for some sneaky foreign cause, not to serve some erroneous high purpose. They did not intend to pull teenagers out of the ambit of their families and into the all-absorbing peer group social life of partying and consumption which now characterizes them. The loosening of the closeness of family life and

of the tight obedience of child to parent came from the shrinking need of families for their children's labor; it arose from
business abundance, from business-achieved prosperity. But as
merchants and manufacturers saw that, first, high school students, then later grammar school children and even toddlers,
had become detached or could be detached and turned into
customers, they went for the kids. Two-year-old American babies test out by marketers to be brand-conscious about the
clothes they wear, and six-year-olds are as attuned to trademarks and logos as an American adult.[7] The more they sold the
children their own things—their own clothes, their own entertainment, transportation and food and drink, the more they
accelerated the building up of youth as a world apart, now dig-
nified by the term subculture.

Business redesigned the architecture of family and youth and
growing up. What may be going on in some of the seldom
visited rooms of the social structure can sometimes surprise,
disconcert and shock. Such is the effect on the adults who found
out that the large record companies were making profits selling
adolescent males compact discs of rhythmic rap ditties which
rhapsodized over the pleasures of physically degrading women.
The once intimate life became a commercially engineered experience, home became a small theme park, manufactured and
sold by the same kinds of organizations which do the same for
the big theme parks. Expressions like "family values," "family-
oriented" or, God save us, "family-orientated" are, if not merchandising tools, then phrases which describe consumer buying
patterns, not the hearth and home suggested in the little nee-
dlepoint tapestries once found framed on the wall above the
fireplace.

The kidnapping of American children began before television. Fifty years ago terms like teenage culture or adolescent
peer group were not in use, but the teenager as a market segment may have been recognized prior to the 1920s. The first
targets were the adolescents. Adolescence itself seems to have
been invented by Clark University president and psychologist
G. Stanley Hall, with the publication in 1904 of his book, with
the wonderful name of *Adolescence, Its Psychology and Its Relation
to Physiology, Anthropology, Sociology, Sex, Crime, Religion and Education*. Up till then people of this age had not been a population

group; a hop, skip and a jump in time and adolescence became a market segment. The now familiar battles over dress codes got underway in the nation's high schools in the early twenties. Rouge, lipstick, eyebrow pencils, high heels were among the consumer items teens were already using. Going into the 1920s educators were reporting in such unlikely places as Indiana that high school students, out till two o'clock in the morning, were "jazzed to death." In 1917 an Ohio high school was telling its parents "that three-fourths of all our low grades and failures are due to the 'social party craze.' " Ten years later the same school was saying, "that social functions leading to 'late hours,' frequent theater-going or any other enterprise consuming much of the pupil's time or enlisting his interests are highly detrimental to good schoolwork."[8] The Lynds quote a Muncie teacher already saying in the early 1920s, "One of the bad features of radio is that children stay up late at night and are not fit for school next day."[9]

With children left to their own devices, the Evil Coachman had no difficulty getting them to clamber on board his conveyance so that, with whip-cracking static, he rose up into the frequency-modulated air bearing his passengers away to Entertainment Land, where they are amused around clock and calendar. Everything is fun, life is a game, Nintendo or other, and if it isn't entertaining, don't do it. If it's Borrrr-ing, zap to the next channel. College teachers with the highest grades in student rating programs are the ones judged most entertaining. When the student grows up in Entertainment Land, of course the best teachers are the most exciting, the ones who put on skits, jump, dance, shout and make funnies. Too young to be true 'taters, they are just little couch spuds in the classroom. The passive learning experience can be observed in the thousands of schools which have their students watch two minutes of commercials every day along with a news program. Study, the children are told by plain implication, is not reading a book; it is being diddled by a TV set, being done to by the box. The authority of school and teacher is brought to bear to instruct children that they are to heed commercials, give them weight and do their bidding. Parents who try to fend off the invasion of mass commerce by refusing to have a television set in their home are compelled by law and custom to send their children

to an institution which sabotages their training and instructs kids to believe the words sung by the jolly, dancing grapes, to give deference to beer commercials which excite and stimulate a life, not of the mind, but of the gonads. The commercial message is that the reward for academic success is getting to make out at the sex orgies on the Florida beaches during college vacation breaks. There's a good reason for scoring high on the SATs.

Getting knowledge is not an activity, something the student does, but something which is done to him (or her); it is passive, it is "experiencial." Behold the new model commercially extruded child as opposed to the old, often imperfect, but nevertheless family wrought version. The student as spectator, the student as customer, consumer and passive spectator. In the past thirty years a generation like no other in the history of the species has attained its majority, the first people never to have known silence.

Born with a loudspeaker button in their ears, less interested in learning, less able to study, taking longer to master less material, students live in perpetual music for they go not with their God but with their Walkman. From dawn to dawn love stories, war stories, crime stories, sex stories, cartoon stories, comedians and schmoozers parade across the retina of their consciousness as the button on the channel changer is touched. A generation reared up closer to the company of the friendly strangers on the screen, whom they see and hear and can never speak to, than to bleeding and breathing humans.

In real time, that has come to mean that children are not raised by their parents. They are raised by television sets, in industrial crèches, at the neighbors who take in toddlers, by scudzy, commercial nursery schools where the johns leak and the health inspector is bribed and by the million and one different expedients hard-pressed parents have devised to keep their little ones physically safe. Mentally and morally the American toddler is on his or her own. In some communities it has been reported that hospitals, hard-pressed business enterprises themselves, advertise special facilities for sick children who are too infectious to go to the day care center. The standard of living which business has taught people to expect can't be obtained by most one-income families, but business has not

brought forth the wealth for working people to pay for good child care.

The consumer-children become aware at a precocious age that business, through advertising and other means, provides them not only with good things, but all things and all thoughts. They know it, they are often a bit cynical about it, but, having grown up in Entertainment Land and never having known the tougher, fibrous reality of nature, they go along with it. Their critical faculties are left undeveloped—thinking is not big in Entertainment Land—they are content to go on buying tickets on the rides in the Theme Park of Life. Deconstructionism and demolitionism are but the acts of the more unruly spirits trying to fight their way through the movie set towns, the artificial forests and the papier-mâché Alps to the exits.

The Evil Coachman took his first carriage load of children to Entertainment Land a long time ago. The children currently growing up there are perhaps the fourth or fifth generation. Each generation has been presented with a yet more complete, more dominating, more beguiling and more captivating edition of Entertainment Land. In the years of Malcolm Forbes' boyhood, the 1920s, the children from upper-middle-class homes such as his were more or less untouched. Now at the end of the twentieth century, even the pinnacled families would find it hard to establish control over the rearing of their children. For the most part the presumption, the hope, that somewhere among the millionaires at least, there is a small group of comfortably fixed people holding out in the last redoubt of good taste and high standards is akin to the myth of the Middle Ages, that the sleeping knight of the forest will come to liberate the serfs. Old money, new money, the Henry Kravises and Brooke Astors listen to the same music that comes out of the loudspeakers in the malls, they watch the same dippy TV programs and go to the same movies. Entertainment Land is not democratic, because it is run by the authoritarian structures of the business corporation, but it is egalitarian. Everybody is there and everybody is getting equally worked over.

A few African-American malcontents have noted that *all* the available culture heros for black youngsters are entertainers. It is less commented on that the same thing can be said for white youngsters. Fame comes to those who wiggle their asses *comme il*

**160**

*faut* to turn on the animal house, who do things with a ball, base-, golf-, foot-, basket- or other, or who warble or prance on a screen. The road to a lesser fame is to be outstanding in one's adulation of athletes and entertainers. The late A. Bartlett Giamatti, the president of Yale University, forsook that *infra dig* position to better himself as the "commissioner" of baseball. When he made the move, not one disgusted sound could be heard, as the media jury exclaimed how wonderfully American, how man of the people it was, as if we didn't have enough men and women of the people already. As rap singers might say, "We got the massy, what we need is classy."

The idea of constantly applied effort, unremitting effort, the social value we now associate with the Japanese, was the norm in the United States before the Evil Coachman began his sinister runs to Entertainment Land. Only hobos and millionaires were couch potatoes then. It was a making, producing, toiling, inventing culture. No one reached in and took without that awareness that "man," to use the expression of the time, was making abundance flow. The entertainment society of our epoch was aborning then, but other values remained powerful. Scientists, science and engineering, as the original source of material blessings, had a place in the public consciousness that we reserve for basketball players and musicians of the more pelvic persuasion. In 1928 Herbert Hoover was elected President under the soubriquet of "The Great Engineer." A glamorously successful career as a mining engineer was a promise that the voters would have a doer, a maker, a producer of wealth directing the nation. Two generations later a movie actor held the same office, and thereby hangs a tale of two nations and two ages.

When Albert Einstein's ship, *Rotterdam*, docked in New York in 1920 it was akin to the arrival of the Beatles a world and time later. Reporters and photographers and thousands of the nameless were there to greet this gentleman who spoke not a word of English and was a citizen of a country that the United States was still technically at war with.[10] A reception at City Hall was followed by a number of triumphant appearances capped by a visit to Washington and the White House, after which one newspaper ran a headline declaring that, "EINSTEIN IDEA PUZZLES HARDING, HE ADMITS AS SCIENTIST CALLS."[11] The name Einstein has

gone into the American language along with rocket scientist as a synonym for genius, but as the century ended, American culture had changed so much that not one person in the galaxy of reigning celebrities was a scientist. It is not surprising that there should be a steady decline in the number of young Americans interested enough and willing to do the work to become scientists.[12] In the 1980s, bowing less to science than to his collector's desire to own the detritus of fame, Malcolm Forbes paid $220,000 for a letter from Albert Einstein to Franklin Roosevelt discussing the possibility of building the atomic bomb. Thoroughly modern Malcolm evinced little interest in science.[13] Like many another American of his time, he was content to take what it could do for him and pass on.

For the last thirty years, native-born, entertainment-happy Americans have increasingly lacked the interest and the stick-to-itiveness to go into the hard sciences and engineering. In recent years more than forty percent of the doctorates conferred by American universities in mathematics, physics and computer sciences have been awarded to foreign-born nationals, the great majority here on temporary visas.[14] More than half of all doctorates awarded in engineering are now conferred on foreign-born nationals; likewise over half of the associate professorships at American schools of engineering are held by foreign nationals. Simultaneously, applications by American nationals for admission to engineering schools now constitute a minority of those applying.[15] People come from abroad to take the places once held by Americans, and let us hope that, after they complete their training, they stay, but the plain superiority in the standard of living and the pleasantness of daily life which America once enjoyed over the entire world is not so obvious now. A growing number of countries have one approximating our own and a lower crime rate to boot.

Such an anomaly. At the same time that the sciences push ahead, and the life sciences—biology, genetics, cytology and so on—explode every-which-way into new discovery and accomplishment, the society as a whole is in growing danger of not being able to sustain itself. At the rate we are going, we won't be able to run, much less repair, the machines our parents and our grandparents invented and passed on to us. We may become barbarians in our own house, brute primitives wondering at

our own possessions and the magic they make, uncomprehending Ostrogoths with no conception of what goes on under the lids and covers of the machines we depend on for our health and comfort. Warning: Do not remove the back of this set; if it breaks, if it starts to smoke or begins to pop and spark, unplug it; if you can at least do that, throw the contrivance out and get another.

The reasons for the decline in the quality of schooling are not the topic here, but whatever the other difficulties, children of the Evil Coachman, children whose parents also accepted a ride in that chariot, are increasingly ineducable. Entertainment-addicted kids who don't do schoolwork because it's dull, boring and bothersome are tough cases even for teachers who hope to teach them statistical mechanics by doing Frank Sinatra imitations. It has reached that point in the high schools. A recent study of a Texas high school reports that, "To get students to learn history, one teacher played a version of 'Jeopardy.' Another teacher in an honors English course, instead of having the students read *The Scarlet Letter* one year, showed them a video of it." The same book quotes teachers in the high school, which does *not* draw its pupils from an inner-city, gang-permeated, hell-hole community, saying, "It still amazes me when I give a test in grammar and the kids can do it . . . It used to be the other way around. I used to be surprised whenever they didn't know it . . . They like to have cars. They like stereo speakers that are fancy. They like to go skiing, they like to wear good jewelry . . . Having fun is what it's all about . . . These kids don't take responsibility, or don't know how . . . Kids used to worry about where they were going to fit into the world. Kids today don't seem to worry if they are going to fit in society, because they don't give a hoot . . . Twenty years ago I was working my kids to death, and now I have to remind my seniors to use capital letters and put periods at the end of sentences . . . They don't seem to care about their grades. They don't seem to care about each other . . . They seem to care about having a good time . . ."[16] The Evil Coachman has taken these wooden heads for a real ride.

Paying athletes to play on college football teams was prevalent in the Ivy Leagues before the turn of the century, but that was rich boys' stuff. The capture of the nation's high schools

and colleges for commerce and entertainment begins in earnest immediately after the Great War of 1914–18. By the middle of the 1920s the fun and excitement of basketball and football, always pushed by local retail merchants, were taking over everywhere. In the middle of the Depression, Muncie, Indiana, coughed up hundreds of thousands of dollars to build a 9,000-seat arena for the Bearcats high school basketball team; in 1937, 120,000 people in Soldier Field, Chicago, watched two high school football teams play each other.[17] Thus fifty years ago, captives already of the all-entertainment culture, parents and school board officials were putting money into providing spectacles that should have gone into buying augers with which to drill holes in the children's wooden heads. In our own era Texas high school football teams travel to away-games in chartered jet airliners.[18] But while the shit-kicker mommies and daddies have had much publicity about putting entertainment in front of education, in far off, supposedly staid, supposedly rock-ribbed and practical Downeast Maine, a high school in the Penobscot Bay region puts more money in its raggedy-ass football team than it spends on books.[19]

Big-business people cannot be blamed for starting the sports mania, but since World War II they have cashed in on it. As with the radio, the appetite for listening was there, the fault was how it was exploited. Coaches everywhere and at every level of play have become an integral part of local and national advertising. McDonald's prints ads on the back of the tickets at Louisiana State University, the University of Denver sells advertising space to beer companies, the University of Southern California has an endowment fund to pay for the football coach. Corporate sponsorships of collegiate athletics are endemic as this study makes clear: "It started in the mid-1980s when a number of companies began sponsoring bowl games and such hybrids as the John Hancock Sun Bowl and the Sea World Holiday Bowl appeared on TV to perplex New Year's viewers. . . . Then the venerable Sugar Bowl became the USF&G Sugar Bowl. . . . San Diego State University has been a leader in the scramble for this new form of revenue. The school sells each home football game to a different business, including, in 1988, Texaco, Sea World, El Cajon Ford, and Smith Barney, and it also has three full-season sponsors, one of which, Agua Caliente

Race Track, has a very problematic ownership history."[20] Hundreds of millions of dollars have gone into building new stadiums and arenas. A joint with the name and distinction of Cleveland State U. has spent almost fifty million dollars on its playpen. Add the interest on the loans to build these places and the money taken out of education budgets for entertainment is stupendous. And it *does* come out of the education budget, because, regardless of the ding-dong propaganda coming out of the director of athletics' office, all, yes, all athletic programs are net money losers.

The bankers, the construction companies, the advertising agencies, the clothes manufacturers, the beer corporations, the tire companies, the hardware industry, the automobile companies, the corporate raptors, peck, peck, peck, feeding off the livers of the nation's schools and colleges. The damage is immeasurable. Test scores tell nothing because the country grades itself on the curve, a statistical device used in many schools to establish a passing grade by looking at the class's aggregate score, so that the poorer the overall performance, the more the passing grade point is dropped downward. They are strip-mining the society; they are the social equivalents of the California companies who used the high-pressure waterpower to dissolve hills and mountains to get the gold. Strip, take and move on, with the land, with minerals under the land and the people walking on top of it.

Not that they intended to, not that it ever occurred to them, and not that they would give a damn if it did occur to them, nevertheless businessmen are subverting the basis of the country's technical competence. The great lizard is eating its own tail, breaking its own dinosaur eggs and making omelets of its own embryos. Well, the beast is hungry and unable to think past its next meal, although it is a pea-brained reptile indeed that eats its own seed grain.

After the nation's children were turned into indolent slushheads, the temples of the high culture were stormed and taken over for business purposes. The country's executives beheld institutions like the formerly august New York Metropolitan Museum of Art and decided that, to use their lingo, they were staring at a poorly deployed asset. Its return on investment was pitiably low, so they made it into a whorehouse. The mighty

Met hung the red lantern between its Corinthian columns with the publication of a brochure entitled *The Business Behind Art Knows the Art of Good Business.*[21]

Henceforth it would be used as a merchandising device. Its exhibitions would now be decided upon after consultation with such places as Bloomingdale's department store. The results of such a course were predictable with such shows as "Twenty-Five Years of Yves Saint Laurent," followed by the damned English hunting nonsense with a show put on by Polo/Ralph Lauren and entitled "Man and the Horse." Debora Silverman summed up what was going on with these nicely pointed words: "The 1980s mass market moguls are cultural cannibals; they absorb the historical materials of art-museum exhibitions for the purposes of advertising, public relations, and sales campaigns. Rather than the domain in which to express the moral brake on conspicuous consumption, the museum becomes the extension of the department store and another display case for the big business of illusion making."[22]

And the museum was up front in pushing its new mission in life. A circular letter sent out to prospective customers explained what the Met can do for you: "Many public-relations opportunities are available through sponsorship of outstanding special exhibitions at the Metropolitan Museum . . . Learn how you can provide creative and cost-effective answers to your marketing objectives by identifying your corporate names with Vincent Van Gogh . . . Canaletto . . . Remington, Fragonard, Rembrandt or Goya . . ."[23] This got an answering echo from Willard C. Butcher, the Chase Manhattan Bank's CEO, a man who was standing his watch on the poop deck as the bank wallowed into some of its more recent messes, but then Chase has a story sad enough to make strong men and investors weep. Quoth CEO Butcher: "We like to invest in established cultural institutions as well as emerging groups and, when possible, we like to bolster our investment with advertising, marketing and public relations activities which help the arts and the thousands of individuals . . . who are part of the Chase community."[24] You betcha you do, Cap'n.

Malcolm, in a courtly way, agreed that the use of art for the greater good of Bloomingdale's and retail sales generally was a worthwhile aim. "As a prime beneficiary of the cultural as well

**166**

as the economic growth of our society, business has a responsibility—a selfish one, if you will—to encourage the development of the arts," he wrote.[25] But what the hell did Malcolm care what happened to the arts? "My interest is not that of an academic collector," he told a reporter who might have suspected as much, "I didn't grow up exposed to old masters. My father didn't found the Mellon museum."[26]

The Mellons gave to museums, not took from them. In comparison to the mingy-stingy millionaires of today—excepting a few like Walter Annenberg—they do look like Medicis in the munificence of their gifts. How they got some of the princely sums they bestowed on us is another matter. Toward the end of the 1920s the Mellon-owned Union Trust of Pittsburgh joined a syndicate of banks which peddled fifty million dollars' worth of Kreuger & Toll debentures. Kreuger & Toll was a Swedish firm which was supposed to have worldwide control of the safety match business. A debenture is a bond issued by a company, backed up only by the company's promise to pay back the money it has gotten from the people who bought the bond. In other words it's a handshake, no-collateral loan, and if Kreuger & Toll didn't make good, the debenture buyers could whistle for their money. It was a 1920s version of a junk bond, and, boy, were Kreuger & Toll's debentures pieces of junk. Union Trust, which said it had examined the company and found its claims justified, sold these pieces of paper at ninety-eight dollars apiece; before long you could buy the same piece of paper for thirty-two cents. After the dust settled, the investing public learned that Union Trust had not bought these debentures for itself; they had simply sold them to their customers. For the money the bank lent to Kreuger & Toll, it had demanded solid collateral.

The bonds stunk so badly that an angry B.C. wrote, "Any crook who issues spurious money is sent to jail for a long term. But any Tom, Dick or Harry can issue spurious bonds or stocks without fear of punishment . . . They do these things better in Britain. There security buyers are protected by law. There the issuers of prospectuses must swear that every fact and figure is strictly true. If events prove any fact or figure was not true, the offenders are slapped into prison." B.C. forbore to mention

**167**

which of the powerful Mellon family he would like to have seen in Leavenworth.[27]

Ivar Kreuger, "the Match King," with whom Americans had invested and lost a quarter of a billion dollars, blew his brains out. It wasn't the foreigner who had jobbed them, but American outfits wearing the fanciest of pants—the Mellons, Lee, Higginson in Boston, Dillon Reed. They told the sheep Ivar was good for the money, but when the time came it wasn't a sharing but a shearing which they got, suckers.

Everybody with an engraved letterhead was out with the clippers. Citibank—called National City Bank then—had salesmen working out of sixty-nine district offices located in all the major cities ringing doorbells in the better neighborhoods peddling foreign bonds, the same damn, soon-to-be-worthless South American bonds the same banks would peddle a second time, fifty years later.[28] What comes around . . .

The latter part of the twenties heard a complaint familiar to moderns, viz, that far too much money was going into the pockets of Jazz Age yuppies, Wall Street brokers, lawyers and the ancillary flotsam who slosh in their wake. Dishonest schemes and wasteful imbecilities were popping up in great numbers as they do when people forsake their vocation to run a business and go play in the big casino instead. The House of Morgan took up with the Van Sweringer brothers, two incompetent, probably corrupt real estate developers, and staked them to a railroad empire and stuck investors with the cost, none of which they got back after the Van Sweringers went bankrupt. Corrupt managers of investment trusts, the 1920s name for mutual funds, loaded up on doggy stocks their crooked confederates couldn't sell anywhere else. As a result, when the crash came, investment trusts and the small investors took a much worse beating than stocks in general.[29] They had neglected to heed the aphorism of perhaps the crookedest, most colorful and most ingenious man to traverse Wall Street's narrow pavements, Daniel Drew, the mid-nineteenth-century cattle drover, steamboat operator, gold market speculator and railroad financier: "Anybody who plays the stock market not as an insider is like a man buying cows in the moonlight."[30]

There was the sniff of stealing in the air. Smart people and honest people could tell no good was going to come of it. For

two years before the great bust, B.C., who was both smart and honest, was warning that the party of the good and the just must reach out and yank the brakes. As early as 1927, he was writing pieces that said stock prices were "dangerously high"[31] under headlines like "STOCK RISE STILL OUTRUNNING BUSINESS RISE."[32]

One of the Milken types of the 1920s was Jesse Livermore. Like Milken, who in his prime seldom ventured out-of-doors, preferring to work through the spooky hours of night, Livermore protected his privacy. The doormen and elevator operators in his office building were instructed to deny such a person as Jesse even existed. Jesse was a stock pool artist, among other things. In confederation with other major market players, Jesse connived to drive the price of a stock up, then take his profits, leaving the members of the genus *Ovis*, who had bought in late and high, to offer up their fleece another time. A 1928 pool on Radio, as RCA stock was called then, successfully drove the price per share up sixty-one dollars in four days. Since only the pool members knew when the price was going to stop climbing, only the pool members knew when it was time to take one's profits and bail out.[33] (The major difference between then and now is that, the pool being legal then, investors often knew it was being run—you could read about it in *The Wall Street Journal*—and knowingly bet on when the pool managers were going to let the price of the stock collapse. In our era pools are illegal, therefore underground, therefore harder for small baa-baas to learn about, and therefore easier to profitably run.)

Jesse was one of the most famous bears of his age, meaning he made his biggest killings when the price of a stock was going down. Needless to say in late October 1929, Jesse got very rich as a lot of other people got very poor. Ultimately, Jesse got very poor, also, finally falling on his sword à la Kreuger, in the men's room of the bar at the Sherry-Netherland Hotel. Nowadays, they go to jail but they get to keep the money.

Before everyone got poor, they got rich, and sang the happy song their grandchildren, some of them working for Wall Street firms with the same names a half a century later, ought to have sung in the giddier days of the 1980s:

My sister sells snow‡ to the snow-birds,
My father makes bootlegger gin, . . .
My mother she takes in washing,
My God! How the money rolls in!

Within two weeks after the market collapse B.C. was writing a piece about 1920s greed. It could be today's editorial on "1980s greed" complete with new bromides for the '90s: "Many . . . had become obsessed by the notion that old-fashioned virtues had ceased to be virtues and that a 'new era' had dawned, an era in which the easiest and surest way to fortune was to merely buy stocks . . . and sit back and see them increase bewitchingly in market value. Bewhiskered axioms of the 'nothing without industry' theme excited only derision . . . The postwar generation had learned a trick worth dozens of these. They were cocksure they had discovered a royal road to ease and boundless wealth, namely stock speculation. . . . Well, there will be a return to first principles. The weekly pay envelope will cease to be ludicrously unimportant . . . Patient plodding, stick-to-itiveness, energy, enterprise will assume their old-fashioned aspect . . . Attention to the daily task will displace attention to gambling."[34]

Trinity Church, the historic Episcopal parish which anchors one end of Wall Street and which is reputed to be New York City's largest landowner, opened up the 1930 equivalent of a hot line to counsel the afflicted and, let's hope, contrite stockbrokers. As the decades rolled past the lessons were lost, but the underlying facts, moral and social, which caused B.C. to write them had not changed.

‡ That's what the stockbrokers of the 1920s called cocaine.

# TEN

# Nutmegs
# and Dynamos

**T**HE OFFICIALLY promulgated legend has Malcolm and his brothers having to work at the magazine during the hard days of the Great Depression, and, while it was true, the family was a long way from going on the dole. The boys had also had to work before the market crash, for B.C. did not want his sons to grow up spoiled. To his credit, Malcolm was careful not to suggest that he was required to do much more than open subscription renewal envelopes down at the office. He recalled B.C. coming around to check how much was coming in and, during the toughest period, the magazine had to skip one paycheck a month.

Although the *Forbes* of the 1930s was an emaciated thing compared to the magazine of the 1920s, the Forbeses were not within a moon shot of the financial devastation which wrecked the childhoods of millions of less lucky people.[1] B.C. was able to

send his sons to the best prep schools and colleges during the worst years.

But even the comfortably fixed felt the weight of the thing. Malcolm remembered his mother's reaction when he fell off his skates and broke a tooth. It was the day of Franklin Roosevelt's first inauguration. The banks had been going bust so fast that the states had closed the ones which were still healthy to prevent runs on them. On that morning in March of 1933, there was literally not a single bank open in the United States of America. You can understand Mrs. Forbes' reaction to Malcolm's accident: "When I came home! The despair on my mother's face when she had to take me to the dentist—'Here's another bill we don't need.' There was no sympathy for my painful hurt. The break was sharp enough but the nerve was exposed. The real pain came from the expression on Mother's face: 'My God, the banks are closing. We're in the depth of the Depression . . . struggling to make ends meet. And now you have to go to the dentist and here's one more bill to be argued about.' "[2]

One of the most salient differences between the early 1930s and the early 1990s is that in the former period what was happening to the country was awful but obvious. Even to people as relatively well fixed as the Forbeses it seemed as though the world was falling to pieces. In the 1990s, what happened with the banks may be awful, but it's not obvious. The pain was masked by the anodyne of government protection, but so also was the extent and even the nature of the damage. In the early 1930s business and everybody else took their lumps. The Hoover administration did make an effort to bail out the banks, but, given Herbert Hoover's principled reluctance to do such things, the effort was too late and too small to matter. The banks took their hit and went down by the thousands. The cost to the depositors, who lost their life savings, was indescribable. It scarred two generations, but the losses were finite and calculable. Many of the culpable bankers paid for their crimes and stupidities, and in these matters stupidity is a crime.

In the latest bank fiasco the crimes were covered over, the damage wasn't reckoned and it is possible that, when all is said and done, the demolished depositors of the 1930s will have paid a smaller price than the protected depositors of the 1990s.

In the 1930s the depositors and the banks were totaled, wiped out, which meant they could start fresh, with nobody owing anybody anything. In the 1990s with the country borrowing unheard of sums to make good the losses, it is possible that the debt will not be paid for fifty or a hundred years. The nation, so far, has scarcely been able to keep up with the interest payments.

The silent crash or what the politicians have called the "soft landing" of the 1990s has further weakened business discipline to the extent that huge banks, insurance companies and other institutions are bankrupt but are kept in business. In 1929–30 the books of the business enterprises were easy to read. B.C. could tell who was making money and who wasn't, who was a low-cost producer and who wasn't, who was bankrupt and who was solvent. The much apostrophized bottom line did not reflect the cleverness of the tax accountants or the ability of the corporation's lobbyists to extract subsidies, but the real state of the company.

B.C. had taken his own advice and gotten out of the stock market before it imploded but he apparently got hit by the after-crash of 1931. How much he invested in stocks and bonds when business revived isn't known. He left a few old Guayaquil and Quito Railway Bonds to the Englewood Presbyterian Church when he died,[3] but there probably wasn't much left of what may once have been a rather grand portfolio. Malcolm was ten in 1929 and spent the rest of his childhood living with what came after the crash. He may have been scared out of the stock market for life. When Malcolm died, he left money, insurance policies and—the greatest part of his fortune—the magazine, the houses and the collections which belonged to the magazine.[4]

This most ardent proselytizer for capitalism appears to have stayed miles away from the risks and hazards of stock and bond market capitalism. You won't hear of Malcolm having gone in with Ivan Boesky and his arbs* to swoop down and destroy an

---

\* If you were hip a few years ago, that's what you called an arbitrageur. An arbitrageur is a person who notes a fraction of a penny difference in what a stock or a bond may be selling for in Chicago and, say, London. He or she then buys in the city where the price is a penny lower and sells in the city where the price is a penny higher. According to certain recondite and impossible to follow theories, arbs perform impor-

innocent carpet company or medical supply house. Malcolm's business interests were centered on the magazine, though he had two land development companies, one in Colorado and one in Missouri. The records suggest even these were conservative undertakings involving little if any borrowing. The Colorado project seems to have made money, the other looks more doubtful, but the two taken together would not appear to comprise any great portion of Malcolm's wealth. Malcolm, despite his public image, was a good businessman of the old school, taking over the family business—which had limped through the 1930s and '40s—and, by dint of hard work, appointing excellent subordinates and a flair for salesmanship and promotion, passing on a splendid property.

At first B.C. thought the crash the work of the Scottish Presbyterian God whose Eleventh Commandment is Thou Shalt Earn Thy Money. But the Depression persisted past the time of reasonable punishment and B.C. saw things transpire which he regarded as plainly and seriously wrong. At first it was God who chastised the lazy, the dishonest and disreputable, but then man began tossing the innocent into the burning pits.

Some of the biggest of B.C.'s "big men," his heroes, were being attacked and laid low. None got laid lower than Sam Insull, the big man in the public utilities industry.

Insull was such a business colossus almost every aspect of him speaks to some modern concern, but none more than his struggle against Wall Street power and speculation. He is a prototypical early example of what became a major theme in the 1980s: a working business forced to bend itself out of shape and even destroy itself to fend off institutional destruction by stock speculators, who had neither the skills, knowledge or intention to run the business themselves.

You have to be a historian or past the age of seventy to recognize Insull's name. In the 1920s, however, he was as well known as Donald Trump and in the 1930s as roundly reviled as Mi-

tant jobs in the market. Let us just say that they are not leeches, merely slugs in the garden of free market capitalism.

Occasionally an overly ambitious slug dreams of upgrading himself into leech status. Such a one was Ivan Boesky, an arb who grew tired of sucking chlorophyll out of the leaves, and hoped to tap into the main stem sap. Since nobody can guess the day to day, or week to week, jumps and drops of stock prices, Boesky did the only thing you can do to make enormous amounts of money in the market very fast—he cheated.

chael Milken, the junk bond peddler. His was the name universally invoked when the speaker wished to call up the greed and
excesses of that decade. Listening to what was being said about
Sam Insull provoked B.C. to take up a cudgel in the fallen
tycoon's defense, although he was anything but blind to Sam's
faults.

"Now that he is out [of his job], everybody is taking a crack at
Samuel Insull. It is natural, it is inevitable that the many thousands who invested in Insull securities which have lost value
should feel bitter," B.C. wrote of the man whose holding companies supplied a tenth of the electric power to homes and
businesses in thirty-two states. "Unquestionably he resorted,
when the pressure became severe, to financial expediencies, especially in the way of inter-company deals, which he would not
have countenanced under normal conditions. Later facts may
prove me wrong, but I cannot believe that Sam Insull was a
crook. Admittedly, he was boorish, high-handed, autocratic,
sometimes ruthless, often insulting. Admittedly certain of his
political activities seemed questionable, although they may have
been inspired by the idea of doing the best possible for his far-
flung companies and their stockholders . . . notwithstanding
whatever may be disclosed . . . Sam Insull was essentially an
upbuilder."[5]

Two years later Insull was an upbuilder no more. B.C. turned
against him, took him off his list of big men and condemned
him to the ring of hell reserved—and perhaps deservedly so—
by the theologians of the work ethic to stock speculators and
other felonious flimflam artists who flourish in the canyons of
Wall Street. By then two presidents of the United States, Herbert Hoover and Franklin Roosevelt, had sent federal posses
out to grab Insull, who had fled the country. Hoover asked
Benito Mussolini to throw Insull in chains and ship him back to
the United States; under Roosevelt the American government
informed Greece, where Insull had next taken refuge, that dollars earned by Greeks in the United States would be frozen in
American bank accounts unless they coughed up Insull. The
Congress of the United States had enacted a special law author-
izing Insull's seizure, and, in a series of moves which prefigured
the fate of Manuel Noriega sixty years later, the American businessman was kidnapped by Turkish authorities, who gave him

to U.S. agents in Smyrna, whence they set sail on the S.S. "Exilona" for the long trip back to Chicago and trial for embezzlement, using the mails to defraud and violating the Bankruptcy Act.

The Insull story is important for us because Insull was done in by the same kind of stock speculation which played such havoc with healthy and productive companies in the 1980s.

His is also a cautionary tale about lynch mobs and how greatness is naked to the nastiest takedowns. On the way back from Smyrna in the spring of 1934, Insull, reflecting on life's little reversals, said to one of his captors, "If two men had walked down Fifth Avenue a year ago, and one of them had a pint of whiskey in his pocket and the other had a hundred dollars in gold coin, the one with the whiskey would have been called a criminal, and the one with the gold an honest citizen. If these two men had, like Rip van Winkle, slept for a year and again walked down Fifth Avenue, the man with the whiskey would be called an honest citizen and the one with the gold coin a criminal.† I find myself somewhat in this sort of situation. What I did, when I did it, was honest; now, through changed conditions, what I did may or may not be called honest. Politics demand, therefore, that I be brought to trial; but what is really being brought to trial is the system I represented."[6]

The system which Insull represented he also called into being, for he not only built up a company but started an industry, and in the process changed the daily life of the nation. This son of itinerant Methodist street preachers immigrated to the United States from London in 1881 and became Thomas Edison's confidential secretary. Like B.C., Insull had gotten his first leg up in the business world thanks to having mastered shorthand. His years with Edison gave Insull a technical understanding of electricity. When at length he was on his own, he became the manager of a small electricity supply company in Chicago. (One dare not call this operation an electrical utility since it served few customers and was in competition with other electrical companies.) Insull gives the lie to the insistent boast of modern MBAs that a good manager can come in and manage any

---

† In the interim prohibition had been repealed and, for reasons which appear utterly goofy to us moderns, ownership of gold had been made criminal.

company with little or no substantive understanding of the nature of the work.

The great system builders have such a close familiarity with the technical nature of the field they're operating in that they are able to do something quite remarkable: they locate the need for a step forward, for a new invention, and then they force it into existence.

When Insull got into the business in the 1890s, there were many companies which were producing electricity for their own use or for sale. They were small-scale, expensive-to-run operations serving few customers. Insull dreamed of huge generating plants serving everybody, an idea which was regarded as fancifully democratic. As he began to carry out his plan, Insull bumped up against the limits of the reciprocating steam engine, which was then used to generate power. To generate the amounts Insull had in mind would require installations the size of downtown Chicago. The only thing to do was to switch to the steam turbine, which in theory could generate enormous amounts of power cheaply but, as Insull's biographer wrote, "the number of tinkerers martyred trying to perfect a steam turbine would populate the army of a second-rate nation."[7]

The engineers at General Electric where Insull went to get a steam turbine developed thought the thing couldn't be done. Insull said that if they wouldn't take the job on, he thought he knew an engineer in England who would. On the off chance Insull might actually do it, leaving GE with obsolete generators to sell, the company told Insull they would try if he'd put up half the development money. In the fall of 1904 the world's first steam-electric turbine was in place at Insull's Fisk Street Station in Chicago ready to be test-fired. Nobody knew if the damned thing would blow up or vibrate into ten thousand pieces of high-velocity shrapnel.

For those reasons Frederick Sargent, Insull's chief engineer, suggested that the boss clear the area.

"Why?" said Insull.

"This is a dangerous business," said Sargent.

"Then why don't you leave?" asked Insull.

"Look, Mr. Insull. It's my job to stay here. I have to. But you don't. Don't you understand, this damned thing might blow up."

**177**

"Well," said Insull, regarding his man and the man's machine, "if it blows up, I blow up with it anyway. I'll stay."[8]

In the early 1880s, Theodore Vail, head of the fledgling Bell Telephone system, did the same thing—found the invention needed to push ahead toward the perfection of a new system. Having conceived of a telephone line between New York and Boston, Vail was confronted with the fact that the iron wires then in existence made mental telepathy a more useful medium of communication. Iron wire is a terrible conductor, and messages sent on it over extended distances are incomprehensible. Silver is good but too expensive; copper is first rate, but at the time nobody knew how to manufacture usable copper wire. Attempts to manufacture it had brought forth strands so soft that in summer the wire wept down into loops between the poles till it touched the ground. Vail found a man in Bridgeport, Connecticut, who had discovered that cold drawn copper wire stayed strong and did not swoon. Given the number of applications copper wire has been put to, this was one more small discovery which changed the world, and Vail, the business executive, had found it first and put it into service.[9]

Not every attempt to force technological progress succeeded. Pierre du Pont, another major figure in the invention of business, came down with an *idée fixe* about the development of an air-cooled engine during his tenure as CEO of General Motors. In the mid-1920s he came within a hair's breadth of causing a business catastrophe for his company by pushing ahead with plans for a production model of the car before the engine was ready. Nevertheless, the great ones, and that would include Pierre du Pont, did not sit at their desks oblivious until somebody from the lab shouted eureka and rushed in with a new widget. Carnegie, Rockefeller, Schwab and famous moderns like H. Ross Perot knew the industry they were running and they knew what it needed to grow.

Insull was remarkable not only for the number of technological improvements he introduced but also because, more than any other single person, he helped to create the huge interlocked systems which are the hallmark of our own times—that union of capital, technology and social organization.

Most talk about businessmen as "men of vision" (and it is usually men they talk about in this way) is claptrap. But Insull

had a vision, a surprising one, in which every home was wired for electricity and every home had electrically powered, labor-saving tools. He envisioned a complete electric world, not only for the rich people, but for everybody. It was a business vision, though eventually it had to become a political one as well. In a justly famous part of Robert Caro's biography of Lyndon Johnson,[10] there is a description of how, thanks to the future president's efforts, the government's rural electrification program brought light and power to the remote dirt-scrabble farms and ranches of the Texas hill country. It is a moving account. Caro describes how the Smith family had wired up their house and then waited and hoped for the day of electricity which never seemed to come:

"But then one evening in November, 1939, the Smiths were returning from Johnson City, where they had been attending a declamation contest, and as they neared their farm house, something was different.

" 'Oh my God,' her mother said, 'The house is on fire!'

"But as they got closer, they saw the light wasn't fire. 'No, Mama,' Evelyn said, 'The lights are on.'

"They were on all over the Hill Country. 'And all over the Hill Country,' Stella Gliddon says, 'people began to name their kids for Lyndon Johnson.' "

There ought to be a similar encomium for Samuel Insull, who, with no help from any government, lit up the cities, suburbs and farms of most of America.[11]

The profitable usefulness of Insull's turbine was predicated on his being able to move huge amounts of electricity from central power stations over significant distances. This could not be done with Edison's direct current system, only with high voltage-high danger alternating current, and that Edison opposed. Insull, as long as he was associated with the Wizard of Menlo Park, had to fight Edison.

Edison's objection to electrical transmission of AC current arose from pique at not having invented the system himself. Presaging the nuclear power debates of our time, he committed himself and Insull to what may have been the first attempt to prevent the commercial-scale introduction of a technology on the grounds it was too dangerous to use. While George Westinghouse went ahead with the manufacture and sales of a prim-

itive AC system, Edison, with Insull in attendance, sponsored a series of demonstrations in his lab to show how lethal high voltage, alternating current is. First several dogs, then a calf and finally a twelve-hundred-pound horse were knocked off by the AC current, as Edison correctly told the world, "The first man who touches a wire in a wet place is a dead man. Just as certain as death Westinghouse will kill a customer within six months after he puts in a system of any size."

As Westinghouse moved ahead selling his system, Edison involved himself with one last demonstration of how dangerous the technology was by associating himself with a project to use electricity, instead of the rope, for executions. For eight thousand dollars the Edison group sold the State of New York an "electrical cap and shoes" and a competition was held to name the process. "Electricide" and "dynamort" were among the names put forward; Edison wanted to call it being "Westinghoused." In the summer of 1890 a wretch was offered up for sacrifice to the apparatus, but the job was botched so badly Westinghouse remarked, "They could have done it better with an ax."[12]

Nevertheless alternating current did not arrive to stay until Insull, out from under Edison and at the head of his own company in Chicago, directed the installation of a number of technical improvements, the most notable of which was the importation from Italy of the Pirelli oil core cable, capable of carrying unheard of amounts of electricity. Insull, like Schwab and others then and the Japanese now, scouted new technology around the globe and brought it back home.

As he moved toward larger central power stations delivering bigger amounts of electricity over greater distances, heretofore unheard of business problems presented themselves. He found himself with an emerging industry in which the start-up costs dwarfed the running costs. Once the power plants and the lines were in, the business cost very little to run; it cost next to nothing to go from low production of electricity to high production, because unlike a factory, no new machines, no new equipment was needed. Thus low electricity sales meant high costs and little profit, while high sales meant low costs and high profit. By the late 1890s Insull concluded he had to run his generators at top speed around the clock, something he started calling "mass-

ing production," which his publicity department shortened to mass production. Evidently the phrase and the idea caught on.[13]

It is our fate today to be under attack from people with bad complexions and rheumy eyes, who lecture us on the free market, the capitalist system and laissez-faire. Instead of making buzz-buzz with their ideological prayer wheels, they should be dramatizing the careers of some of these remarkable business people. There are at least a hundred million Americans who have been taught to think that a businessman is a purse proud old fart who spends his days accepting awards and lecturing people on subjects he knows nothing about. A few writers have given Insull his due, however.[14] One is Thomas Hughes, who has written a worthy appreciation of Insull: "Unlike European utility magnates, he stressed, in a democratic spirit, the supplying of electricity to masses of people in Chicago in the form of light, transportation, and home appliances. In Germany, by contrast, the Berlin utility stressed supply to large industrial enterprises and transportation, but was relatively indifferent to domestic supply to the lower-income groups. In London, utilities supplied at a high profit luxury light to hotels, public buildings, and wealthy consumers. Fully aware that the cost of supplying electricity stemmed more from investment in equipment than from labor costs, Insull concentrated on spreading the equipment costs, or interest charges, over as many kilowatt hours, or units of production, as possible. Much as Ford later pushed the evolving Model T through his production plants as rapidly as possible, Insull processed energy as quickly as possible in his power plants."[15]

Insull's methods of making sure there were customers around the clock to buy his mass-produced power have gone into business language as "load management." Every real-time, on-line service company, from airlines and telephones to computers and pizza delivery, has adopted Insull's approach to its own needs. You have Sam Insull to thank for those jiggling, jumping airplane ticket fares. He came up with the idea when he began charging customers different rates for electricity use at different times of the day.

To switch power from one group of customers, such as home owners and transit lines, to shops and factories, hour by hour

around clock and calendar, demanded a flexibility Insull could only achieve by casting his net wide across city and suburb, farm and field to corral users with a variety of needs. Hence was born the present-day regional power grids, as Insull's activities called into existence a host of companies and products dependent on cheap, universal electricity.

He had to convince people they wanted and needed electricity. In 1909 he opened an "Electric Shop," demonstrating uses for electricity in the home on the first floor and for factory and office on the second. He put out *Electric City*, a free periodical, he advertised electric appliances in the newspapers and opened a string of appliance stores in Chicago's more affluent neighborhoods. In the less affluent ones he had door-to-door salesmen passing out electric irons on a six-month-trial basis. To win blue collar customers he set up installment plans to finance house wiring and appliances, pushing such things as electric hot plates, coffeepots, chafing dishes, toasters and curling irons. He paid tract developers twelve dollars for every house they brought power into and an additional two dollars and fifty cents for each outlet.[16] For several generations nobody in Chicago bought a light bulb because you could take the burned out ones to the nearest Commonwealth Edison office and exchange them for free. In an era when gaslight was cheaper and brighter than electricity, Insull's merchandising paid off. In 1898 his company signed up its ten-thousandth customer; fifteen years later it had twenty times that number.

To pay for the equipment to keep up with his companies' phenomenal growth, Insull needed hundreds of millions, just as today's utilities need billions to pay for increased generating capacity. Insull, however, detested Wall Street and the two great investment banking houses that dominated New York, Morgan and Kuhn Loeb. To escape the piratical tolls levied on money-needy businessmen, Insull decided to end run Wall Street. He took off for England and sold his companies' bonds personally in London, saving untold amounts of money in fees. Extortionate fees are still with us. Only a few years ago Henry Kravis, the Pillsbury Dough Boy of American finance, pulled off one deal which alone netted him more than forty million dollars.[17] This for a little paperwork, taking a few meetings and roaring around looking important, a wee-billy billionaire,

glimpsed, perhaps, bouncing on the cushions in the backseat of a limousine. Power without accountability, these men who answer to no tribunal, who speak to no public, are seldom seen save in the backseats of their black chariots.

Mr. Kravis' outfit also got itself sixty million little ones in the course of scarfing up Owens-Illinois, the glass container manufacturer. Companion hyenas at Morgan Stanley feasted on the liver of the same corporate carcass to the tune of fifty-four million dollars.

Around 1907, ever trying to escape the purposeless costs imposed on productive enterprise by the Kravises of this world, Insull teamed up with Harold L. Stuart of the small Chicago firm of Halsey, Stuart and Company to sell bonds retail to individuals. The bulk buyers, the institutional investors, the insurance companies, the pension funds, the places in the command and control of Wall Street, were avoided as, over the years, Stuart sold hundreds of millions of dollars' worth of Insull utilities bonds to smaller places and individuals.

At the same time Insull started up a company to sell shares of stock in his utilities. Eliminating the middlemen of Wall Street, everybody from meter readers to clerks in the Insull electric companies hit the street peddling stocks. At the end of the 1920s a million ordinary people owned shares in Sam Insull's electric enterprises. In America the difficulty with capitalism frequently isn't a dearth of capital as much as it is a shortage of capitalists. Too few people own whopping amounts of the country at the same time that tens of millions don't own a single share. In his deal, Insull cut Wall Street out and Main Street in.

He was not alone. In 1920 American Telephone & Telegraph had hit a wall. Demand for new phones was unprecedented, but World War I had stopped construction in the Bell System so that the company was in need of gigantic amounts of money to catch up. The board wanted to sell a new issue of stock to raise the money, but the stock market was in shabby shape just then, making it doubtful that selling a new issue would be successful. Even raising the dividend paid on AT&T stock to make it sexier didn't improve things and the board began to fear that if it went ahead the company would be eaten alive by the fees charged by investment bankers for playing middlemen in the sale of the stock.

At that junction the company's young vice president for finance, Walter S. Gifford, destined to be a legendary CEO, piped up to say, fear not, oh, knights of the board table, I shall sell your stock without your having to pay a penny in fees, commissions or other gougings. A somewhat skeptical board agreed for lack of a better plan, and Gifford swung into action. He hit the mass media with a newspaper and magazine advertising campaign announcing a once-in-a-lifetime opportunity for people to crack open their piggy banks and take their savings to the nearest Bell Telephone office and buy themselves a few shares of stock for the proverbial rainy day. People heeded the message, withdrew money from the savings banks, which were paying a paltry four percent, and bought ninety million dollars' worth of Mr. Gifford's stock, thus clearing his shelves of his entire inventory. AT&T became one of the few stocks which a wide public had its money in and was well served by.[18]

Then as now across the country businessmen cursed Wall Street, the bankers and high interest rates. In California A. P. Giannini tried to sell shares of his Bank of America, first named the Bank of Italy, to as many people as possible. In the 1920s B.C. reported interviews with ecstatic barbers and waiters of Italian extraction whose bank shares' market value had quintupled in a few years. It was also Giannini who broke with the idea that only well-to-do people, gentle folk, should have bank accounts. The bankers' class bias against working people was one of the reasons the United States Government for many years ran a small people's saving service through the Post Office Department.

Although he had done his best to stay clear of Wall Street, when Giannini, who was to modern banking what Insull was to electricity, moved east to begin putting together a banking operation of national scope, he was soon in a power fight with the Morgan interests. In the course of the battle, a furious Giannini told Jackson Reynolds, the president of the First National Bank of New York, that he wasn't about to take orders from J. P. Morgan. To which Reynolds, replying with cool menace, said, "Mr. Giannini, you have made a great success. I do not presume to advise you. But if the Morgans tell you to lie down and let them walk over you, if I were you, I would do it."[19]

Beginning with the Civil War the American government has

**184**

found that in times of crisis, it is cheaper to raise money for the patriotic effort by skipping around the Wall Street Venus flytrap to sell bonds directly to the people. The crisis over, Washington reverts to an arcane and complicated system for selling bonds which, in the opinion of those who are qualified to pronounce judgment, is expensive and inefficient.[20] It is a system which makes a small number of people largely rich and in 1991 was the occasion of the great Salomon Brothers government bond scandal. There are so many scandals they are given license plate numbers. The bond scandal was 11C871Aa. It was a doozy, since 11C871Aa may have made it more costly for the United States to borrow to pay its debt, thus resulting in a charge on every citizen. This is the fiscal equivalent of selling the plans for the A-bomb to the Communists. Some might call it treason.

Why should a Wall Street trading house make a fortune selling its country down the river? Why should Michael Milken have taken home a half a billion dollars in his pay envelope in one year? Why should Henry Kravis be allowed to put on a Godzilla costume and run crazy in the streets, an abominable Dough Man chewing up factories, offices and communities?

One reason is the tax laws. Universities and tax exempt pension plans, including those run for government employees, have been made available to Kravis and his ilk to enable them to do their marauding Norseman number on the productive businesses of the society. Save for one instance when the company got caught with too much inventory as the nation went into the trough of a business cycle, Sears, Roebuck never had to borrow money, never had to sell shares to raise money. During its halcyon years the company was able to take care of its money needs for expansion from its own profits, no small feat for an enterprise which needed large amounts of money to finance its operations. Modern tax law makes it harder for companies to do that.

Samuel Insull thought he had the answer to some of the questions, a presumption for which he paid dear. He thought he had found a way to take care of his utilities' need for expansion money without having to stand and deliver to the Wall Street highwaymen. They did not forgive him. He had made enemies who would help bring him down, but from that we

**185**

ought not to impute a perfect Gallahadian character for Samuel Insull. He was no Uncle Fud, but an ideocentric despot, who said he didn't want yes-men around him but preferred to hire Irish Roman Catholics because he believed they were obedient, and avoided hiring Jews and Scots because he thought they weren't. He was as pushy and self-promoting as the most obnoxious of our modern tycoons. When he built Chicago's new opera house, it was so much his project and his idea that the citizens of the city, seeing the great art deco edifice shaped rather like a skyscraper-sized armchair, nicknamed it "Insull's Throne."

Insull's system was premised on monopoly. The load management and financing of his power supply system began in the bottom of the earth where coal to turn the turbines was dug in Insull-owned mines. It was his franchised rights-of-way which brought the wires into millions of homes. Insull gained his monopoly by buying out the competition, but to keep it he understood he had to accept public regulation. He learned early how to deal with all the different forces which impinged on his business. To gain goodwill and keep his companies in continuous operation, Insull accorded union recognition and won himself a reputation as a generous employer. He was paying high wages and running his business on a forty-four-hour workweek long before most.

The goodwill thus gained helped in dealing with governments at every level, from the "gray wolves" of the Chicago City Council to the Federal Power Commission, but a man like Sam Insull wanted stronger bonds than goodwill to make sure he got his way. Midway through the 1920s Samuel Insull had become notorious for his contributions to political campaigns. His operation was recognizably modern in that he contributed to both parties, preferring, of course, to lay the largest chunks of do-re-me on the winners. At length he overdid it and gave so much that he turned a winner into a loser.

In the 1926 Illinois Republican primary—in those days the Republican nomination was the same as election in Illinois—Insull contributed the staggering amount of $125,000,[21] to the campaign of one man, Fred L. Smith, the chairman of the Illinois Commerce Commission, which regulated public utilities in the state. No similar act of corruption would offend a majority

of modern United States senators, who will excuse any action by their confederates, but in the 1920s there were limits. The Senate refused to seat Smith, as Senator George W. Norris, the voice of high idealism and public power from Nebraska, told his colleagues, "It is not a question of Illinois being deprived of her two votes in the Senate, it is a question of Mr. Insull being deprived of his votes in the Senate."[22]

Insull, who was selling electricity cheaper than it had seemed possible and was selling it to millions, who had invented an industry and who had been asked by the government of his native land, Great Britain, to come home and advise them how to do there what he had done in America must have been driven crackers having to behave as ordered by tier upon tier of regulatory bodies.

To this day, many a business person has to face what Insull did, and they resort to the same devices for the same reasons. They are wrong to do it, but often they have more justification than Insull, who flourished before the blossoming of large-scale bureaucratic oversight of business activity. It's beyond the scope of this book to go into the costs and burdens put on business for no good result, but since one of the book's main messages is that business isn't delivering the bacon, isn't coming through with the wealth and the goodies as it did when Sam Insull and his confreres were running things, the one mitigating circumstance business can justifiably plead is government. "Business administrations" may dole out favors to particular businesses, but they have not helped business in general since they have not learned to regulate effectively at a cost which business and society can bear. The problem with the Reagan Revolution is it didn't revolt. The paperwork, the legal costs, the delays and foul-ups were as great from a business point of view when he left office as when he arrived. Yes, the business plaint about government interference is self-serving, but that doesn't necessarily mean it is untrue. If consumer groups and other special pleaders want anything in the long run beside less merchandise of poorer quality at higher prices, they will have to learn that not all business squeals of pain arise from greed denied. The making of the things we need and want, the providing of the services we depend upon and enjoy at prices we can afford to pay, is the obligation of business, but the maintaining of a soci-

**187**

ety to make it possible for business to live up to its obligations falls on all.

When Insull went down, the mob of proper people pulled him to pieces. To the best sort, he was the worst sort. Wall Street destroyed him and the conventional judgment of the time was that the man got what he deserved. B.C., who so often went against the herd, was out in the square shouting with the rest of them that hanging was too good for Sam Insull. " 'Wrecked by Avarice,' " B.C. pronounced, "That explains in three words, what actually caused the collapse of the $2,000,000,000 Insull Utility Empire, engulfing in ruin hundreds of thousands of investors . . . driving the proud, arrogant, dictatorial Samuel Insull into exile—and now culminating in his arrest and enforced return for trial."[23]

As it ultimately worked out, the people who believed in Insull and kept their stock certificates in their bureau drawers—a lot of plain folks did—lost no money. Calling Insull a "veritable Napoleon, creator of a far-flung empire and its czar-like ruler," B.C. accused Insull of "transforming pieces of paper into fabulous profits. Holding company after holding company was organized. Printing presses worked overtime turning out beautiful stock certificates. To himself he allotted at trifling cost, reams of these easily-manufactured tokens of 'wealth,' tokens which a speculation-mad public clamored to buy at rising, soaring, skyrocketing prices."

Insull was involved in the construction of an unfathomable tangle of public utility holding companies, but it wasn't in order to bilk his investors. It was because he was frightened out of his wits that he would lose the control of the companies to a speculative corsair of the Perelman/Lindner/Boesky/Kravis/Milken type. Cyrus Eaton, a market player with a reputation which might worry any CEO, began secretly buying huge amounts of Insull stock and by the summer of 1928 owned at least twice as much of the companies as Insull himself. B. C. Forbes had his misgivings about Eaton, wondering where he got the money to "gobble up utility after utility until he became something of a Napoleon in that particular world."[24] Afterward Eaton insisted he was playing the same kind of game that would later be played in the 1980s by Warren Buffett, a billionaire said to be the best judge of corporate horseflesh on Wall Street. Buffett

finds the best run companies, buys into them without dis-
turbing the management and sits back to let the investment
ripen.[25]

To keep his companies, Insull bought Eaton out, but to do so
he had to borrow the money, putting his stock up as collateral
for the loans. If the price of the stock fell, Insull was obliged to
put up more stock or pay back part of the loans. The Wall
Street stoats and weasels, led by the House of Morgan, con-
spired to drive down the price of the stock of Insull's utilities,
forcing Insull to come up with more and more collateral to
cover his loans until he had nothing left and was ruined.

He might have saved himself. His advisers wanted him to do
so by betting that the price of his own stock would go down,
shorting his own stock, as they say on Wall Street. This was the
same stock he had sold to thousands and thousands of working
people, and Insull refused to break faith with them. It would be
"immoral," he said. "We've got a responsibility to our stockholders. We can't let them down."

Fred Scheel, Insull's chief stock man expostulated, "Mr. Insull, they're going to be let down anyway. Unless we go short,
we can't possibly win."

"Well, we've got to try," is all Insull would answer.[26]

The utilities magnate was a victim of what was called greenmail in the 1980s. A greenmailer is one who, with his confederates, buys five or ten percent of the stock in a company, enough
to frighten the CEO into believing the greenmailers may take
over the company and send him packing, albeit with his golden
parachute. To prevent the takeover, the greenmailer's shares of
stock are bought at a price higher than the same shares are
selling for in the open market. Often the deal includes a signed
contract that the dealer will make no attempt to greenmail
again for a specified number of years. To raise the money to pay
the greenmail, companies today do what Insull did more than
sixty years ago: they borrow. Borrow enough and a once
healthy company is sick with debt.

In the mid-1980s T. Boone Pickens, Jr., and Carl Icahn, both
part of what would have been called the Milken-Kravis Ring in
the nineteenth century or the Milken-Kravis Pool in the 1920s,
swooped down on Phillips Petroleum. After T. Boone had Pickens'd it clean, the Oklahoma corporation was eight billion dol-

lars in debt, which was eighty percent of what it was estimated that the company would fetch if it were sold lock, stock and barrel under the auctioneer's hammer.[27] To come up with the interest payments on such a huge amount of money, all ballast had to be thrown overboard, including the vaporization of nine thousand jobs.[28]

The greenmailer and the takeover artist pay choirs of apologists to justify these rapes and fiscal harassments. Greenmailing and such are "redeploying assets," as the hired academic obscurantists say, meaning "we're taking the money out of this company and putting it where it will do more good." The precise location of where it will do more good is their own wallets. The propagandizing Pickens was roaring around the country at the height of the greenmail frenzy setting himself up as a God-ordained instrument of social justice, if you can believe it. Pickens would tell reporters, "I am the champion of the small stockholder . . . Many American companies are heavily undervalued and I blame their management entirely."[29] To quote such stuff is to refute it.

The robber barons had a violent robustness about them. Regardless of their crimes, their accomplishments were at least as impressive as their villainies, something which cannot be said of Messers. Icahn, Pickens, *et alii*. The journalism of the Vanilla Age in which elevator music and tranquilizer pills kill the capacity for indignation does not convey how revulsive these money men can be.

A case in point: Carl Lindner, a modern practitioner of the greenmailer's art, which may go back as far as the 1860s.[30] Ohio Casualty Insurance and GEICO Corp. are the names of two companies which paid him greenmail. One shudders at what uplifting effect these games may have on the premiums people pay.[31]

Thought to be worth more than eight hundred million dollars,[32] Lindner is a Baptist and at least as public about his piety as was John D. Rockefeller, Sr., the difference being that Rockefeller tithed. In comparison Lindner gives like a miser. Like many rich men, he's sure we're out to get him so he goes everywhere with a bodyguard, even varies his route to work in the morning,[33] but they don't call you a crackpot if you have enough money. Lindner crawls about handing out worthless

coins stamped with "God Bless America" on 'em.[34] The very deserving get cards on which are printed bromides like "The harder I work, the luckier I get" or "Life is hard by the yard, a cinch by the inch" or "Only in America! Gee, am I lucky!"

Luck or knavery, Cincinnati may not think itself so fortunate, for it is on Rhinelander City, the Queen of the Ohio, this green-mailer and takeover artist inflicts himself. He owns the daily newspaper, he has headquartered five corporations there and has had a building at the University of Cincinnati's College of Business Administration named for him after he popped for nearly ten million dollars to build this temple to himself. Perhaps we should be more appreciative but it is a sum slightly in excess of one one-hundredth of a single percent of his known assets. Bow down, O Cincinnati. Though his power in the town must be frightful, a local country club is supposed to have turned down his membership application, a snub which is said to have elicited the following: "The old rich sometimes look down on the nouveau riche . . . but it is better to be nouveau riche than not rich at all." Amen.

This old Baptist greenmailer and his American Financial Corporation have twice been forced to sign consent decrees promising not to commit fraud or manipulate securities in connection with Lindner's Provident Bank in Cincinnati. The accusations were the usual kinds of things, improper loans to insiders, etc. It is of passing interest that the Lindner's executive vice president was Charles H. Keating, Jr., a man who would go on to greater fame as the star defendant in big time legal dramas and as the personification of corruption in the savings and loan association industry. The consent decrees were the ordinary kind the Securities and Exchange Commission lets the Visigoths of the marketplace off the hook with. They come with the boilerplate statement that the signers aren't copping to any plea, and that their assent shouldn't be interpreted to mean that they are guilty as hell. Well, as Lindner, who paid off the mortgage on the church where he and his wife go to Sunday school,[35] says, "Remember the golden rule. Whoever has the gold, makes the rules."

Ah, the aphorisms of the arrogantly rich. "The public be damned,"[36] is a classic, and I like this one attributed to Henry C. Frick or another Carnegie executive: "I have always had one

rule. When a workman sticks up his head, hit it." And in the modern rich/collector school of wealthy swagger is Malcolm's "He who dies with the most toys wins."[37]

Several of Lindner's former business associates are convicted felons, notably Victor Posner and Michael Milken. Before the roof fell in at Drexel Burnham Lambert one of Milken's confederates at the firm remarked that Lindner and Milken, "just love each other to death." Guilt by association is looked down upon by civil libertarians, but if you see three small children with crumbs on their faces and the cookie jar empty, you are entitled to your assumptions. These guys were lending each other money, doing deals back and forth, sharing the cookies in their jars, so to speak.

Speaking of cookie jars, Lindner was able to put his Baptist scruples aside long enough to attend Milken's famous Predators' Ball, the annual bacchanal and deal-doers carnival where the curdled cream of American and perhaps world finance disported themselves in the Diamond Jim Brady tradition. The journalist Jonathan R. Laing wrote of him that, "Lindner hardly seems the type to attend the yearly Drexel Burnham High Yield Bond Conference in Beverly Hills, let alone receive star billing at . . . the Predator's Ball. Yet show up he does, and even delivered a formal pitch this year (1988) for his new broadcasting concern, Great American Communications Co. Square old Carl, 33rd degree Mason, the apotheosis of the Midwestern yokel in the midst of all those swingers. You'd sooner expect Lawrence Welk to show up at a heavy metal concert."[38] When there is money to be made, there are principles to be bent, if not—heaven forfend!—laws to be broken.

In 1980 Lindner played his small profitable part in the events leading up to the First Executive Corporation/junk bond disaster of 1991,[39] the largest such failure then recorded.[40] Milken got the start-up money for this effort to base an insurance company on the solid foundation of junk bonds from Lindner and several others, but we may presume that by the time the thing crashed he had scuttled elsewhere.[41] Such is the dossier of a modern greenmailer/takeover artist.

The public relations rationale for the greenmailer and takeover artist is that this is the best way, sometimes the only way, to

shake up or replace a lazy, incompetent management which may be doing right by themselves but not by the stockholders. No shortage of rotten managers exists, the corrupt fruits of blood favoritism and frat-jock patronage, but the greenmailer and the takeover artist don't pick their targets by studying companies to find those in need of improved management. The victim company is selected because circumstances make it possible to grab it, shake it, squeeze it and discard it. If it should turn out that the disemboweled company ends up with a superior manager running it, well, get out a press release on it.

When Insull was driven from office by Cyrus Eaton, no man alive could run an electrical utility as well as Samuel Insull. At one of Insull's trials, Eaton testified to that effect.[42] As Insull's wealth was pulverized by the bear raiders out to destroy him and seize his companies, he fled, pursued by clouds of accusations and prosecutorial spirits who claimed he had defrauded the people. As he was brought back to America in chains, B.C. intoned, "Thus did 'love of money' prove in very truth 'the root' of the evils that have befallen the proud, imperious Samuel Insull, captive about to be brought to the bar of justice."[43] The people never bought it, however. Insull was tried, and then tried again, but it was impossible to find a jury which would vote to convict him. Insull was the kind of guy who gave capitalism a good name; he had cut ordinary people in on capitalism, let them have a share, and he had, by any known measure, made the lives of millions of people easier, healthier, more comfortable—better.

Doubtless Sam was insufferable. Moreover, he was a political corruptionist on a grand scale, which makes him no different from a number of other men whose names now identify some of our most important schools, hospitals and museums. It is hardly news to remark that the corruption continues in our own time on at least as large a scale. The difference between a Sam Insull or a Collis P. Huntington and the bunch passing out bribes now was that the first got the job done, and getting the job done earns no little forgiveness. The second pocket the money, but they don't get the job done, and for them, no forgiveness is possible.

The men who had brought Insull down could boast of having discharged the best man for the most important job in one of

the nation's most essential industries. They went on to be given testimonial dinners while Insull, without assets save for his pension, left America after his acquittal to live on until he dropped dead of a heart attack in the Paris metro in 1938. His story demonstrates past peradventure that any relationship between the depredations of greenmailers and takeover despoilers and good management and business efficiency is accidental. Yet the fact that raiders have been unable to convince a broad public that their enrichment is an unalloyed social good has been a vexation to some of them. At length Carl Icahn, one of Michael Milken's unindicted co-connivers, a man who had for years railed about the inept and selfish management of the companies he preyed upon, took it upon himself to show the world how it should be done. Taking control of Trans World Airlines, Icahn went ahead and botched the job. At this writing after some years of Icahn's direction TWA is a dying cow.

In the end Icahn revealed himself to be what people had taken him for, a man with a talent for the smarmy exploitation of the anomalies of the market in stocks, preferred and common, bonds, debentures, zero based coupons and all the other pieces of paper that the world of stock jobbery refers to as their "products." Today's reality is they no longer even give you a handsome, steel-engraved certificate when they hornswoggle your money out of you. You get a blip on the screen and a printout.

Put up against some of the most lurid market players of the past, Icahn is a dwarf. He can't compare with Jay Gould, the most loathed and feared market operator of the nineteenth century, who, thanks to a corrupt relationship with Ulysses S. Grant's brother-in-law, was able to corner the gold market and create turmoil in the markets of Europe as well as the United States. For all that, Gould was perhaps the first person to understand that the railroad system of his time, which consisted of literally hundreds of half-bankrupt, underimproved companies, thousands of miles of parallel streaks of rust, had to be replaced by well-financed and competently managed trunk lines. He then proceeded to go out and do it. In the process he frightened into existence other trunk lines organized by men like Vanderbilt who did it also, if for no other reason than to

chase Gould off. Gould aspired to something higher than Wall Street shrewdness.[44]

There is a strain in American culture which admires a certain kind of horse trading shrewdness, the Yankee peddler selling wooden nutmegs, but when petty dishonesty and mingy sharp practice are done with hundreds of billions, the results are less amusing than they are devastating.

# ELEVEN

---

# "The Play-things of Speculators"

WHETHER OR NOT Jay Gould had anything like a vocation, many of the greatest business people had and still do. The intuitive judgment most of us have that a life of Wall Street chicanery is often shameful, shady and almost intrinsically dishonest is more often than not correct. The paper professions, the perfidious clericals, the investment bankers, their accountants and lawyers, spend no small sums hiring professor/propagandists to convince us that computer models show that Wall Street services are of the highest order and necessity, but Rockefeller knew better. "I have always opposed putting Standard Oil shares on the Stock Exchange because I did not want them to become the play-things of speculators," quoth John D., Sr., himself, in 1917; "It was better that all our people concentrate their attention on developing the business rather than be distracted by the stock ticker . . . To this day our shares are not listed on the New York Stock Exchange."[1]

The generation coming up after Rockefeller felt the same way. Bernard Baruch, one of the most successful speculators of this century's first three decades, was anything but proud of the way he got his money. "The speculator yearned to be known as a 'creator of true wealth, not (of) money but of things useful,' " his biographer wrote. "Personal wealth through speculation was not enough without the societal esteem attached to the man recognized as a builder. Great men did more than watch their millions multiply. We are told by Baruch that his father was surprisingly unimpressed by his son's wealth; he asked, "Now that you have money, what are you going to do with it?" The physician wanted to know how wealth could improve the speculator if the speculator could not improve the society."[2]

Malcolm was the antithesis of the nomadic wrecker-profiteer, going from situation to situation to spoil and speculate wherever an opening presents itself. He was wedded to the real business of publishing. Not much older than seven when he began putting out a family newspaper in the basement of the house in Englewood, he was seventy when he commenced his last publishing venture, the unsuccessful magazine *Egg*.

In between, while in grammar school, he put out a paper with the aid of a hectograph apparatus. At the two prep schools he attended, Hackley and Lawrenceville, he started newspapers, and he was still at it at Princeton where he founded a periodical named the *Nassau Sovereign*, a respectably serious undergraduate publication which continued in existence for some years after Malcolm's graduation before fading out. While he was doing basic training in the Army, he put out a paper for his outfit. In the brief period after graduating from college and going into the service he acquired a small weekly paper in rural Ohio.

After recovering from his war wounds, in 1949, he attempted, with B.C.'s financial backing, publication of a lavish six-times-a-year periodical called *Nation's Heritage* at the stupendous price of $30 a copy or $150 per subscription. This too was a flop, but, when it came to his chosen field of publishing, Malcolm hung in there, so it was entirely in keeping with his vocation that, many years later, he bought *American Heritage*. He also bought the *Social Register*, whose profitability is unknown, and

toward the end of his life he was able to add a string of weekly newspapers in New Jersey to his publishing group.[3]

Malcolm, then, was not simply in business, he was in the publishing business, as Carnegie was in the steel business, as Sears was a merchant and as William Gates, the Microsoft man, is in the computer software business. They were not businessmen but a certain kind of business man, men sufficiently wedded to their industries to make lifetime career commitments. This is not to say that a person, particularly a younger one, shouldn't move around until he or she finds the right location. Often, in times past, the best men started off in one industry, and moved to another where they discovered their métier. Insull began in electrical equipment manufacture before going to public utilities; Rockefeller began in groceries, got into oil and stayed there; du Pont went from chemicals to automobiles.

It is possible that at some point or other Malcolm could have sold the magazine and, by investing the money in one thing or another, died richer than he did, but his business was publishing. If business people, or companies, turn themselves into corporate table-hoppers going in and out of a succession of industries, it is less likely that any of the companies will be effectively managed. These restless soldiers of fortune may die marginally richer, but Malcolm did okay, staying put and doing one job well. The roving banditti of business, who buy a company and hold it and sell it, the speculators à la Dough Boy Kravis, or the executive quick-change artists who go from company to company, argue that the constant switching of people and money in and out of a business leads to higher profits and greater wealth and prosperity. This is the never solve a problem, just leave it school of conducting business, and, ultimately, the landscape is littered with problem businesses and a diminishing number of successes.

Nevertheless, the idea persists that a competent person doesn't need to know his business to run it well. This is the ideal all-purpose manager, who, armed with what the charlatans and optimists call the "science" of management, can step in and run any company in any industry.

Thus Alfred P. Sloan, Jr., of General Motors is most revered as the manager *par excellence*, the man who is thought to have invented management by the numbers, the person who turned

the art of directing these organizations into a transportable skill which can be trucked from one company to another with no real knowledge of the substance of what is done. Sloan, who, with Pierre du Pont, brought the General Motors Corporation to the pinnacle of its success, is used as *the* example that business is shifting "assets" around on a computer screen, that all you need do is have the right ROI—return on investment, a term popularized at General Motors—and the rest of the story is pure profit.

The historical Sloan didn't believe that for a minute. In truth his view was the same as Carnegie's. He had the same sense of calling about his work, the same fascination with it, dedication to it, absorption in it. "Speculation never had any attraction for me," he said more than fifty years ago, sharing our contemporary disdain for the parasitical professions. "Other than a few professional operators, who has really got ahead by stock-market trading? Naturally, I like to see General Motors stock register a good price on the market, but that is just a matter of pride. Personally, I consider its price fluctuations inconsequential. What has counted with me is the true value of the property as a business, as an opportunity for the exercise of management talent. I have been most fortunate in being connected with a successful enterprise and I have gained by sticking to it through all the vicissitudes of changing conditions. When any man has formed an association in the early stages of a developing business—one that is producing something of benefit to the community or performing some useful service—his road to fortune, I believe, is clearly defined. He should help make it a success. Stick to it."[4]

Those are the words of a man who was in the car business. As a large GM stockholder himself, he didn't pull his money out when General Motors had a couple of bad quarters or tell himself it was no longer possible to make money in the automobile business in the United States. Ignoring whatever might be the fluctuating judgment of stock market analysts, Sloan judged GM's profitability not by quarter to quarter jiggles, not even by annual reports. GM was set up to reach target goals—average levels of profitability over five-year periods.

The upbuilders, as B.C. would say, his big men, had a tertiary interest in the price of the stock. In the 1990s a CEO is judged

by the price of his company's stocks and bonds. In Sloan's day, and before him, in Carnegie's, the notion would have been thought outlandish. In their day a CEO was judged by how well he ran his company, how good the profits, how low the costs, how fine the product or the service and, occasionally, even how well he treated the employees. In our era, few executive talents are more prized than the ability of a CEO to dazzle the anthropophagic stock analysts, who make the buy, sell or hold recommendations.

The hired professorate, who thicken the air with the abracadabra talk of quackery worthy of the woodcutter in *Médecin malgré lui,* speak learnedly of the Wall Street finagler as "an instrument of the efficient distribution of resources via the mechanism of the capital markets." Which is Ph.D. doublespeak for saying that the stock manipulators and the bankers get money to the people and the enterprises who can use it most productively. Half a trillion dollars in bad loans, rotten stock flotations and junk bonds, fraud and peculation give proof, if proof is needed, to the truth of such nonsense.

American industrialists have long done their best to stay away from Wall Street when they need the money for new equipment, research or expansion. Men like Carnegie did not want to vitiate their control in their enterprises by selling shares in it or borrowing and having restrictions placed on them by the lender. For years Carnegie paid next to no dividends, but it takes a strong CEO to put the profits back into the company. Certainly, Carnegie's refusal to distribute them had something to do with Henry Frick, a large but decidedly minority stockholder, and Frick's fury toward the little steel master. At their last savage meeting, Frick told Carnegie, "For years I have been convinced that there is not an honest bone in your body. Now I know that you are a god damned thief." Nonetheless, instead of dividing the profits up among Carnegie's stockholders, they went back into the business. What the stockholders missed in dividends they made up in the soaring value of their shares.[5] His protégé, Schwab, while building up Bethlehem Steel, went nine consecutive years without paying a single dividend, explaining that, "If dividends are paid, the stockholders to that extent receive directly and immediately their share of the earnings. If, however, the Board of Directors . . . decides not to

pay dividends, but to reinvest the earnings in the business, the amount so reinvested enhances the intrinsic value of the stock . . . No one can reasonably deny that the reinvestment of those earnings in the business in lieu of paying them out in dividends increased the intrinsic value of the common stock."[6] Plowing the profits back into the company resulted in much more money for Schwab's stockholders, as he used the funds to make Bethlehem a leader of the world's steel industry. A giant in the service industry sector, Sears, Roebuck and Company, was also built by putting earnings to work expanding the company and increasing its value to its owners and the world. What we have been seeing in recent years is that when companies are boarded and captured by the raiders, the money vanishes into thin air.

Putting the money back into the enterprise isn't business penicillin. Nothing is, alas. Some businesses have start-up and early expansion costs which can't be taken care of by immediate profits. The utility industry is one; the airline industry is another, and, in times past, such was the case with the railroad industry, which is why government often subsidized it.

Nevertheless much of the yakkity-yak about "capital formation," i.e., saving up a wad and putting it to work in a business, is but noise from organized stock jobbery to get their hands on more money to fritter away on a scale of waste and frivolity matched only by the larger organs of government. There is good reason that industrialists struggled so hard to stay out of the hands of bankers and brokerage houses. If they could retain their earnings to put back into the company they could retain their sanity and efficiency.

Hence in the early years of the century General Motors went for some years without paying a dividend.[7] At American Telephone and Telegraph, that autocratic visionary Theodore Vail endured criticism for withholding dividends in order to put the money back into growth and research.[8] Old man Watson at IBM found a cute way to put the money back into the company *and* pay dividends according to his son, Thomas, Jr.: "Dad's idea for financing IBM's growth was to plow profits back into the business. That was not easy to do, because he also believed in paying substantial dividends to IBM's shareholders. For years Dad relied on smart accounting to get around this di-

lemma. Instead of paying dividends in actual money, he paid in stock, so that if you held one hundred shares, you might get another five shares at the end of the year."[9] IBM stockholders, thus abused, grew to become very, very happy and wealthy people, and, as they got rich, the company they owned served the nation and the world as few others.

This history suggests that the corporation tax, however sexy politically, is a bad idea. Let corporations keep their profits to put them back into the enterprise. During the *l'age d'or* of business growth and productivity, that is how most companies financed their expansion. By taxing corporate profits, business people, who might otherwise avoid it, are forced to go to the swine and kine of Wall Street to raise money, and anybody delivered into the hands of the parasite professions will not be set free until drained of life and left for dead on the downward slope toward bankruptcy. And when you study what has happened to scores of productive, profitable businesses, these words are a mild exaggeration at best. Get rid of the corporation tax. Its disappearance will not cure American business of all which ails it but it will help a little. A little is a lot, because a healthy society is attained by doing many little things well. As for the lost tax money, it can be recaptured through income tax on the dividends which will ultimately be paid out. And when the stockholder sells a share of stock—worth more because the company has become worth more—there will be a tax on the profit.

(Parenthetically, the Greedy Guts party wants to cut the "capital gains" tax, the tax levied on profits made from the sale of stock. The rationale is that a cut would "stimulate" investment. A cut in the capital gains tax is more money for the stock swindler community, not more money for investment. Leave the money in the hands of people who do the real work, not in the pockets of the now-you-see-it-now-you-don't boys. By the same token, one can junk instruments like the Small Business Administration, by which politicians, salaried civil servants and dogoodnik dufooses make idiotic and/or corrupt investment decisions.)

Nothing is automatic, however, and in an era of dumbo CEOs it does not follow that letting them keep the profits means that they will do anything productive with the money.

The low IQ bizocrats running some of our major corporations really shouldn't be trusted with allowances of over five dollars a week.

Starting in late 1989 and throughout most of 1990 the genii who run the Tenneco Corporation took money out of the company treasury to buy back its stock from its own stockholders at more than fifty-five dollars per share of stock. That's all they could think of doing with the profits from this natural gas company. They spent three hundred million bucks on this project and then, my dears, in June of 1991 announced they would be *selling* nine million of the same shares they had bought a few months previously for thirty-six dollars a share, for a net loss of something near one hundred and eighty million dollars. The concern's chief financial officer, the CFO, explained that, "We didn't anticipate the recession and its impact on our business," but, of course, that is what he is paid to do. If you and I mess up to the tune of a couple of hundred mill, well, we aren't business people, we're not paid large salaries to plan ahead and get it right.

But incompetence abounds. It may take an electron microscope on some occasions to distinguish between stupidity and criminality. One wonders if the idea, in the case of some buy-backs where top-ranking officers have been awarded large blocks of stock, isn't to cash in and amscray, leaving the company to the Chapter 11 knackers. For whatever reasons, between 1984 and 1990 the glamorous Lee Iacocca spent almost two billion dollars of his company's money buying back stock at one third more than he needed to pay. In truth, the money he was frittering away on stock repurchase was ardently needed by Chrysler to develop new car lines.[10]

The list of capitalist fools who haven't the foggiest idea of what to do with their capital is too long for enumeration. But one more tale of men in the boardroom with seven and a half watt bulbs illuminating the bleakness behind their eyes. This story concerns CBS.

In 1985 Ted Turner indicated an interest in buying CBS. Turner is the William Paley of the present era, Paley being the man who started CBS, and who was the outstanding broadcast executive of his own time. By 1985 Paley was very old, very crotchety. Still on the board, but no longer the CEO.

You might have thought that the news that Turner was knocking on the door would have caused the CBS Board of Directors to break out the Taittinger. They had had five presidents since 1970 and were now on their sixth without finding an adequate successor to Paley; the company was adrift without strategy, policy and direction, and here came the man who could supply all three plus imagination, dynamism and a record of successful business derring-do. So what did they do? They jumped out of their pants and reacted as though the Florida serial killer were downstairs with a bouquet of American beauty roses, asking for a date with their daughter.

They decided to borrow a billion dollars for the sole purpose of putting the company far into debt, to make it unattractive to Turner. They then took the billion and bought back CBS stock. These junior J. P. Morgans had put their company a billion dollars in debt to prevent its being run by the most competent, most able, most successful CEO in their industry. If they'd had the sense they were born with, they would have paid Turner a billion dollars to come in and run the place. And as a reward for this dunderheaded coup these jerks get put on the A list of New York's tonier dinner parties.

No incident better illustrates the contrast between these irresponsible wastrels in the boardroom, who have no dedication to their enterprise, and B.C.'s upbuilders, the Insulls and the Sloans and Watsons. What a thing to do! To spend hundreds of millions of dollars to deprive your company of the best talent, strongest leadership and the sharpest vision, to use the cliché these types are so fond of using when they give each other distinguished service awards and accept unearned doctorates. This is social treason, a betrayal of stockholder, customer, consumer and the society. In its own way it is as much sabotage as placing a bomb in the luggage compartment of an airliner, and the motives for both acts are equally indefensible. Apparently, little more than pride, power and pique were behind CBS's repelling of Turner. The gossip of the time—and nothing has come to light since to contradict it—was that they thought Turner wasn't part of their gang, that he was too pushy, too vulgarly entrepreneurial, that his politics were a bit off-key. He was too strident a figure. Some of them may also have suspected that the first thing he would do on taking over would be to

drop them and scores of highly paid incompetents off the top floor of Black Rock, as the CBS headquarters skyscraper is called.

There was one more turn in this CBS soap opera. Hard times came to Black Rock. The billion-dollar debt had to be paid for. Expenses had to be cut, including—may Zeus divert his gaze!—the corporate helicopter which took Paley, the aging Baron of Broadcasting, to and from Manhattan and his estate at Southampton, Long Island. The battle which should have erupted in the boardroom over the imbecility of turning away Turner was at last joined over the one question they all were competent to understand, private perks and personal pampering.[11]

Instead of Turner and the best in the business, CBS did get a new boss, Laurence A. Tisch, a real estate guy, your ordinary billionaire schlockmeister, neither better nor worse than a score of other men who got into real estate after World War II. Tisch bought himself a large chunk of CBS stock and had himself crowned CEO/Generalissimo.

In the business press, which tends to slobber over anyone with a couple of billion bucks to rub together, Tisch is hailed as a heavy-head intellect, though it would have taken a special kind of genius not to get rich in real estate in those years. From real estate Tisch went on to speculate in such things as oil tankers and insurance with a cunning for numbers which may pass in some circles as a substitute for the constructive genius which brings forth the flow of goods and services that lead to national prosperity. Without attempting to assess how high or low the Tisch IQ may be, it is safe to say he isn't a Ted Turner. A nickel-nursing nut who behaves as though he'd escaped from the set of Molière's L'Avare, Tisch has run his company so as to personify penny-wise and pounds foolish.

While losing hundreds of millions by paying too much for the rights to broadcast various sports events, he hired an efficiency expert to cut costs, a meteor named Ed Grebow, who prowled Black Rock, clipboard in hand, to discover that the dispensing machines in the women's lavatories were selling Tampax below cost. This resulted in a four-hundred-dollar a month loss for the corporation, but by raising the price from a nickel apiece to a quarter, CBS was able to move the item from the red to the

black. It was rumored that other CEOs were laying traps for Ed's services, but Tisch prized him too highly to let him go.[12]

Nevertheless at a few hundred dollars a month, CBS would have been a long time getting down the road to the next billion. So the company passed GO and collected two billion by selling CBS Records to Sony, leaving Tisch sitting on top of an emaciated but cash-rich CBS, a corporation big in the bank and small in the brain. At board meetings, reports have it that the directors joined hands and danced around Tisch, singing, "Larry, Larry, what are you going to do with the money?" At first the farsighted captain of industry put the money in United States Government Treasury Bills, a strategy which yielded so much interest it represented forty percent of the now enfeebled CBS's profits. At length, after more dancing around the boardroom table, Tisch was able to come up with an idea—the same idea he had before: he would buy back yet more stock from the stockholders. In due course the company's capital hoard was reduced by seventy percent, money which might have been spent on the business, if there had been anybody around with an idea about how to do that.[13]

There are two schools of thought about a company buying back its own stock instead of using it to build up the business or giving it to the people who own it in the form of dividends. One school says it's just stupid, the other says it's crooked. During the Great Depression some companies took advantage of the low stock prices to buy back their stock, a subject discussed in *Forbes* magazine by Benjamin Graham, a professor at Columbia University whose influence on investors like Warren Buffett, who served as his acolyte, cannot be exaggerated. Graham, whose name is still invoked wherever serious investors gather, seemed to regard a company's repurchasing its own stock as no better than simple theft: "The prime reason for accumulating the surpluses in good years was to make possible the continuance of dividends in bad years. Hence the absence of earnings is in itself no justification for stopping all payments to shareholders. To withhold the owners' money from them by suspending dividends, and then to use this same money to buy back their stock at the abnormally low price thus created, comes perilously close to sharp practice . . . all these strange happenings flow from the failure of the stockholder to realize that he occupies

the same fundamental position and enjoys the same legal rights as the part-owner in a private business. The panoply and pyrotechnics of Wall Street have obscured this simple fact."[14]

Since Professor Graham is no longer with us we can't know if he would think Professor Tisch had or had not come perilously close to sharp practice, but what he said about companies which stuff their safes with money and don't share with owners has a certain applicability today: "The grotesque result is that the people who own these rich American businesses are themselves poor, that the typical stockholder is weighted down by financial problems while his corporation wallows in cash. Treasurers are sleeping soundly these nights, while their stockholders walk the floor in worried desperation."[15]

The typical stockholder is a rare bird, hard to find and sparse in numbers. The Department of Commerce and the Bureau of the Census have no figures showing how many people own how much stock. It is frequently said that millions of Americans do, but reliable information on property ownership is not kept, in accordance with the silent policy which makes tracing the patterns of wealth and therefore power as difficult as possible. All studies show that in the premier capitalist nation there are damn few capitalists.

You would never know it from watching network television where the market averages are given without fail every night, thereby creating the optical illusion that huge numbers of people have a direct material interest in learning what the stock market did that day. The Public Broadcasting System offers three or more hours a week of stock market news and nonsense. Such concentration on a subject of remote concern to the broad public isn't owing to perversity or obtuseness. Broadcaster and sponsor understand that the small minority which does have a direct material interest are the folks with lots o' money to spend.

An Internal Revenue Service study concluded in 1986 that most of the corporate bonds and stocks owned by individual persons, not pension funds and the like, are in the possession of the less than two percent of the population whose net worth is over half a million dollars.[16] Another study, also done in the 1980s, concludes that ninety percent of the personally owned corporate stock in the United States is owned by ten percent of

the households.[17] Suffice it to say, as in Benjamin Graham's day, there appear to be a lot of people who own only the fewest shares of stock but the very paucity of the number of their shares impels them to "walk the floor in worried desperation." They can ill afford a loss.

Graham was writing in the Great Depression, an event or condition which led B.C. to summon up all his resources, material, moral and spiritual. It nearly ended him, and did end him in the sense that in his last years B.C. Forbes, who died in 1954, was a tamped-down man, not exhausted, not disillusioned, but used up; the fire was no longer there. The same can be said for American business. It began to lose something in those years which it could not recapture. Fewer remarkable people came to the fore, but some of them should be named to emphasize the point that, though we have slowed down, we haven't yet—thank goodness—stopped: An Wang, Estée Lauder, William R. Hewlett, David Packard, William Gates III, Thomas Watson, Jr., Herman Lay, Edwin Land, Steven Jobs, Juan Trippe, Arthur Levitt, C. R. Smith of American Airlines, Frederick Smith of Federal Express, Sam Walton, Ray Kroc and many others. It is disconcerting to realize that an alarming number of these men and women are of the immediate post-World War II generation.

As the decades succeeded each other, it became obvious that the marvelous engine has been losing velocity, has not been kept in repair and certainly hasn't been doing for America what it did in the past. The rise in the standard of living in the fifty years after 1930 did not come remotely close to the jump forward it had attained in the half century commencing in 1880. If business had been able to continue at the rate it had been going up to 1930, there would be no homeless, there would be no slums, there would be no welfare ghettos, there would be no pollution problem and the national landscape would be greener and happier than most of us now believe it will ever be. The gray fatalism, the hope in tiny gains and microscopic improvements, would not be the recurrent maximum expectation. Public people wouldn't be formulistically prefacing everything they have to say with, "There are no quick fixes, there are no easy solutions," which we know translates into "I have no fixes, quick or slow, I have no solutions, easy or hard." Well, in

that case, the unstated apodosis goes, "So, what the hell! Why try?" It is not the spirit which built the nation. That was a spirit which animated people to say grandiose things and go out and get the job done.

Government action, war spending and regulation have played their parts in the sinking into the fudge and sludge, the shrinking growth, in the oozing downward of the national subsidence, but both are outside the scope of this book and neither explain the bad management, the bum decision making, the low energy levels in the high places of business, the complacence, the living with low standards, the propensity of managers to blame everybody else for their problems—the unions, the moral fiber of their employees, the Japanese, the Democrats, the Republicans, even welfare mothers. The heads of half the CEOs in America are simply knots tied above the neck to keep their bodies from falling apart.[18]

The Soviets have thrown off the dead weight of their *nomenklatura,* the privileged higher-ups who got all the goodies. We have yet to recognize our business *nomenklatura.* In our politics a movement is afoot across the nation to limit how long someone can hold public office. In business, in the organizations which provide us with food, clothing, shelter, comfort and care, the man at the top can hang around as long as a Supreme Court Justice or Fidel Castro. No commonplace utterance is more laughable than the big businessman making his speech about how the U.S. Government should be run on business principles. It *is* run on big-business principles, viz, overstaffing, bureaucracy, sloth, sloppiness, routine, lack of accountability, failure to follow through, waste, rigidity, tunnel vision and an addiction to the use of the hold button.

(Apologies and gratitude to the business people and their companies to whom the above does not apply. They are keeping us afloat, but they are too few and too small a proportion of the whole to give us the progress and abundance we need.)

The Soviet Union was a case of not producing at all. The last quarter of a century in America has been a case of not producing enough, not enough invention, not enough jobs, not enough houses, not enough competent people. Everybody's dancing, everybody's parked permanently at the movies, everybody's figuring out how to spend money, not how to make the

stuff you spend it on. The United States is not about to collapse, it is subsiding, inch by inch sinking downward, but enough inches gets you a foot and enough feet gets you a yard. Not a crash but a slide.

Inequality in wealth and income was canceled out or at least muted in the past by the hope and realistic expectation that for white people first, and non-white people more slowly, things would get better all the time. They did too, they got better by any and every measure, but now after a generation in retrogression the hope has grown feeble, the expectation has come to seem a fantasy. America is no longer baking the ever-expanding magic pie and everybody knows it.

Social peace, order and security depend on the magic pie. Now the faltering management at the bakery is imperiling tranquility at the bottom of the social pyramid, poisoning intergroup relations. As there is less and less to look forward to, more angry words are exchanged between competitive minority groups. Quotas, affirmative action programs, job and contract set-asides for minority group members, while debatable in the best of times, become collision points in a society in danger of moving from a politics of plenty to a politics of scarcity.

In the golden years American business wrote itself a dishonorable record of fostering racial and intergroup hatred. The steel and packinghouse industries, for instance, made a minor specialty of using African-Americans as strikebreakers. During the 1919 steel strike the United States Steel Corporation paraded black scabs through downtown Gary, Indiana, as a demonstration to white mill workers of how easily they could be permanently replaced. For business interests wanting to use racial hostilities to divide and control, the policy paid off in Chicago in July of that year with a week of race rioting which left thirty-eight people dead, over five hundred wounded and more than a thousand homeless.[19] The riot's cause, according to everyone who has ever studied it, was competition for jobs and homes. The nasty frictions of our own times have the same cause, and only the terminally fatuous can beguile themselves with the thought that a more advanced America is now immune to such homicidal rages.

Inciting intergroup violence, using child labor and killing employees by knowingly making them work in unsafe circum-

**210**

stances were some of the not-so-pretty practices common in the years of business's wildest growth and greatest accomplishment. Nothing can be said in mitigation of things which are wrong *in sese*, but it should be added that business's success created the material foundation for eliminating such practices. Business's failure will assuredly restore them.

If costs cannot be cut and profits maintained by good management, better products, higher quality, effective merchandising and increased efficiency, then business people will make up for their failures by taking it out of the hides of their employees. How the employees will protect themselves, or if they will be able to, is problematic. This generation has seen pension programs jettisoned, health insurance dumped overboard, fringe benefits dropped, as corporations with failing track records and little imagination try to strengthen their balance sheets by chopping personnel costs and doing scant else.

Chopping is butchery, not skillful management, as per the layoffs at companies where some people, given expensive severance packages, had to be rehired as consultants. Meat-ax layoffs are a sure sign of boobery in high places. Nine times out of ten when you read that the such and such corporation will be laying off X thousand people in the next two years, it's panic, not efficiency at work. Be assured that, without regard to who does what with what result, corporate planning has simply plucked a number from the sky, cranked it into a computer model to see what that may do to the balance sheet for the next few years and then run with it. It bears remarking that the management making these cuts is also the management which hired thousands of unnecessary people. They're too out of touch to distinguish between the necessary and productive employees and the drones hired for the purpose of empire building, prestige and the need to have a chorus of supernumeraries larger than a Metropolitan Opera Company production of *Tannhäuser*. The Wagnerian chorus performs many functions besides singing the CEO's praise. It supplies the CEOs and lesser great men with people to open limousine doors, close limousine doors, impress fellow CEOs with one's superior importance, agree with the corporate leader and in all ways possible to pander to his primary drives.

Unless business's horn of plenty is filled up again, child labor

will grow—it never went away entirely—as work for people of all ages becomes more dangerous, more demanding and less financially rewarding. One group will pit itself against another in a swelling cacophony of ugliness. The recent arguments over discrimination, reverse discrimination, quotas, etc., are a taste, as government officials try to find a fair way of being unfair, to aportion out five jobs to six qualified people, three places in medical school to four suitable candidates, three houses to five deserving families. A meritocracy can only work if the places exist once people have qualified to fill them. Civil rights leaders, lawyers, Supreme Court judges, rank-and-file protestors and jailees are given credit for knocking down the laws and court decisions which erected Jim Crow. Without taking credit away from the brave and courageous, it would never have happened—none of it—if the wealth had not been manufactured in such huge quantity that people could back away from snapping at each other and competing with each other even to the death of personal liberty, even to keeping some people in near bondage. As long as there were not enough good jobs for the whites, the blacks were going to be consigned to swabbing out America's urinals. The fifty-eight years between *Plessy* v. *Ferguson* in 1896, the Supreme Court decision making racial segregation an inalienable right, and *Brown* v. *Board of Education* in 1954, the decision making it an inalienable wrong, were the years in which so much wealth was produced that Americans could cut each other a little slack and begin the work of making the Bill of Rights real. If the wealth diminishes, the rights may soon do the same.

Whether the rights survive undiminished, the almost-rights to money and services accorded one group or another will certainly be curtailed and may finally be all but abolished. We have been party to the spectacle of human ills at war with each other. The AIDS army marching for more money, and being counter-attacked by the Cancer navy and the cardiovascular disease air force. The lesser diseases of the kidney, colon and liver vie with each other for alms. Public figures of one sort or another are on the air warning that the cost-benefit calculus of neonatological and gerontological medical care makes it necessary to agree on a space-age way of exposing the sickly young and feeble old. Like ghouls rifling the bodies of the dead, organized groups

**212**

prowl the society looking for weaker groups' benefits to take for their own. An upcoming struggle is predicted between the people under forty or forty-five, who have been losing the most ground, and the people over sixty-five, who are the one statistical category which has seen its lot improve in the past generation. But that's not going to last much longer, as can be seen by their having their medical benefits, step by step, lessened or eliminated. The campaign to degut Social Security is underway, and its success would have far-reaching consequences in a society where half the working population has no pensions. The retirement income of millions who do have some form of private pension comes from programs designed to supplement Social Security, not replace it. If there were mean streets in the days of milk and honey, brace yourself for what is to come in a time of decline and scarcity.

In the 1920s, B.C. repeatedly published articles about the difficulties ordinary employees had to confront. In 1929 *Forbes* carried an article entitled "Gouged by Doctors—Hospital Cost Far Too High for Patients of Moderate Means—The Need for Business Leader to Step in." A second called, "When Medical Gougers Exploit the Sick," tells the story of a man who had to come up with a hundred and fifty dollars cash before the doctor would perform an emergency appendectomy. Only by borrowing half the sum from a neighbor was he able to have the operation. *Plus ça change*, eh? How about those lawn sales and raffles to pay for a heart operation for the neighbor family's daughter?

Year in and year out B.C., whose personal experience had robbed him of all illusions about the salubrious nature of long hours and low pay, editorialized for decent compensation, paid vacations and the like. If his son lacked his moral imagination, he had his decency. Malcolm was a good employer. He paid well, lent small sums interest free, had a free health fitness program which included a well-appointed gym on the roof and did many other things for *Forbes* employees which were generous and thoughtful. This didn't include carrying drones, misfits and incompetents. By all accounts during Malcolm's years the magazine was a well-run place. When a nearly overabundant prosperity came to it in the seventies and eighties, it did not overstaff as so many companies do when the money starts coming in.

**213**

When the good times ended in 1930 and the wealth stopped flowing, there were calls soon enough to foreshorten everybody's rights. B.C. saw the connection between prosperity and liberty as the material basis for personal tolerance and laissez-faire vaporized, and as the times worsened he worried about the *dirigiste*, even fascist, solutions rising on all sides. Americans, businessmen in the lead, called for a dictator. Gerard Swope, the president of General Electric, was urging that the free market be suspended and replaced with government-administered state capitalism. Sizable chunks of business opinion just gave up on laissez-faire and the free market. The United States Chamber of Commerce backed Swope's plan, which was outlined by B.C.: "All industrial and commercial companies, with 50 or more employees, and doing interstate business, may form a trade association which shall be under the supervision of the Federal Trade Commission or a bureau of the Department of Commerce or some Federal supervisory body specially constituted. These trade associations may outline trade practices, business ethics, methods of standard accounting and cost practice, standard forms of balance sheet and earnings statement; collect and distribute information on volume of business transacted, inventories of merchandise on hand, simplification and standardization of products, stabilization of prices and all matters which may arise relating to the growth and development of industry and commerce in order to promote stabilization of employment."[20]

Herbert Hoover, however, called the business plan for prosperity, "the most gigantic proposal of monopoly ever made in history."[21] It was, he said, an attempt to "smuggle fascism into America through a back door."[22] He was right and B.C. knew it. In the 1920s he had written to warn American businessmen impressed by Mussolini's ability to get things cleaned up and accomplished that Italy was a police state.[23]

Hoover's principles kept him on course but once the horn of plenty gave out, many a businessman forsook the principles he'd sworn by one or two years earlier. In the face of scarcity, the first thing businessmen wanted to jettison was the free market. Against adversity, rights, liberty, principles crumple. Everything depends on there being enough to go around because desperate people can't be relied on. One such was a desperate

George P. Torrence, president of the Link-Belt Company, whom B.C. quoted saying, "President Roosevelt should appoint a dictator for each major crop—wheat, corn, oats, cotton. These dictators should be responsible to, or themselves for, the Federal Farm Board. Each dictator shall have the authority to limit acreage."[24] He was not alone.

B.C., frantic and confused, exhorted and beseeched, first one way, then another. Sometimes he gave in to the desire for a strong hand: "Wanted: A Financial Napoleon able to command and lead the nation."[25] Sometimes it was an old-fashioned capitalist hero, as in his "Open Letter" to the fecklessly ineffectual J. P. Morgan, the younger, in which B.C. pleaded that, "The American people feel they have a right to appeal to you, the present head of a House of Morgan, infinitely more gigantic and powerful than the House of Morgan in your father's day, to come forward at this hour of unprecedented unemployment, distress, discontent, and assume the leadership your father unquestionably would have assumed before conditions had been permitted to become as grave and ominous as they are at this moment."[26] In another issue in the same year of 1932, B.C. assured himself and his readers that, "Recovery Is At Last Within Reach If We Exercise Willpower."[27]

Sometimes he scolded and demanded: "Snap out of it! Snap out of it. Gloom has reigned long enough. It is time to drop cowardice and exercise courage. Deflation has run an ample course—to carry it much further would mean needless destruction, criminal destruction. The country is sound at the core, sound politically, sound financially, sound industrially, sound commercially . . . The season for fresh planning, new enterprise, hard work, driving force, initiative, concentration on business is here. Let's go. Snap out of it!"[28]

In the weeks of near despair he would do things like print couplets from Oliver Goldsmith's *The Deserted Village:*

> Ill fares the land, to hastening ills a prey,
> Where wealth accumulates and men decay.[29]

Others joined him at the barricades. Thomas J. Watson, Sr., IBM's founder, contributed a piece to the magazine entitled, "Every Man Must Be A Salesman."[30] In line with such thinking the frantic editor embraced National Sales Month during which

the nation's estimated five million salesmen were to give the country a goose toward prosperity, each by booking two extra orders.[31] At one point the poor man was reduced to running an article by Julius Klein, Assistant Secretary of Commerce, with a headline over it which read, "New Business Will Arise!—A Storehouse of Facts for Men Who Seek to Utilize Nation's Latent and Enormous Buying Power—The Example of Miniature Golf!"[32] Another time B.C. mournfully informed the readership that Alfred P. Sloan himself, the Chairman of the Board of General Motors, in one of whose company's real estate properties *Forbes* had its Detroit office, had told B.C. he was cutting the magazine's rent because prices on everything were going down and staying down.[33] Still another issue found a distraught B.C. exclaiming, " 'Tis indisputable that there has been a great breakdown in the functioning of our existing go-as-you-please, mutually destructive system. Chaos, involving appalling unemployment, cannot be permitted indefinitely without inviting social upheaval."[34]

As seems to happen whenever a severe business downturn occurs, a hullabaloo broke out over the inordinate salaries of conspicuous executives. In 1930 a fight erupted over the million-and-a-half-dollar bonus B.C.'s friend, Charlie Schwab, had paid to Eugene Grace, the president of Bethlehem Steel. B.C. took pen in hand to defend his pal[35] but the times were unfavorable to executives paid ducal fortunes for their services. The fight over Grace's money went to court in a stockholder suit where the businessman was put on the stand and asked to explain his titanic bonus—the equivalent of possibly thirty million in modern money.

"The factor used to determine my bonus is one and one-half per cent," Grace answered.

"One and one-half per cent of what?" the examining lawyer pressed him.

"I don't know," Grace replied with more regard for secrecy than public relations, but for all his arrogance, he had been brilliant at his work.[36] A knee capper of a boss, as hard a one as you will find, he had a gift for the business, he had a calling. Eugene Grace was a steel man.

We're again in a period when businessmen's salaries are being questioned, their emoluments held up against a life increas-

ingly frayed and pinched for the salaried millions and their compensation compared to what the CEOs of foreign firms are taking home. Americans like the idea of the big jackpot, but the big winners of the past won for everybody. They didn't scoop the dough off the table and keep it all for themselves. They left everybody, the whole society, richer, and how many CEOs are doing that now?

# TWELVE

---

# The Platinum
# Pickle

**H**IDING THE TRUTH about what the CEO is paid still goes on. Then as now the non-salary compensation is the easiest to play games with. In theory the statements, usually called proxy statements, about the condition of the company sent every year to shareholders, include what the nominal owners of the company pay its officers, but penetrating the legal-accountant double-talk is next to impossible. The practice is called "proxy obfuscation" by one expert in the strange little field of executive compensation.[1] It is calculated that one year H. J. Heinz Co. Chairman Anthony J. F. O'Reilly was the recipient of stock options worth about one hundred and twenty million dollars.[2] Knock off weekends, holidays and vacation time, and you are contemplating a guy who is bringing home about a half a million dollars a day.

If it should turn out that Mr. O'Reilly has been maligned, that he makes only a quarter of a million dollars a day, he must

understand it is not character assassination which did him in, not the malice of others, but his own obscurantist proxy statement. If a person is paid a hundred million dollars, he ought to be man enough to get up in public and admit it. (Pardon the sexist phraseology.) It may be asking people too much to have the courage of their convictions, but they ought to have the courage of their paychecks. Let's have a little bragging and carrying on here! When they told him that he was worth a couple of billion dollars expressed in modern money, Sam Insull, who really wasn't particularly interested in getting embarrassingly rich, said, "My God! I'm going to buy me an ocean liner." That's more in line with the spirit we're looking for, although perhaps it was just this attitude problem which brought Insull to an unhappy end. (For the record, O'Reilly's millions are tied to the performance of this stock and he must wait a couple of years before he can cash it in.)

Mr. O'Reilly has a reputation as a hard worker, but a lesser man might be inclined to ease off after a week or two at those rates. The great objection—beyond questions of taste and a doughty republican sense of the fitness of things—to paying these men (they are virtually all white men) such stupendous salaries is that such compensation is a disincentive to work. The standard quote in those respectful magazine profiles is, "I don't do it for the money." Yeah, well then, why isn't a man like Mr. O'Reilly a Trappist monk? Like hell they don't do it for the money.

When Julius Rosenwald was looking around for his successor at Sears, Roebuck he specifically ruled out men who had already made their pile. He even ruled out his son, Lessing Rosenwald, who was an above-average business talent. Money is a basic red, white and blue motivation, but the reason Andrew Carnegie kept the salaries of his executives low was that he knew if you pay them kettles and vats full of money, they don't work as hard, they don't apply themselves as much, they don't do as good a job. Americans have seen that with their professional athletes. Despite the bulldiddy about how they play for pride and for the team and the hometown, the incontrovertible truth is that nine out of ten of them stop giving a hundred percent once they get their three-million-dollar contract. What is true of instant black millionaires from the ghetto is true of

instant white multimillionaires in the better suburbs. Pay them these huge amounts of money, but only after the day is done, when they're getting their gold watch and going off to Palm Springs for twenty years of golfing and gassing with the other retired millionaires. Notice how few executives can make a success twice in a row? Once the rip cord is pulled on the gold parachute, they seldom can move on to another company and score a big success. Playing for pride ain't the same as playing for money, and they have all of that they can piss away and then some. The plainer the office, the fewer the perks and the frou-frous, the less money they have to buy things to distract them, the greater the hope the CEO will stay focused on his or her work. The CEOs set the example of working the longest hours, displaying the greatest dedication, being the most self-sacrificing until the Big Pay Day, the huge, good-bye bonus.

Instead the *average* pay of CEOs in large companies is seventy to eighty times greater than the *average* employee. Put in dollars that means a clerical person will be paid, maybe thirty-five thousand dollars, and the top boss will be getting about three and a half million. That's the average—the average of what the people in the packing department and the executive vice president take home. The discrepancy has got to make people feel worthless, unimportant. It is a screaming inducement for employees to say to themselves, "Why should I put out? Let him do the thinking. I'm fly speck material. Okay, buddy, you make eighty times as much dough as I do, I'm gonna make sure I put out one eightieth of what you do." In a society which heaves with a feisty, not to say aggressive, egalitarianism, a person making eighty times the average of his subordinates either has to be one of those Napoleons of business B.C. was on the lookout for or he will demoralize his own organization. Either he proves he is worth his money and wins their respect, or he is going to have a corps of people leaning on their brooms. Given the quality of many of the CEOs who used to go to Malcolm's parties to get their heads turned and their pockets picked by the advertising department, broom handles is a growth industry.

Employees do seem to be less resentful of an owner than a non-owner-employee CEO. Malcolm's people didn't have it in for him at all. Ownership is a well-respected value in this soci-

ety; people concede one has a right to do whatever one wishes with one's own property. The non-owner manager, however, is perhaps still a fellow employee even if he does bring home an O'Reilly-sized paycheck. Malcolm further defused the demoralization of his Maharajah way of spending by constantly doing nice things for people. Inside the company and out, a job well done won you a congratulatory card from Malcolm, or flowers or some other nice touch.

Nevertheless, Malcolm did his best to keep his net worth his own secret. These hugely paid men are aware what the knowledge of their outsized compensation can do to the morale of their own companies. That's why an Anthony O'Reilly will make it next to impossible for a lay person to figure it out. He has a reputation as an able manager, whether he's one hundred and twenty million dollars' worth of ability we'll let others decide, but at those pay levels an executive should not be moonlighting. This is a guy whose paycheck ought to cover the rent and shoes for the kiddies, but, in addition to being in charge of all 57 varieties of pickles, plus the catsup, plus everything else at the enormous H. J. Heinz company, he also served on the once fancy-pantsed board of Allegheny International with such tony personages as Jean-Jacques Servan-Schreiber, the eminent French author, Richard M. Cyert, the president of Carnegie-Mellon University, and Alexander ("I'm in charge here") Haig, former Secretary of State, former White House Chief of Staff, former commander of NATO, former everything.

Men like O'Reilly don't serve on other companies' boards of directors for the money. Most directors only get about twenty-five thousand dollars plus other bennies, pocket change for most of them. Often they join boards for the same reason that, like Malcolm, they troop from place to place stooping to pick up honorary degrees. It suits their fancy, it tickles their *amour propre*. It's what big shots do, and they're big shots, aren't they? They join because they want to get other CEOs to join their boards. Or they join because there's a banker or a potential somebody they want to make a deal with on the board. They join boards because one of the CEOs that they regularly play golf with asks them to. (The net efficiency of business would pick up ten percent if we could turn the golf courses of America into cow pastures.) Sometimes they join boards because they're

too stupid to know any better. They're confused, overstimulated, underreflected, running here and there in their jets, getting from the condo in Colorado to the condo in the Alps to the castle on the Rhine. If you go back over the record of the biggest investment swindlers and Ponzi game operators of the era —men like J. David Dominelli in San Diego—a surprising percentage of the people they took to the cleaners were big-shot businessmen, too crazy even to know how to intelligently invest their enormous salaries.

Despite the fancy people sitting on its board, Allegheny International took a tailspin into Chapter 11 bankruptcy. Neither the speculators, nor the arbitrageurs, nor the raiders, nor the greenmailers nor the takeover artists bear the onus for the smashing up of this valuable and productive company, which makes products we use and want—electric blankets, toasters, coffee makers, mixers, barbecue grills. The company was wrecked by bad management, and bad management alone, and it was the job of the one-hundred-and-twenty-million-dollar man, the platinum pickle, and his distinguished fellow board members to prevent that.

The story is a sadly familiar one. It features that business folk figure, the out of control CEO, with his fleet of jets, self-dealing loans at two percent (and still not paid back, or so it was alleged), a skyscraper in Houston left standing empty at a cost of a million dollars a month, tens of millions lost in oil and gas drilling, an industry about which Allegheny's management was virginally innocent of knowledge, and so forth and so on. Every Mad Ludwig seems to have done one thing which people remember him by. In Allegheny's case, CEO Robert Buckley is remembered for flying the corporate executive corps to some lush and distant spot where they enjoyed a luau, the centerpiece of which was an ice carving said to cost ten thousand dollars. You gotta sell a lot of coffeepots if you're going to eat like that and Allegheny (brands Sunbeam and Oster) didn't.[3]

Failing all else, the Board of Directors should have stepped in and stopped this nonsense, but evidently they did nothing until they read about how he was running the company whose operations they were charged to oversee in *Business Week* magazine. Then they took action; then it was too late. Hi! Ho! the Derry-o, to bankruptcy court we go.

As many words of wretched business school prose have been written about Boards of Directors as any topic you may name. Cries for regulation and legislation and litigation are uttered, re-uttered and re-re-uttered. A few of the ideas have merit. Recruiting more outside directors, who aren't company employees, makes sense, and that has been happening. Making sure the CEO is *not* the Chairman of the Board would help and perhaps it should be required, but no reform, no regulation, can make up for people who don't do their jobs. Not so many years ago, angry stockholders of crashed corporations started suing members of boards for non-doage, mal-doage and mis-doage of duty, so the board members got their companies to take out insurance policies to protect them against the costs of such suits. When men and women in high places fail in their major business responsibilities, they must be called out for it, loudly and publicly. They must be jeered, hooted and booed, they must be made to walk in shame. They must be shunned, kicked out of their clubs, laughed at on the "Oprah Winfrey Show," belittled on "Donahue," made to understand that men —and the men are the malefactors—who put their companies on the rocks, who fail as board members, are a disgrace.

This is not an area for more government regulation or legislation. That will make the lawyers still richer and impede effective managers and board members from doing their business. These dodos, whose derrieres we are trying to put to the fire, are proper conformists who will crinkle up and die from ridicule and ostracism.

Since the Japanese began to outsell them and the balance of trade turned negative, the lords of the nation have been preaching the moral fibers–work ethic sermon to the underclass, the lower class, the working class, the middle class, the sophomore class and every other damn class, millions of whom are up at dawn breaking their asses, holding down two jobs, hustling, moving and hoping to hell they'll catch a break so they can pay their kids' orthodontist's bill. Now let us see the board members, the top people, get their fannies off the society page and their tushes out of *People* magazine and take them down to the office and put them to work.

Allegheny belongs to a class of companies which, Mad Ludwig at the helm, were steered straight onto the rocks and down

into bankruptcy in a matter of minutes. There are thousands of such firms in Davy Jones' locker, and those failures touch us every day as society comes up short in the things we need. There are even more companies whose managements don't kill them, but merely ruin their health, turning them from robust breadwinners into chronic invalids.

No company better epitomizes the zombie corporation than Navistar, once known as International Harvester, and once one of the premier businesses of the world. Founded by Cyrus Mc-Cormick, a classic tinkerer, the young concern was incorporated in Chicago as the McCormick Harvesting Machine Company in 1847, and in 1851 the famous McCormick reaper was given a medal at the London Crystal Palace exhibit. A J. P. Morgan-managed merger brought the McCormick company together with several of its competitors to form International Harvester, which held control of eighty percent or more of the agricultural equipment market.

By 1911 with manufacturing plants in Canada, Sweden, France, Germany and Russia, International Harvester had made itself one of the pioneering multinationals. More than forty percent of its profits came from overseas, while at home its network of dealerships—a distribution, sales and service marvel —helped make American agriculture the wonder of the world.[4] By 1917 IH was the seventh-largest company in the United States.

Across the years the company was a leader in developing new equipment and new products. The Farmall tractor, which was born in 1922 and knocked Ford out of agriculture, was so ubiquitous it became emblematic of the last, large rural generation. In the late 1940s, the company reached its apogee. The largest manufacturer of agricultural equipment and trucks of all kinds, an important force in construction equipment, the Harvester was doing over a billion dollars a year in sales—a stupendous figure then—and was employing a hundred thousand people or more. Its labor relations were horrendous, as they had always been, but on balance International Harvester was a big plus for America. It was also on its way down.

If it is true that happy families are alike, but miserable ones come in a million shapes and sizes, so also with good management and bad. Even so it appears that more often than not, the

screw-up manager is the manager who doesn't know his business, the antithesis of a Sloan. Yet most of the men in the procession who brought International Harvester to grief had spent their careers with the company.

Harvester wasn't brought down by a single Mad Ludwig. It takes work, a kind of dogged negative dedication, to ruin such a property. Harvester had great resources in talent, organization and money, and it took a procession of numskulls over decades of stupidity to turn this business diamond into a lump of coal. The varieties of errors, blunders and miscalculations are impressive.

Right after World War II, when the company should have been reviewing the bidding and figuring out what to do in a changed world, it fell a victim of affirmative action. Fowler McCormick, grandson of the founder, was made Chairman of the Board in 1946, and from the available accounts he was off safari-ing or meandering about a meadow somewhere until the board canned him in 1951.[5] He must have been gawd awful, because people of his pedigree are ordinarily unsackable regardless of how disastrously they screw up.

Look, for instance, at David Rockefeller. For years Rockefeller was the *bête noire* of both the far right and the far left, which took it as an article of faith that he was the central spider in a globe-embracing financial conspiracy. Perhaps he was, but he neglected to include the Chase National Bank, of which he was the chairman, in the plot. During his years it fell far behind its competitors, wending its way from blunder to blunder while its ostensible leader was off being a world personality. The board never fired David, who—glory be!—lost the race between retirement and destroying his bank. At length he left Chase to other hands scarcely more competent, so that at Chase, even with its longtime absentee manager gone, the personnel and organizational changes which ought to have been made, weren't, as the place went into its era of post-Rockefellerian foul-ups.

Malcolm tamped down some criticism of Rockefeller in his magazine, but there are limits to what money and power can do as the members of the Politburo learned in 1991.[6] On the occasion of Rockefeller's retirement *Time* magazine reported that the right school and the best voice coach would get you farther

at Chase than banking acumen. It quoted one Wall Streeter as saying, "He ran Chase like an exclusive club. Bank officers tended to worry more about how many oils from the Chase art collection they had on their walls than about profits."

In the 1970s as Chase fell farther behind its great rival Citibank and lurched from fiasco to debacle, the famed Chase Manhattan tower came to resemble an Aztec altar upon the stones of which vice presidents were split open and offered up to the Money God. The Money God wasn't propitiated, however, because the bank continued to lose money and so many vice presidents were pushed off the roof that *Time* reported that, "For years the standing joke in banking circles was that Chase Manhattan Chairman David Rockefeller kept firing the wrong person."

The descent from awe to ridicule was completed when Ron Rosenbaum, one of the best of the business journalists, told his readers that David Rockefeller was having Lifestyles of the Rich and Famous parties. "Yes," he quoted Robin Leach as explaining, "he gives little cocktail parties and then everybody toots into the television room to watch the show. Then they all go to dinner."[7]

Unless the dipsydoodles get into your bloodstream and make you mess up, running a bank so as to produce a successful, if not showy, annual report is routine. Running a company like International Harvester, which manufactured, distributed, financed and serviced hundreds if not thousands of products of precision and complexity around the planet, is a different matter. You gotta know your onions.

IH's management didn't. In fact it never got near the onions or the wheat and the barley, which is a drawback if you're selling agricultural equipment. Its smaller rival John Deere began to steal a march on IH. "One of the good things about Deere," recalled a disillusioned IH executive, "is the geographic awareness, because most of their corporate executives live on a farm or near one. (IH execs) ride down to work at 400 North Michigan Avenue on the train; they don't see a farm except maybe once a year when they take a vacation . . . Deere's (located in Moline, Illinois) got farm all around it; those guys walk through a history of agriculture before they get to their office. There's a different mentality."[8]

The Deere people understood that history was making the small family farm vanish and acted accordingly, as the company adjusted its dealer network and brought out larger tractors, combines, etc., for larger scale agricultural operations. Harvester didn't. By the time IH woke up, their customers' once legendary brand loyalty was a thing of the past and, in a misbegotten moment, trying to play catch up, the corporation resorted to theft. It appropriated the engineering for Deere's revolutionary corn-harvesting machines, an act which later cost it millions of dollars in damages and the shame of hearing a federal judge tell its executives their company was guilty of "an exceptional case of willful infringement."

International Harvester was losing out to the competition by failing in research and development in some areas, but it was ahead of the competition in others. It came up with a new line of construction equipment which was lighter, cheaper and better, and a few years after that it brought forth the DT-466 diesel, said to have lapped the competition on power, quality and fuel consumption. But Harvester failed to bring these new products to market successfully. Chaos within the organization hampered it, as did the failure to allocate money where it was needed. Huge sums were spent where there was no market, or invested in plants and products which ought to have been closed down. Money was dumped into HI home appliances, a brand known only to rural America even as the population of the countryside was disappearing. The years passed and hundreds of millions were lost, as the various constituent parts of the troubled company warred with each other and floundered because top management couldn't do it right. In 1962, for instance, the company spent one third of its factory improvement money on its Wisconsin Steel subsidiary, which contributed five percent of IH's profits. After putting untold more millions into the steel company, Harvester sold it in 1977 for a comparative pittance in a leveraged buyout* financed by—can you imagine?

---

* Unless you have been absorbed in a love affair or in your work at the genetics laboratory for the past fifteen years you know what a leveraged buyout is. For lovers and biologists the term refers to a no-money-down or very low-money-down purchase of a company, the rest of the price being supplied by lenders. The lenders may be a bank or may be people or institutions buying "junk bonds," so called because repayment is problematic. Because the bonds are risky the interest rates on them are very high. When the Mafia charges such interest rates it's called loan sharking and their dons

—David Rockefeller's bank. Within three years the new, debt-sick steel company went from bank to bankruptcy.

By the end of the 1970s the jig was up. Poor in cash, rich in confusion, management began selling off chunks of the company it couldn't run, and then found it couldn't run what it had left. In the 1980s it lost billions and the losses continue into the '90s, as the half-dead, half-alive, corporate corpse fluctuates a little one way, a little the other between red and black, plus and minus. In 1991, down to about a quarter of what it once was, Harvester suffered the indignity of being dropped from the list of Dow Jones Industrials. The prices of the stocks on this imperial list are put in an algebraic Mixmaster and the resultant sum is the famous Dow Jones average, which people refer to when they say the stock market is up or down. Only the mightiest companies representing Business America at its best are on the list, and being dropped is like being drummed out of the corporate elite, or worse yet, kicked out of your golf club.[9]

In 1986 with the aid of an "identity consultant," International Harvester changed its name to an eight-letter word randomly generated by a computer, which had nothing better to do one afternoon but name doodles. What kind of a gelatinous, uncertain, dare I say un-manly, management needs to hire an identity consultant? Nevertheless International Harvester, once a name of commercial and industrial glory, would be no more. Henceforth the shrunken successor organization would be referred to as Navistar. Skunk cabbage by any other name still stinks. Call it Eau de Monay, call it Sents-sational, Inc., call it Essence de Lucre, it smells like hell.

In the early 1980s name changing was the corporate rage and there were more than four thousand of them in five years.[10] The most irksome were the ones which abolished the landmark names, as what was once the Carnegie Steel Company, and then United States Steel Corporation, was reduced to USX. It was as though the CEOs themselves knew they were pygmies, dwarf goats, rubbing their tiny horns against the legs of heavy, ornately carved desks where the big men once directed great enterprises, their names unrecognized, yet their

---

are put in the penitentiary. When the Dough Boy or Salomon Brothers or Morgan Stanley sell you one, it's called investment banking and their dons are put on the cover of *Fortune* magazine.

presence always with us across the national landscape which sprang from their hands and brains. Alexander Cassatt (Pennsylvania Railroad), Julius Rosenwald and Robert Wood (Sears, Roebuck), Walter Chrysler, Harvey Firestone, Glenn Martin (airplane manufacture), King Gillette (razors), Bernard Gimbel (retailing), Henry Flagler (Standard Oil and real estate development) and more, more, more. The old names had to be removed by heirs repudiating a heritage too difficult to live up to, too intimidating to contemplate. With the names of the past erased, no standard of accomplishment remains, no memory of great things done.

In its thrashings around International Harvester turned not only to identity consultants but to management consultants as well. Booz, Allen & Hamilton, Inc., came up with a plan in which the company was segregated into five, more or less free-standing, divisions. It failed.

Descriptions of the Booz, Allen plan suggest that it was mightily influenced by the organization of General Motors, which is not surprising. Since World War II, companies from Sandusky, Ohio, to Yokohama, Japan, and back were modeled after mighty GM. Copying GM was the mad fad of the time. Copying isn't the same as understanding, but in business the herd-seeking business person is as crazy to feel the comforting, compacting bump of bellies on either side of him or her, as the most peer group intimidated teenager. Just let me be able to say, well all the other fund managers went long on that stock, all the purchasing agents bought that model pump, all the soap companies raised their prices. Let's not get caught out there alone. There isn't a human being in American corporate management who has to be told what the initials CYA† stand for. One of the anomolies of America is how there can be so much talk about individualism and so few individualists.

The management consultant fad for GM was sane compared to some of the other ding-a-ling ideas people in charge of multibillion enterprises have used to juice up the old bottom line. Companies drop their executives on deserted islands with a rusty fish hook and a pack of matches in the belief that survival training will teach their people how to increase market share;

† Cover your ass.

other firms send their management to sit under the tinkle of cut-glass mobile structures as Himalayan mystics encourage these lost children from the corporate world to sing chorales in praise of money.[11]

If a company is going to copy anyone, Sloan and GM at its zenith are what should be studied, provided that it is understood there are no formulas to be learned and mindlessly stamped on to the organization. GM had an approach which might have helped International Harvester if it had been modified, adopted and amended, but that wasn't done. More recently, American managers spent a lot of company money on airfares to Tokyo whence they returned clutching vials of what they thought were miraculous corporate antibiotics. Just-in-time inventory control, production teams, robotics, etc., all have their place, if a manager has the judgment and intelligence to find it.

The organization and modus operandi invented at General Motors in the 1920s—though not widely appreciated for another thirty years—were the last signal accomplishment in the making of business in America. GM had learned how to run a giant-scale, technologically advanced multiproduct organization; it succeeded in making the thousands of different suborganizations comprising General Motors mesh together to help each other and reinforce the health of the whole enterprise. When you recall the complexity and variety of what General Motors was doing, you can appreciate why other managers looked at it as the eighth wonder. It was such a stunning one that no business school, no text, no consultant was left unmarked by what Pierre du Pont and Alfred P. Sloan, Jr., did. Pound for pound, person for person, nothing compared to GM.

Du Pont and Sloan took over direction of the corporation in 1920 when it was on the verge of collapse. The company had been put together by William Crapo Durant, a man of considerable entrepreneurial genius who was handicapped by a planet-sized, disorganized ego which made it impossible for him to manage the various auto manufacturers he had assembled. Although GM wasn't as big then as it would grow to be, it was a huge company and no single part of it was working in harmony and cooperation with any other. As a result, although the vari-

ous units had been repeatedly warned not to build up inventory, the company hit the 1920 recession with over two hundred million dollars of unsold automobiles. Most of the company's debt came from borrowing money—not for new plants or equipment, but to pay for the tens of thousands of unsold motor cars.

Some years before, the Du Pont Company, more by happenstance than by plan, had been sucked into buying stock in General Motors. In the crisis it was in danger of losing its investment, and to forestall this unhappy event, Pierre, the du Pont family's reigning business genius, was forced to hie himself to Detroit to take over running what was then the nation's largest industrial snafu. In the snarl of GM vice presidents who were running around like disoriented cockroaches emerging from an insecticidal bath, Pierre made contact with Alfred Sloan. Sloan was an engineer who had manufactured roller bearings and sold them to car manufacturers back in the days when they were still putting wagon wheels on the horseless carriages. Sloan had grown up with the industry, loved it madly and knew it cold. When Durant bought him out, Sloan stayed on to work for GM. He and Pierre both had the kinds of minds which could contemplate one hundred thousand apparently disconnected parts and see how they could be fit together to make a whole.[12]

It was these two men who figured out how to run a megaorganization. Considering how many different parts, made of different materials by different design and process, go into a car, it is a wonder anyone can make one automobile. Du Pont and Sloan were ultimately making one automobile every few seconds, millions of them a year, in endless shapes, sizes, colors and quality. In addition to the automobiles, at its height GM was also the leading manufacturer of refrigerators for the home and the developer of the gigantic diesels which brought an end to the age of steam railroads. At its apogee, with over eight hundred thousand employees, GM was as big as an army, but an army is made up of people who all do the same thing, at the same time at the command of hup! The GM army was composed of salespersons, scientists, assembly workers, mechanics, bookkeepers, etc.

The details of the GM story have been told well and often

enough not to bear repeating here. Suffice it to say that du Pont and Sloan invented a method for combining centralization and decentralization, to get the benefits of both without the drawbacks of either. They accomplished this feat by devising the first major change in the way business organizations were put together since Daniel McCallum. They created a series of freestanding divisions for the various makes of cars, for the diesels, the trucks, the refrigerators, automobile bodies, everything GM turned out. Each of these divisions was required to make a profit, even when providing parts and equipment for each other. What they created, in effect, was a not so little capitalist Soviet Union, a corporate country of its own, but they didn't make the mistake the Soviets made of failing to insist that each producing unit also be a profitable unit. To keep the system honest, any GM unit was entitled to import from outside of GM if someone else was selling what they needed cheaper.

To avoid an inventory disaster, impose other goals and controls and to make sure all the units took full advantage of what was available to them through the GM system in the form of research, engineering, sales, finance, etc., du Pont and Sloan drastically modified the hierarchical chain of command instituted by McCallum. The organizational chart no longer looked like a pyramid because, in between the divisions, various working committees were created. A GM organizational chart of the late 1920s was still vaguely pyramidal—they didn't fall into the trap of eliminating individual responsibility and authority—but it also had the look of a honeycomb, the cells of which were the many working committees. The committee system permitted the top people to concentrate on the overall questions without losing contact with the day to day necessities.

The other change which made this huge, multiproduct, even multi-industrial organization possible was the system of accounting which du Pont brought with him from the family company and perfected at General Motors. One of the things that separates the free trade commercial era from the business era is cost accounting. This is not the same as bookkeeping. There are Babylonian clay tablets which record the financial doings of some grain company in Old Testament times. Basically, bookkeeping is writing down what comes in and what goes out. The first article describing how to keep double entry books, which is

fancy bookkeeping, was written by Fra Luca Pacioli, who lived from 1445–1514, and the Italian merchants and bankers were probably using the procedure far earlier. Even that was more than many American manufacturers and shopkeepers needed during the country's early days. Pioneer concerns like the textile mills would only add up their books twice a year. It was enough to know that there was more in the purse at the end of the day than there had been in the morning. It wasn't until the 1850s that the first managers, specifically J. Edgar Thomson of the Pennsylvania Railroad, began to get interested in what it actually cost to supply the service. And wouldn't you know it? A man named Fink, Albert Fink, a civil engineer working for the Louisville & Nashville Railroad, first worked out the precise formulas for reckoning what it actually cost to move a ton of freight from one place to another. Thanks to Fink, we still pay more per mile for short hauls than long ones.[13]

That's what cost accounting is—the careful analysis of what it costs the company to get the work out. The idea is to break the work down to the smallest useful unit and figure out what the costs incurred are. In complicated modern enterprises, this can be tricky, demanding the collecting and crunching of all kinds of information a bookkeeper has no use for. A failure to understand costs correctly or misallocating costs can lead to expensive botched decisions and money-losing practices. The bookkeeper will pick up the money losses soon enough, but won't be able to explain where, in the long train of complicated activities the company is engaged in, the losses are occurring.

It seems obvious to us, but it wasn't obvious to the people on the other side of time. Many men of the business generation after Fink's still didn't get it, as the steel men wondered at Carnegie's high levels of production which wore his furnaces out while they husbanded theirs. But old Andy, with his railroad background, had applied cost accounting to his own operation and knew that his methods were cheaper. Nevertheless, it was the turn of the century before the notion of depreciation found its way into companies' cost accounts.‡

‡ For those who stoutly resist any knowledge of the ways of business, depreciation is the loss suffered through wear, tear and obsolescence on your machines or your factory or whatever else you may use in your business which is subject to the depredations of rust and worms.

At GM, du Pont and another executive he brought with him from the chemical company, F. Donaldson Brown, introduced an array of cost accounting innovations,[14] but the one which was to be the most widely picked up by others to the worst effect was something called return on investment, or ROI. ROI is another idea which strikes you as simple enough once somebody else has come up with it. It means calculating how much money has been put into a given endeavor and then what kind of interest it is paying back in the form of profit. Making such a calculus around a gigantic and complicated place like GM is not a simple task, but Brown, who, like Fink, was an engineer and a cost accounting fiend, did it marvelously well.

Brown was able to construct a system in which the return on investment of each of GM's many divisions was reckoned, thereby giving management a tool in deciding who was efficient and who wasn't, which subdivision needed more money for new equipment and which needed something else. Dull, dull, dull, but it was the final tool needed to run a company which grew to eight hundred thousand employees, the greatest industrial organization in American history and the most profitable. So, don't knock return on investment.

You can, however, knock what happened to ROI. After Sloan was gone from the scene, the methods he and his collaborators had used were reduced to a nullity by the bizocrats who followed them. Return on investment was perverted into a meaningless, formulaic exercise as one close student of the company wrote: "A typical investment case at GM might look like this: An executive submits a plan that produces a 15-percent return on investment. Then something changes in the market place . . . However, rather than evaluating the changes and adjusting accordingly, the numbers are reworked still to yield a 15-percent ROI. Over the years, operating people . . . have learned how to make the numbers 'come out right.' "[15] That's what they did in Russia; they made the numbers come out right. It was the reality which was all wrong, but nobody looked at that.

Inside GM and out, the stupid, the lazy, the dishonest and the negligent began to act as though Sloan and his co-workers had stumbled on a formula for success. Learn it and apply it. Make the numbers come out right, and kid yourself into thinking that, by an alchemy nobody understood, the result would be

a good car and a profitable organization. Nothing could be further from the truth, but business schools, business people, business publications missed what Sloan had really done and what he had clearly told the world he had done. They concluded that if we make the numbers come out right, we're all going to get filthy, muddy, slimy rich. From near and far they came to GM to imitate. ROI became another incantation like free market. Say it enough, and you're pure gold.

Misunderstanding the nature of the GM accomplishment, sensible people came to believe great enterprises could be run by studying digits on the pages of a printout. By the late 1980s a few accountant-scholars realized that a good idea had been run into the ground and took pen to paper: "After 1925 a subtle change occurred in the information used by managers to direct the affairs of complex hierarchies. Until the 1920s, managers invariably relied on information about the underlying processes, transactions, and events that produce financial numbers. By the 1960s and 1970s, however, managers commonly relied on the financial numbers alone. Guided increasingly by data compiled for external financial reports, corporate management—the invisible hand—has 'managed by the numbers' since the 1950s."[16] In other words guys who didn't know, in the vernacular of Gasoline Alley, baked beans from Shinola about the business itself were seeping into the companies and corporations everywhere; financial pod people, numbers' aliens from the accounting department, were slipping into the CEOs' chairs and taking command.

The belief and practice of method without knowledge of substance have lodged themselves everywhere. Teachers are instructed in teaching "methods" with the assumption that they will be equipped to teach any subject, regardless of their ignorance of it.

The country is rife with people who have no firm grasp of any concrete branch of human knowledge, but who are trained in such gaseously dubious skills as communications, policy analysis, facilitation, empowerment and development. It is a world abounding in such imprecise terms as referral, coordinating, consulting, expediting. In this dark borderland between useful effort and outright quackery, where fat government, slack business standards and schlock social science meet, the word most

often heard is *process,* an endless coming to be, an infinite promise, never carefully stated, never fulfilled. Process makes going through the motions an end in itself. On this misty terrain we meet the professional administrator who is said to be able to run any institution without competent understanding of the nature of its work and the professional manager who can do the same with any business.

Men like du Pont and Brown did, of course, work in two separate industries. Some of the knowledge and technique won in the chemical industry were transportable. Certain skills and procedures are applicable, when adjusted to fit a different industry and a different company, when the person doing the applying knows the substance of what's going on. Be it cost accounting or many other techniques, a general body of business knowledge does exist and can be taught, but lacking a thorough grounding in a particular industry and company, the results will be poor. Managing by the numbers, whatever the numbers, is managing for low profit.

Sloan used the numbers but he didn't manage by them. He could use them effectively because he knew the automobile business. He knew Henry Ford, he knew Walter Chrysler, he knew 'em all, sold 'em all roller bearings before he got to GM, and, on top of it, was an MIT-trained engineer himself. He was anything but a guy "from financial" with no idea of what transpired under the hood of the gas buggies he was manufacturing. What is more, once he had the new system in place, Sloan stayed in touch with every aspect of his business. The man never stopped working: ". . . I made it a practice throughout the 1920s and early thirties to make personal visits to dealers. I fitted up a private railroad car as an office and in the company of several associates went into almost every city in the United States, visiting from five to ten dealers a day. I would meet them in their own places of business, talk with them across their own desks in their 'closing rooms' and ask them for suggestions and criticism concerning their relations with the corporation, the character of the product, the corporation's policies, the trend of consumer demand, their view of the future, and many other things of interest in the business. I made careful notes of all the points that came up, and when I got back home I studied them."[17]

Note, please, that Sloan didn't come into town and have the dealers meet him in the Presidential suite of the most expensive hotel. He went to their places of business to see firsthand. His regimen was a day-in-day-out grind, sans flunkies and frou-frou, but as the football coaches say of their harder-working morons, he had a "blue collar work ethic." Indeed he did. By his own description, there was a period when he arrived at the office at 8 A.M., left at 6 P.M., Monday through Saturday, fifty-two weeks per annum. No vacations, no holidays, kiddies. In fact he had no kiddies. No hobbies either.

Such a life is not for everybody, nor should it be. Only the smallest number are called to the life of labor and self-denial that was Sloan's, who left his fellow citizens the once miraculous General Motors Corporation, and such other benefactions as the Sloan-Kettering Hospital. Nevertheless the topmost people must be ass-busters, fanatic in their dedication, and wise in their use of the power entrusted to them, strong and unbending in the accomplishment of their work, soft and understanding in their use of other human beings. If they can't reach Sloan's level, they must do at least as well as Malcolm, who was good, if not spectacular at his work.

It is a high standard but the society gives them, in return, power and riches, and it *is* the society which provides them with everything which makes their companies possible from the legal framework, to the education of their work force to the roads on which the company trucks travel. It is not too much to ask that, in return, they do their jobs well and humanely. Or are we to conclude that the bromide about responsibility going with authority and privilege is merely pap for the populace?

Management by the numbers would be bad enough in and of itself but a shift occurred in business accounting which would have momentous consequences. From the time when Fink devised it, through the time when Sloan and Brown put it to such good use, accounting was a management tool, a means of isolating costs so that they could be lowered, a means of analysis so that managers could see the advantages of taking one path versus taking another. Return on investment was not devised for outsiders, for market analysts, for the portfolio managers of pensions funds or for the likes of the Dough Boy and the other high finaglers of low finance.

It was strictly an internal management device, and it was used differently than ROI and similar measures are used now, when they are checked out quarter by quarter on the calendar. Sloan and his people looked at five-year segments. The stock market goes crazy when the accounting numbers jiggle around, but Sloan and Brown knew that there would be years when the return on investment was going to be lower than it might have been. They would even plan it that way, because they were focused on what would be best in the long term for the magnificent enterprise they had done so much to build.[18] It would never have occurred to them to react to month by month fluctuations, whose meaning, if any, was unknowable.

But today, return on investment and similar measures are primarily of concern because of how they will affect the price of the company's stock. As late as 1945, Perry Hall, a legendary managing director of Morgan Stanley, an outfit responsible for launching more than one stock issue onto the market's choppy waves, was saying that only ten percent of American corporate financing came from selling stock.[19] Expansion money came from profits.

As the stock market became the be-all-and-end-all for CEOs, cost accounting ceased to be a tool of management and became a tool of finance. The important statistical measures were kept primarily for people outside the company—the stockbrokers, the IRS, the Securities and Exchange Commission and to satisfy the standards of the certified public accountants.

Certified Public Accounting and cost accounting are not the same and have different origins. The CPAs arrive on the scene essentially to protect the interest of stock- and bondholders, to ensure their investment is as advertised. Much of the first impetus for CPAs arose from the concern of British investors, and the first major CPA firm, Price, Waterhouse, was an import from England.

Cost accounting grew up inside American businesses as an adjunct to the art of management. It had different roots and different purposes, and has, alas and alack, been largely blotted out by the CPAs.

The attendant abuses and distortions in cost accounting were made more prominent by pegging CEOs' annual compensation to the price performance of his and, once every blue moon, her

company's stock. Such incentives, which seem engineered to encourage executives to find ways to boost the price of the company's stock, do nothing to boost the company.

In biz language here are the names of some of the gimmicks CEOs use as listed by Thomas Johnson and Robert S. Kaplan: adoption of more liberal accounting conventions, switching from accelerated to straight-line depreciation, changing from deferral to flow-through for the investment tax credit, lengthening depreciable lives, capitalizing previously expensed items, assuming higher rates of return on pension fund assets, amortizing past and prior pension costs over a longer time period and switching from completed contract to percentage of completion method for long-term contracts. Thus you can feed crack cocaine to the stock while the company with those funny little factories in Keokuk, Iowa, and San Jose, California, can be half-dead and dying.

Numbers aren't collected the same way for stock market players and other outsiders as they are for efficient management. Cost accounting was replaced by stock market accounting, which increases the likelihood that the CEO isn't going to understand what's going on in his company. Some of the zombie corporations we see hobbling along collapsed because the management didn't know what the real costs were, and in what departments, divisions, offices, shops and work clusters they were incurred. They weren't collecting the right information, their books were set up wrong.

Strange and screwy things can happen when the books are set up wrong; nut-ball practices of the kind we associate with the government become the order of the day. In one corporation highly salaried engineers were ordered to benches to run ordinary production machinery because the numbers said it was cheaper to use them than low-wage, blue collar workers.[20]

Although computers have made it possible for management to know the step-by-step costs of an operation for a few pennies, few of them bother to collect the information. There are tales of subordinate managers who have taken to using their own PCs to keep track of costs. It's as though the repudiated Communist party factory managers from the Soviet Union had snuck over here, donned capitalist rubber masks and taken over. Long live failure!

Corporate HQs have been known to close low-cost, efficient plants and keep the high-cost, less efficient ones running on the basis of misleading printouts. Indeed the suspicion is about that many companies may have committed large errors in computing their labor costs, thus involving them in the wasted expense of moving various operations abroad. Exporting American jobs overseas at a loss out of garden variety stupidity is social treason.[21]

Even as the numbers veered off from reality, they began to be treated as though they themselves had a tangible existence. A billion dollars' worth of "assets" was no longer seen as a social organization where large numbers of people performed a vast number of variegated and skilled tasks. Assets, equity, P/E ratios, ROI and fifty more terms used in the "capital markets" became real in and of themselves.

Something of the kind had happened in the 1920s when people were delirious over "paper profits," and it happened again, on an even greater and ever-growing scale, in the years after the Second World War. The numerical abstractions and giddy flittings from last year's hot new idea to this year's surefire conceptual winner, all so dear to the novelty-loving investment banker, business school visionary and overheated stock salespeople corrupted too many executives. Even while they were talking about their hands-on style, bosses lost touch with their own businesses and the nation found itself with a managerial crisis on its hands.

# THIRTEEN

# King Harold
# and the G-Theory

WILLIAM ZECKENDORF had delusions of grandeur which led him to see himself as Lorenzo the Magnificent rather than Big Bill the Builder. It was pure Zeckendorf to say to one of the Rockefeller brothers, "Nelson, don't you think it is about time that the modern Medicis began hiring the modern Michelangelos and Da Vincis? I plan to go into a great building program on a national scale, and I'd like to put together an architectural staff that could provide new thinking."[1]

History had fated this modern Medici, the man who thought up Century City and Lincoln Center, and projects almost as grand in Washington, Denver, Philadelphia and elsewhere, to do his work in the architecturally dismal 1950s. But he did go with I. M. Pei, the best of a school of architecture which does not rival that of the Italian Renaissance.[2]

What Zeckendorf is remembered for is not his buildings, but his prestidigitation with numbers. He opened up the Age of

Numerology with the introduction of what he called his Hawaiian Technique, so named because he was surf fishing there when God sent him the inspiration which would first elevate and then destroy him. The Hawaiian Technique was a way to finance real estate purchases which, in his words, "often could make two plus two equal to four plus one plus two plus more."[3] When numbers no longer stand for real things, you're adding by a different kind of arithmetic. Zeckendorf's method of calculation would be used repeatedly over the coming decades as Boesky and the Dough Boy and the rest of them assured the world that they had made, by virtue of the insights given only to genius, "two plus two equal to four plus one plus two plus more." Oh, yeah.

The precise steps Zeckendorf took to pull off his loaves and fishes operation need not detain us, but to get something of the texture of how these guys work—Milken, Kravis, Pickens, any of 'em, in jail or out—the following passage by Zeckendorf himself explains the Hawaiian Technique.[4] Even if you don't understand some of the terms, you'll pick up the underlying meaning if you let yourself tap dance to the confidence game rap: ". . . considering only the land, I determined that $250,000 of the total million-dollar income of the property should go to the ground rent. This ground rent, since it must be paid before any other expenses, is the safest of all possible incomes to the property. Capitalized at the rate of five percent, therefore, the ground should be worth five million dollars . . . since ground income is so sure, a mortgage on the ground . . . would be even more secure. I would have little trouble finding an insurance company or pension fund willing to take a four-percent return for such a safe risk and could therefore sell them a mortgage on the ground for three million dollars which would eat up $120,000 of the land's total income. The remaining $130,000 of income capitalized at the rate of $6\frac{1}{2}$ percent would be worth two million, and for this sum I would sell the land to an institutional or individual investor."[5] Thus two and two are made to yield a lot more than four or so the hocus-pocus will tell you.

When you hear a financier, banker or industrialist talking like that, call the bunco squad and run like hell. For all his smarts, and Zeckendorf was a pretty smart man, his kind of

arithmetic works best when the trade winds are blowing in his direction. His intricate schemes demand that all the high-range predictions come true. A little stormy weather, a dip in business conditions, and the trouble starts. At the end of the 1950s, business did slack off and Zeckendorf, finding he couldn't keep up with the payments, redoubled his borrowing from the men he called "my Shylock money lenders."

For all his drawbacks, Zeckendorf was a business person of energy and entrepreneurial imagination, not dissimilar to businessmen of the 1890s and early 1900s who commissioned Frank Lloyd Wright and Louis Sullivan to build their palaces of commerce. His ability to see castles and cities unbuilt where slums and weedy railroad yards stood played him false by beckoning constantly farther until his own enthusiasm delivered him into the power of the money monsters. He lacked prudence, but prudent men only see things as they are, not as they might be.

This was still a period when home buyers got six percent mortgages, which helps explain why there were more of them then, and when healthy companies could borrow money at four and perhaps even three percent. The wounded Zeckendorf, however, was paying twenty-four percent to André Meyer of Lazard Frères. He could have gotten the money from Al Capone for less than from Meyer, whose name to this day is usually preceded by the adjectives legendary or great. That congenital simpleton David Rockefeller hailed this French émigré toad as "the most creative financial genius of our time in the investment-banking field." So be it, but Felix "The Fixer" Rohatyn,[6] Meyer's protégé and legman at Lazard Frères, may have come closer to the mark when he said, "André could peel people like bananas."[7] Well, it takes one to know one, but it is assuredly the case that, after dealing with Monsieur Meyer, many a man must have walked away acutely conscious of no longer being covered by skin.

Meyer and Rohatyn went on a mergers and acquisitions spree. They were a high-finance Bonnie and Clyde, going from one town to the next shooting and looting. Meyer was described by a fellow Wall Streeter as a man with an "almost erotic attachment to money. Just to have it, to feel it, to be in possession of it gave him an enormous kick." Meyer, who is dead, apparently thought that money alone endows its possessor with

respectability, and he was probably right. But Rohatyn, who is a character out of *Bonfire of the Vanities,* preferred playing the part of a wise elder. Some years ago, when called to account by Emmanuel Celler, then Chairman of the House Judiciary Committee, for the merger orgy of the 1960s, Felix the Fixer owned up that it was not a desire to see greater prosperity and productivity in his adopted land which drove him to play his part in bringing about that great shipwreck, but a passion for pelf shared with his mentor, "the most creative financial genius of our time."

ROHATYN: I think we are much more an effect than we are a cause . . . The majority of these transactions are not transactions that would not have seen the light of day without us.

CELLER: Profit is a great motive, isn't it?

ROHATYN: Yes, Mr. Chairman.

CELLER: It is a motivation of most of these transactions, isn't it, one way or another?

ROHATYN: Certainly, Mr. Chairman. We run our business to make a profit.

CELLER: Wouldn't that be a part of your motive to bring about mergers?

ROHATYN: Certainly, Mr. Chairman, we certainly like to be involved in these transactions because, as you say, they are profitable for us.[8]

A Lazard Frères modus operandi was to have one of its partners get on a corporation's board and involve the company in a merger, bringing large fees to Meyer and his associates. Rohatyn tried it with William Paley, the founder and builder of CBS, as this incident, told by Sally Bedell Smith, illustrates:

At a luncheon in late 1979, Rohatyn tossed out the annual report for Bausch & Lomb, makers of contact lenses. Paley was captivated by the look of the report; handsomely produced, it exuded quality.

"It may not make sense, but it's a good company, the right size and range," said Rohatyn.

Leaning back in his chair, Paley mused, "I think it could fit."

"Why?" asked Rohatyn.

"We are in the TV business and people need good eyesight to watch TV," said Paley.

"Maybe we should do this."[9]

Paley didn't, but the confreres had better luck with Robert Sarnoff, chairman of RCA, whom they enmeshed in a series of idiotic mergers which finally cost him his place. Robert Sarnoff had the job thanks to another affirmative action placement. His father, David, was a legitimate Big Man, a true pioneer and major force in the building of the broadcast industry, whose only serious business mistake was making sure his son took over from him. In the 1960s RCA-NBC went out and got itself a real estate company (Cushman & Wakefield), a rug manufacturer (Coronet Industries), an auto rental company (Hertz), a book publisher (Random House) and Banquet Foods, this last being the occasion for one of Sarnoff's successors to remark, "We became the biggest chicken pluckers in America. The problem was our technically trained managers didn't know how to manage chicken plucking."[10]

But what won Felix his sobriquet the Fixer was the relationship he and the confreres had with International Telephone and Telegraph (ITT) and its CEO, Harold Geneen. Geneen was the stoutly determined son of English immigrants; his father had gone broke when Harold was a lad, thus giving him an extra prick of desire to make good. This Geneen did by making ITT into a many-billion-dollar corporation by the process of consuming hundreds of other corporations. Harold Geneen became Mr. Conglomerate.[11] He was called the General Patton of Industry and countless, naive children from schools of business studied "the G-Theory of Management." The G is for Geneen, not for good.

Meyer's biographer described how Geneen found the companies he pounced on: "He (Geneen) would carry with him the ponderous Moody's manual of industrial companies and casually leaf through it on airplanes as though it were the latest Agatha Christie thriller. During meetings with his staff about possible purchases, his acquisitions people would wheel in a shopping cart full of annual reports for Geneen to peruse. Geneen's technique for sorting through these reports never varied: he would start with the financial statements in the back and then work his way to the front, where he found out what it was the company actually did. Yet as hard-boiled as Geneen usually was, his judgments sometimes had their quirky side.

Once, he was given the annual report of a key-maker to look at. He seemed intensely interested for a few minutes, but then suddenly tossed the report aside and said to his aides, 'What's next?'

" 'You don't like it?' a staffer asked him.

" 'No, I don't,' Geneen replied. " 'Did you happen to look at the chairman's picture? I don't like his eyes.' "[12]

Geneen may not have been good as a CEO, but he was good with numbers. He'd spent his whole life in accounting, finance, reading reports, his bookkeeper's eye zipping up and down columns of figures. By the time he became the King of ITT, there was no trick Hard Driving Harry didn't know to make the numbers come out the way the stock market loves them to look. His proudest boast was fifty-eight consecutive quarters during which his books showed growth. His financial huffery and puffery blew ITT up to number nine on the *Fortune 500* hit parade. When the General Patton of Industry retired, it was supposed he would be the first person since the Virgin Mary to make the direct assumption into heaven.

Before he could do so, the press, which had vastly inflated Geneen's reputation, began to tear it down. By 1985 *Time* was running a story entitled "An Incredible Shrinking Giant" in which it said, "ITT was the most voracious of a new breed of corporate giants that came to be known as conglomerates. Under the leadership of Harold Geneen, Wall Street's original Pac-Man, ITT gobbled up more than 275 companies; at one time the corporation produced everything from hydroelectric turbines to Twinkies . . . After taking over from Geneen in 1980, Chairman Rand Araskog tentatively began to shed some of the conglomerate's less profitable divisions; last week he announced that ITT was going on the corporate equivalent of a crash diet. In the coming months, it plans to sell more than a dozen subsidiaries . . ."[13]

When companies are translated into numerical symbols as quantifiable assets, their essence, that they are social organizations, is overlooked. The turmoil, fear, upset and disruption within an organization when it is sold, and often sold again, hasn't been measured. One of the companies dumped by the new boy at ITT was Avis car rental, sold to a company in which William Simon, a former Secretary of the Treasury, was in-

volved. In a span of about forty years the company had eleven different owners.

A few months after the *Time* article, *Fortune,* a publication often reluctant to print a bad word about a big corporation, observed that Geneen's record profits came at the cost of these companies' futures.[14] Years later the off-loading of companies continued.

This was not the first time that *Fortune* had suggested that the General Patton of Industry didn't know which end of his tank the bullets came out of, that the modern miracle manager had gotten it all wrong. In the May 1975 issue of *Fortune,* Carol J. Loomis broke a story saying that Geneen had spent a billion and a half dollars buying the Hartford Insurance Company without having been able to correctly construe its books. Geneen was ignorant of the company's "yellow peril," the unfortunate name the industry at that time used to denote liabilities lurking down the road and hidden in something called "Schedule P" of the annual report. "Harold Geneen does not really understand these matters himself! That mind-boggling fact emerged from an interview," Loomis wrote. "Geneen said he was not familiar with 'Schedule P;' that fact, itself very startling, made the questions more difficult to frame." At first, Loomis recounted, Geneen couldn't accept that he was staring at a surprise loss of more than one hundred million dollars, but she said, "Then he seemed to be coming to a horrified realization that it might be true."

Ain't that a pistol? A man pays a billion and a half dollars for a company and can't answer the reporter's questions about it because he doesn't understand them.

Something else Geneen and Rohatyn didn't understand was that the Hartford takeover would detonate an antimonopoly outcry which embroiled them with the Justice Department, the Watergate scandals and a congressional investigation. It also involved them with a contretemps with the IRS, questionable deals in Italy, Liechtenstein, outfits with suspicious sounding names like Eurofund and Mediobanca. Also part of the intrigues was Charlie Engelhard, a friend and neighbor of Malcolm's, a hugely rich man, said to have been the model for the Goldfinger character in the *James Bond* stories. Eventually Charlie, who was up to his eyeballs in precious metals, literally ate

himself to death consuming Hershey chocolate kisses, but not before the grossly obese centimillionaire tried to depose Malcolm from his New Jersey state senate seat and almost succeeded. Geneen and Rohatyn got no kisses from anybody. Instead the Securities and Exchange Commission leveled the most serious accusations against them, not dissimilar to those which would put Ivan Boesky behind bars a generation later.*

Jim Cook, a writer on *Forbes*, was another who wondered out loud about the new, heaven-sent formula for getting rich without working: "The question then is not: Is conglomeration a viable corporate strategy? The question rather is: How do you tell a good conglomerate from a poor one? Or, to put it another way: How does a conglomerate go about making an acquisition worth more than it paid for it? . . . The answer is supposed to be in what it has become fashionable to call synergy—the so-called 2-plus-2 equals (at least) 5 effect. . . . If synergy exists, each corporation involved possesses an unrealized potential that a merger permits to be realized . . . Conglomerators . . . suggest that synergy can convert a prosaic business like metal products into a glamorous one . . . Is this not often—as the critics argue—a financial illusion, made possible primarily by the extreme leveraging of commons earnings through the issuance of convertible preferreds and debentures? Even worse, is it all done with bookkeeping?"

The same issue of *Forbes*, November 1, 1967, which carried Cook's penetrating questions, also contained an interview with the Junior Watson of IBM in which, in the more courtly language CEOs reserve for each other, he says the same thing: "The conglomerates baffle me. We have turned down dozens of companies outside the area of computers . . . We know how to run a computer business. We know nothing about running other kinds. Yet I see Thornton and Geneen doing well. So there must be some top managers who are good at just management. But at IBM we think we are only good in business machines."

In 1973, more than five years after Cook had asked whether it was all done with bookkeeping, after the market had done one of its swan dives and the air was heavy with predictable

---

* The charges were not pursued.

remorse, as it would be yet another time in the early 1990s, *Fortune* answered the question. Yes, the magazine said, "Financial reporting was governed by such elastic rules that only an expert dogged enough to dig through the myriad footnotes in corporate reports could get a glimpse of where genuine profit growth ended and artful accounting took over . . . the most damaging result of the conglomerate merger era was the false legitimacy it seemed to confer on the pursuit of profits by financial manipulation rather than by producing something of genuine economic value. Some conglomerates specialized in using adroit but legal tricks to fatten their profits, and the example has been widely emulated. By temporarily seducing much of Wall Street with earnings growth based on accounting gimmicks, conglomerates may have, for the long run, weakened public confidence in the securities market."[15]

Everything which was decried then is decried now. It is all still with us, even synergy, which Andrew Carnegie saw through a century ago when he remarked: Put all your eggs in one basket—then watch the basket.

Synergy asserts that yes, there is such a thing as a free lunch if it is done under free market auspices. Lunch is free when you steal it. A deal-steal works like this: one or more of the Dough Boys spot the corporation to be heisted, round up the gang—lawyers, accountants, consultants—and suborn somebody on the inside by giving him a cut. That somebody is top management who knows not only where the bodies are buried but also where the boodle is. With the company's shares hypothetically selling at $10, its stockholders are offered $12.50, although the insiders know that, properly packaged, one can resell them at $30 per share by breaking up the company into parts. Thus, when the heist is pulled, the shareholders will have had $17.50 stolen from them for each share they own and are forced to sell. (The mechanics of these robberies are such that one is forced to sell.)

Benjamin Stein, writing in *Barron's*,[16] explained the sheep-shearing mechanism with pithy clarity: "LBO's work for the same reason that pawnshops work: because the pawnbroker/manager/LBO financier knows as a matter of certainty that he will be able to resell or repackage your watch or your company for more than he paid you for it. Why do LBO practitioners

make a great deal of money? Why do people who shoot fish in a barrel reap a great many dead fish? . . . In America today, the looting of one's own stockholders and the financing of such transactions, has become as important a route to wealth—perhaps more so—as any other route and certainly the most certain."

Synergy was one of the things peddled by Steve Ross when he put together Time Warner, that lumbering, debt-soaked, behemoth of entertainment and communications. By an alchemic process, unknown to science but familiar to faith healers, the magazines, the movie studios, the cable television comprising this misbegotten corporate enterprise were to work on each other and demonstrate once again that two plus two equals whatever silly number will stimulate the greed needed to reel in the suckers who put up the money to make the deal go.

To get these scams underway, two things are required, a gizmo and an abracadabra man. In the 1920s it was guys like Ivar Kreuger, in the 1950s and '60s it was guys like Jimmy Ling: and in the 1980s the abracadabra man was Michael Milken, residing at this writing in the federal penitentiary, although it would take a microscope and a prayer to distinguish him from the men teeing off this very minute at the five most expensive golf clubs in America.

An adoring press finds a way to celebrate the abracadabra man's genius. They couldn't say enough in praise of Jimmy Ling, maker of a multibillion-dollar conglomerate once called Ling Temco Vought, next LTV and now called broke, to the great pain of its employees, its investors, its creditors and its pensioners. This from *Newsweek* in the late 1960s when Jimmy had his mojo working to inflame imaginations and render common sense comatose: "In one short decade, he has dazzled Dallas and Wall Street alike . . . The man who worked this miracle looks more like a pro football quarterback than a business genius. Daily workouts hold his powerful 6-foot 2-inch frame down to a tightly muscled 200 pounds and he walks with the spring of an athlete. When Ling talks, however, all doubts about his calling vanish. At the approach of an inquiring outsider, Ling shoots from his chair as if spring-propelled, extends a powerful hand, fixes the caller intently with his piercing black eyes, and begins a tireless, non-stop, explanation of his methods

and goals."[17] Jesus! They come right out and say he is a miracle worker and nobody giggles.

Athleticism is prized in our biz-heroes. If they are morally muscle-bound and brutishly insensate, it is believed these qualities make for a better bottom line. As evidence we offer this about the CEO of Greyhound, which appeared in *Fortune:*[18] "John Teets has pummeled and punished his body into superb condition, and loves to talk about it . . . 'I'm tough,' Teets admits, 'tough like leather, with just enough give to take a beating all day long and not shatter . . . I've got a senior executive whose wife has two lumps in her breasts. I don't want to know about it. I do it so when I weigh a business decision, I don't have all that luggage that a guy's wife isn't well.' " Go, team!

Because Michael Milken, the grand prestidigitator of the junk bond era, was a furtive and secretive man, the business press painted a dark, magic picture of a silent man, in his cabinet, turning cow pies into gold. Like Stalin and Churchill, and doubtless other famous men, good and bad, he labored the midnight hours through.

The Milken gizmo was better than synergy. His gizmo was a book called *Corporate Bond Quality and Investor Experience* by an unknown professor of the dismal science by the name of W. Braddock Hickman. His *chef d'oeuvre* was published in 1958 and reportedly sold 934 copies, but according to Milken it contained a secret more wonderful than anything you'll find in the Book of Mormon. The latter only promises life everlasting; the former vouchsafes riches without end. For years he waved the book in the air, used it as his proof and his sales piece, and everybody said, Amen, bro, but nobody read the damn thing. It was the good book and it said in it, in words precious beyond price, that all you have to do is buy cheap crap—junk bonds,† so called because they're the high-risk borrowings of companies which don't have enough money to pay off their debts.[19] That's the ticket to the dream Alhambra where naught is to be heard

† Celebrity varlets like Michael Milken made a specialty of peddling this kind of loan. The junk bond pays a high rate of interest to those who buy it because it is a gamble that the company issuing it will generate enough income to pay it back. If resorted to in moderation and purchased by high rollers who know what they're doing, the junk bond can have a small but useful place in the world. We have come to know the costs when the bonds are sold by confidence men, road agents and other rascals to pension funds, insurance companies and retirees.

but the hollow clunk of golf ball dropping into cup. And in the evening the houris of the nineteenth hole offer a choice of anything on a silver platter as the Dow Jones ascends to a million. Tsk! And they say it's the socialists who believe you can get something for nothing. At the welfare office, hard times and food stamps have taught them it just ain't so, but on Wall Street they still believe you can live the good life without having to work for it.

The hard-working, ordinary business people, the executives who do bust ass—and there still are hundreds of thousands of them—are suckers for the abracadabra men. They go for the pitch not necessarily because they're greedy. Many a business person is profit-motivated, but *not* greedy. They go for the pitch because they are optimists, they are boomers, boosters and ballyhooers, because they have to be. The heart and soul of business is a hopeful optimism which believes, with no solid evidence to support it, that the other guy's word is good, that he will stick to the letter of the contract, that the delivery will come in on time, that the parts will fit together, that the loan will be approved, that the people in the machine shop will do it right, that the new machine will live up to the specs in the brochure, that the ad will pull, that the new product line is right, that the competition doesn't have something better, that the government isn't going to shut 'em down and, above all else, that the customers will come in the door with money in hand. There is good and sufficient reason why business people go wild about criticism and pessimism, why they sing pep songs to each other, why they love the positive and hate the negative, why they cherish enthusiasm and why they are always up for the next person to soft-shoe through the entrance with a happy smile and a nutty idea which might just work, Harry.

These people are easy marks because they want to believe. When it doesn't work, and the thing comes crashing down on them, they treat it as an unfortunate Saturday night drunk, pick themselves up and start over again. But these aren't episodic binges. What started in the Zeckendorf period, the mesmerized belief in loaves and fishes, in two and two equaling improbably large numbers, is essentially the same con run slightly differently over the years.

The nomenclature is new, but there is an underlying same-

ness between what a Milken, Icahn and Kravis have been pulling in recent years, and Daniel Drew's racket a hundred and
fifty years ago. Drew (1797–1879), a storied, born-again, illiter-
ate Methodist hypocrite, found out early the way to fleece the
sheep scientifically and repeatedly was to have control over the
issuance of a company's stocks and/or bonds and make the market in them, that is, be the person people come to when they
want to buy or sell these pieces of engraved paper. The Erie
Railroad, that company which played such a large part in the
history of business, was his chosen instrument for this work. As
they said at the time: "Daniel says 'up'—Erie goes up. Daniel
says 'down'—Erie goes down. Daniel says 'wiggle-waggle'—it
bobs both ways!" How about Dough Boy says "Up"—RJR
Nabisco goes up, etc.?

Perhaps the most devilishly creative man to trod the length of
Wall Street, Drew is credited or blamed for inventing everything from short selling to stock watering. Though he never
went to jail, he died bankrupt—let the Dough Boy take warning
—and left many a contribution to Wall Street lore and legend,
the best remembered of which, anent short selling, may be:

> He who sells what isn't his'n
> Must buy it back or go to prison.

Without poetry, the modern method is simple: phase one was
conglomeration, redeploying assets in the 1950s and 1960s for
the most efficient use of capital. That's the way the professors
they hire as apologists talk. Gigantic companies providing thousands of unrelated goods and services but guided by master
managers would take us up to a stratosphere of prosperity. Instead the conglomerates wound up in a bathosphere of debt,
mediocre aimlessness and bankruptcy.

Phase two brings de- or dis-conglomeration via the leveraged
buyout and the junk bond. De-conglomeration was necessary,
the professors explained in the 1970s and 1980s, to redeploy
assets for their most efficient use. What was joined together for
efficiency, was then divorced for efficiency. Thomas Lee, testify-
ing before a congressional committee in 1989, about his six-
hundred-million-dollar leveraged buyout of Hills Department
Stores, Inc., called the procedure the "re-entrepreneuring of
America." Hey, baby! Free market, entrepreneur, initiative,

**253**

lick-spit, bootstraps and hot shots, *numero uno* vrooming down the highway toward a state of capitalist perfection. Two years later Hills Department Stores did the famed belly rotation and it was bankruptcy bloat, specifically Chapter 11.[20]

Sometimes one and the same company conglomerated and then turned around and dis-conglomerated. Such was the story of Beatrice, once a wonderful, low-overhead, no frills, high-profit food company based in small Chicago headquarters. It was the kind of place that didn't have a boardroom because the old-time CEOs understood that you can rent a nice place to have a meeting once a month a whole lot cheaper than having a gonif of a corporate interior decorator design you something at three quarters of a million dollars.

Then, as ill-luck would have it, Beatrice got itself a real, rootin'-tootin' Ludwig. He put up a framed cartoon in the new and expanded headquarters, showing a CEO meeting with his fellow executives and saying, "All of those opposed signify by saying, I quit."[21] The company had no sooner gotten rid of this winner than the big Dough Boy, Kravis his very self, came along and bought Beatrice so that capital/assets could be efficiently redeployed and the re-entrepreneuring of America might continue. In furtherance of that cause, he installed a whiz-bang by the name of Kelly. The next intelligence offered to those followers of the thrill of business victory and the agony of business defeat came in *The Wall Street Journal.* A Beatrice executive was quoted as saying of the new, efficient CEO, "He needs good short-handle broom guys for day-to-day operations. If he's by himself, I'd wonder if his mail is being opened." Another major division head also spoke up: ". . . sometimes a month or more would go by and we wouldn't even talk. Not only did he not tell us what to do, sometimes I couldn't get him to voice an opinion about what we were doing."[22]

In general, statements by high-powered executives, whether from newly purchased companies or old-line losers, that waste is going to be eliminated, unnecessary staff will be cut and a new and winning approach is being installed are best listened to in the same spirit accorded similar words uttered by a) the mayor, b) the governor or c) the President. At Sears, Roebuck, once *the* glory of American merchandising, but now a demi-semi conglomerate into insurance, real estate, stock brokerage,

etc., they hit with one such statement about every six months. They've been doing it for years, but Sears is a candidate for the corporate death list—another once great company which has flamed out and is on its way to becoming a black hole.

After a company has been conglomerated and dis-conglomerated, sucked and resucked, and left for dead in the bankruptcy court, the biz-animals come out, shimmering a cold silver in the dark. These are the workout artists, as they are called, people whose occupation is corporate necrophagia. On Wall Street, the money pooled to invest in collapsed junk bonds, ruined banks and wrecked manufacturers is called "vulture funds." One such investor is thirty-nine-year-old Leon Black, who made his first fifty million at Drexel Burnham Lambert, Michael Milken's company, doing leveraged buyouts and junk bonds. Mr. Black made good his escape unindicted, his fortune intact, and hopes, through his vulture fund, to dine well on the carcass and carrion of the business dead. Mr. Black even elicited a retch or two at *Forbes* magazine, where they have strong stomachs. "In his second career," the article said of Mr. Black, "he plans to get rich all over again cleaning up the kind of financial messes he helped create. Like a polluter going into the pollution cleanup business, Black does bring a certain knowhow to bear upon the subject."[23]

"Restructuring isn't as profitable as mergers and acquisitions," said one businessman, who conceded there comes a point when there isn't enough left to do more than make soup. "We're dealing with companies with limited amounts of cash."[24] Nonetheless, the lawyers, the bankers, the brokers, the arbs, the consultants, the accounting firms, the spectrum of the parasite professions, all those incriminated in the *trahison des clercs,* have made billions on the structuring, restructuring, re-re-structuring, interment and burial of God knows how much productive capacity. No one can count the houses not built, the sick not served, the children ill-served, the medicine not distributed, the jobs not created, the parks not cared for, the science not done, the necessities and the luxuries foregone because of the monumental disloyalty of those who put profit above country.

The positive damage can be traced, added up and described. Thanks to *The Wall Street Journal,* which consecrated several months of Susan C. Faludi's time and published her long article

on page one,[25] the consequences of one, enormous, leveraged buyout were documented and described.

The company, the Safeway grocery store chain, was the victim of a leveraged buyout in 1986. This was not an example of the stumbling, consumptive corporation in need of new management, new capital and new life. To the contrary, in the years immediately preceding the attack, Safeway's profits had doubled, its dividends had gone up each time and the price of its stock had tripled. As Ms. Faludi wrote, "But all that wasn't enough for takeover-crazed Wall Street, where virtually no company was invulnerable to cash-rich corporate raiders." By all accounts this was not a company in need of having Henry Kravis buy it up and take it private, but the Dough Boy went ahead and did it, loading the company with debt. Wholesale closings and firings followed, as the new Safeway, transformed from a healthy, useful and profitable social organization, was turned into a desperate place struggling to pay its debts and stay alive.

Ms. Faludi went out and found the people they fired. She told of James White, thirty years a truck driver for Safeway, who on the first anniversary of his dismissal, "told his wife he loved her, then he locked the bathroom door, loaded his .22-caliber hunting rifle and blew his brains out." She told of Patricia Vasquez, a systems analyst, fourteen years with the company, one of those employees who skipped lunch to get the job done. After she was told that the reward for doing her job well was to be thrown out the door, she "packed her service citations in a cardboard box and left looking pale and drawn. The next morning her two young children found their single mother on the bathroom floor, dead of a heart attack." Mr. Quigley's wife, a diabetic, couldn't take the news; her blood sugar shot up and she was soon dead. When Mr. Morrison, fourteen years with the company, lost his job, his fiancée walked out on him—she didn't want to be with a guy who didn't have a job. He got another job, but the Dough Boy got that company too, and they fired him again. This time Mr. Morrison lost his house.

Then there was the case of Mikhail Vaynberg, a refugee from the old Communist Russia, who was a refrigeration engineer at Safeway and instituted changes that saved the company more than a million and a half dollars. They fired him and, get this,

when he asked for a letter of recommendation so he could get another job, the new owners told him no, "you might use it to sue the company." First you get Stalin, then you get Henry Kravis.

For all that, there are no mobs out on the street calling for Henry Kravis' head. Nobody's heard of him—an anonymous man who sits in his office and tells the flunkies, buy this, and a woman dies in California, sell that, and a family is ruined in Texas.

Susan Faludi was given a Pulitzer Prize for her article, and seldom was one as merited, but though the news of her prize was widely printed, the contents of her story were not discussed. Well, you see, *The Wall Street Journal* is a competitor. We can't give competitors free advertising. So do your own story on death by leveraged buyout, murder by junk bond. No, what's the point? That story's already been done. They did it in *The Wall Street Journal*.

One reporter and one newspaper can't get such a story out. Even now, after books like *Den of Thieves* and *Barbarians at the Gate,* the injury to individuals and the nation is not understood. It will take everybody going after such a story in the same way that the AIDS story has been pursued to bring home the enormous damage which has been done.

# FOURTEEN

# Honky Tonkin'

THE STORY of the damage done by business barbarians should be pounded home day after day after day, week in and week out. It isn't, because American journalism is commercially driven to entertain, not scold. Can you imagine NBC, owned by General Electric, denouncing corporate cruelty by others? What about ABC? Its single largest investor is Warren Buffett, the Chairman of the Board of Salomon Brothers. CBS is in the hands of real estate speculator Laurence Tisch. They might well put the story on the air once—they probably would —but once is not enough. Matters like this demand crusaders who scream, shout, yell and repeat until a new social norm comes into force.

When the automated workings of a commercially run mass media fail to protect the people on the *Forbes 400* list, they turn to the public relations industry. Spin doctors do not find their origins in politics, as you might be led to believe by the snotty

cracks TV reporters make about flacks in the pay of politicians. Spin doctoring began with business. Its first prominence derived from John D. Rockefeller, Jr.'s publicity man, Ivy Lee, sent to Colorado to do damage control at the Ludlow Massacre of 1914, where the wives and children of striking miners were killed by the authorities. It was during that episode that "Poison Ivy," as some called him, made an enduring contribution to the culture. He invented the phony front group for his public relations ploys. It would later be widely copied by the Communists and others.

Hill & Knowlton, one of the largest public relations firms, got its start keeping other people's employees in line by helping to crush strikes. The company was closely connected with Thomas Mercer Girdler, who ran what he himself called "a benevolent dictatorship" while head of the Jones & Laughlin Aliquippa works and the Pennsylvania town of the same name during the 1920s. John L. Lewis, the founder of industrial trade unionism, described Mr. Girdler, who went on to become the CEO of Republic Steel, as "a heavily armed monomaniac, with murderous tendencies, who has gone berserk."[1] The description has not been more than halfheartedly contested, and Girdler's company was the source of much of Hill & Knowlton's business for years.

Carl Byoir, the founder of another of the largest public relations companies, commenced his business career with "Nuxated Iron, 'a high-priced iron tonic of low cost and little value'; Seedol, a bowel tonic; Kepmalt, a weight builder; Viaderma, a rub-on reducing compound; and finally Blondex, a hair dye." From there he went on to manufacture illusionary public sentiment for the Great Atlantic & Pacific Tea Company in order to deflect hostile legislation. In the course of doing so he invented what is now called "grass roots lobbying," that is buying, creating or convincing local groups, real or letterhead, to send letters, make phone calls and do other things to influence public officials. An experienced operative can create the impression that a vast number of people are exercised over one issue or another. Over the years public relations firms have come to know grass roots lobbying is often as effective and less visible, and therefore less controversial, than political contributions by corporations or individuals.

There are limits to everything, as was the case when Michael Milken's public relations firm tried to retool his image to keep him out of jail and his company, Drexel Burnham, out of bankruptcy. His spin doctors tried grass roots lobbying on the judge who was deluged with letters from people writing on Milken's part, and they tried everything else. Under the eyes of the invited media, the p.r. flacks had Milken and some of his co-workers, as avariciously antisocial a group to assemble outside of a penitentiary, take slum children to Sea World in San Diego, pizza parties in Salt Lake City, a zoo in Philly and a circus in Dallas. The reclusive Milken, who hates to touch human flesh, was made to personally lead nearly two thousand inner-city kids to a baseball game, where he bounced one of the little bastards on his knee. The most grotesque was the bringing of black and Hispanic kids to the Drexel trading floor of a Saturday morning to watch a magician perform—not one of the people who worked there, but an Actors Equity magician. The law prohibiting taking minors to a house of ill fame was suspended for the day, but is there no limit to the allowable exploitation of little people unlucky enough to be born to impecunious parents?

Kravis, needing only an ambiance of deference and approval, has not had to avail himself of the services of a Hill & Knowlton, for he and his fellow businessmen are the beneficiaries of a permanent public relations campaign. It stems from the think tanks, that business invention which has turned paid propagandists into disinterested scholars, and which ceaselessly persuades us that the activities of men and women like Henry Kravis are such stuff as the American Dream is made of. Think tanks like the American Enterprise Institute probably supply most of the experts appearing on all the radio and television talk shows in a year; the nation's daily press is sodden with free columns distributed by such places. The American Enterprise Institute, sustained by bucket-sized contributions from business people, came from something called the Committee on Economic Development, which was once the propaganda department of the National Association of Manufacturers.[2] It is, in a larger sense, one more front group, a very successful one indeed.

Business requirements and business dogma dominate the

whole culture, the pop/mass culture, the high culture, the academy. A generation ago we saw the last of the long line of famous free-lance intellectuals who could pick business up by the nape of the neck and give it a good shake. Paul Goodman, Dwight Macdonald, Edmund Wilson, C. Wright Mills, and before them Henry Mencken and Edgar Lee Masters, and before *them* the ill-tempered aristocrat, Henry Adams. Once there was a place for the thinking outcast, an Emerson and a Thoreau. They were the prophets, the seers, nay-sayers in the hallelujah chorus. They were the voices of heterodoxy, and now there is no place, no podium, no television station to broadcast their dry sarcasms, their raillery, their contemptuous anger at the shoddiness of the intellectual product. Now there are twenty professors on hand taking money to explain that when Henry Kravis does his *Four Horsemen of the Apocalypse* routine on a company, he is "purging" business of wastes, the Ex-Lax, you might say, of the capitalist system.

In the *Forbes 400* list, Kravis[3] and his cousin and business partner, George Roberts, come in at around the half-a-billion-dollar level. A big payday, but Malcolm's adoring friend John Kluge, who puppy-dogged his yacht in the wake of Malcolm's here and there around the world, had larger ones. If liquidated, which is not a bad idea, Kluge, according to the magazine, would be worth more than a centipede can count on his fingers and toes or something over five thousand million dollars. It has been broadly suggested that he swindled his stockholders to possess much of these riches, but his would not be the first great fortune which does not stand close scrutiny.[4]

The *Forbes 400,* now an annual publishing event, and a profitable one for the magazine, was Malcolm's idea. True, his father had published a list in 1918 with the headline: "AMERICA'S THIRTY RICHEST OWN $3,686,000,000—ROCKEFELLER HEADS LIST WITH $1,200,000,000."[5] Throughout his life, Malcolm was at pains to recognize what B.C. had left him. Because he was a self-deprecating person, people discounted Malcolm's repeated statements that the best thing he ever did was to be born the son of the right man. Even when it was conceded that the magazine had been started by his father, B.C.'s enduring influence in shaping it is seldom recognized. Nevertheless, in this as in other things, Malcolm improved on his inheritance.

B.C. published a list once, one which was lacking in the detail, size and packaging of what Malcolm brought forth as the *Forbes 400*.

He did it against the passive resistance of his staff, which went through the motions the first time Malcolm ordered it up, then announced it couldn't be done, and only did it after Malcolm said it would be done. Office lore has it that Malcolm told his people, "Don't tell me what can be done and what can't be done. I own this magazine, I say do it, you go ahead and do it. Get someone on it full-time, take whatever money it costs. I don't care if you take a year, I don't care what it costs. Get a senior editor on it and get a reporter on it, a researcher on it full-time."[6]

It took more personnel than that before it was done. Wealth loves secrecy and sniffing out millionaires all over the country, trying to get a line on them, demands dogged, investigative work. Information on who owns corporate America is largely unknown. The law stipulates if a single person owns more than five percent of a corporation it must be made known, but as repeated scandals concerning the "parking of stock," that is hiding it under another name, show, even the five percent rule is probably widely evaded. Reporters who have worked on the *Forbes 400* say that the billions, perhaps trillions, of inherited money are especially hard to trace. A society where power is money and money is secret is a society in which power is unaccountable and irresponsible.

Gigantic organizations, with influential power at every official level, organizations which can come and go, flattening communities, bestowing prosperity and taking it away are like a four-legged god worked in gold from biblical times, a big god, many times higher than a little person, a god with a jeweled, monitor-eye in front of whom lights are made to wink and disks whir and the people scurry. Organizations which can cause social and familial disruption, which can cause sickness and death, which can arrive and ruin the earth, these huge entities are the property of invisible, unnamed people. They cannot be called to account, cannot be made to answer for their uses of property.* It is not given to see who owns and who controls; from

---

* The beneficiary owners of corporations are protected from having to answer for the crimes committed by managers in their pay. Limited liability, as it is called, was in-

time to time a glimpse is offered of the front men, the spokes-persons, the CEO with the media coach, or the $450-an-hour, no-comment lawyer. To the people touched by such corporations, America is a forest of megalithic shafts, high, hard and flinty, their triangular tops pasted over with the picture of a human face.

Americans have been trying for a long time to find out who holds the money which controls them. Moses Yale Beach's *Wealth and Biography of the Wealthy Citizens of New York* was issued in 1845, and from that time forth compilations of one sort or another saw the light of day, but the only list comparable to the *Forbes 400* appeared in 1892 when the *New York Tribune* published the first installment of its "American Millionaires," series, which, it said, was put together with the help of fifteen hundred people around the country. The millionaires were categorized geographically and by the source of their wealth, quite an undertaking. Ten years later the *New York World* did an "Almanac" of millionaires which was almost as inclusive.[7]

Both papers got involved in this expensive undertaking because of the tariff controversy, the question being whether or not men were getting rich by profiting from protected industries. Malcolm, on the other hand, was practicing what has come to be called list journalism. We see it everywhere in an age when few are able to read a sentence containing a relative clause. What Malcolm wanted out of the list and what he got in spades was publicity and low-grade, amusing controversy such as Bob Hope's writing to the magazine to protest his overvaluation: "If my estate is worth over $50 million, I'll kiss your ass."[8]

Going down the *400* list, even with Mr. Hope omitted, one reads the names and suspects that the drones, sad sacks and

---

vented to encourage people to put their money in large enterprises without having to worry that they might personally have to pony up if the corporation went into debt. Over time it has come to mean that managers can run unsafe places of work, poison people in the vicinity, commit any kind of injurious act and the people who directly profit from it are shielded from having to make good the damages. Only the corporation can be sued, and, if forced to pay, the stockholders lose accordingly. Too little, too late.

In the 1860s limited liability made sense; in the 1990s it has become unlimited license. A corporation should not have limited liability in perpetuity, but for stated periods of time and subject to halfway decent behavior. The owners of barbarian corporations should have no more protection for the irresponsible use of their property than the average automobile owner has for his.

simpletons easily outnumber the workers and producers. Perusing the *Forbes 400*, the reader is persuaded that we need a much stiffer inheritance tax, something that might restrict people from passing on—in their lifetime or after death—more than twenty or twenty-five million. While keeping us stocked up with a good number of relatively rich people, that would unlock some of the old money and get it circulating. A little of it might even fall into the hands of an entrepreneur who would know what to do with it.

Some of the rich, who are always feeling put upon, cheated, paranoid and just generally bitchy, objected to having their names appear on the *400* list because it would a) subject them to kidnappings; b) incite thieves to steal their art works instead of their children; c) encourage the tax collector to come calling; and d) tell money raisers on which doors to knock.[9] Mingy, stingy, angry and frightened, their reaction was predictable. Of more interest were the ones who wanted to be on the list and be on it big. Some wanted on because they like to be the Big Billionaire from Baton Rouge, but others understood that ranking on the list brought with it commercial advantage.

Surely, it was for that reason that Donald Trump pressed the magazine's editors to be assigned billionaire status. "His attitude was, he wanted to be at a billion and then let's negotiate from there," was how one of them described his behavior.[10] The bankers read your name in the *Forbes 400* and call you up to ask you if you'd like two or three wheelbarrows full of money. On this subject you can take Trump at his word when he said, "The banks call me all the time. 'Can we loan you money? Can we this? Can we that?' " They were lending him on his signature, no collateral, lending him a hundred and twenty-five percent of what the mortgaged property could have been resold for, even more.[11]

Without a doubt getting on the *Forbes 400* list has helped many another swing a deal. But the *Forbes 400* itself is not to be sniffed at. In a nation where the ownership of wealth is concealed and therefore the controls of power can be seen only deductively, the magazine's annual survey constitutes the largest body of information on rich people available to us. Even the IRS studies the list to get some handle on who the hell owns America.[12]

We know who doesn't own it. Most of the people who live in it. Half the population is here, you might say, as long as it can pay rent. One percent of the adult population owns about four trillion, repeat trillion, dollars' worth of property. The rest, the ninety-nine percent, are those of us whose worldly goods consist of a car, a house (with the bank and finance company, of course), plus a little money in a savings account and a little less money in the checking account. Some of us have a retirement plan, and if our employers don't steal it, that's worth something too. But stocks, bonds, Treasury bills, the exotica of investment, almost none of the middling million Americans own such things or ever will.†

From a business point of view, few of us are in business. We are without capital. With but small exaggeration you can say that ten percent of the population more or less controls a hundred percent of the wealth. If the wage earner(s) loses his or her or their job(s), the average family has enough money to last three months before it is tapped out.[13] Then it is relatives, friends, the church, selling the car or the house or let's go test the safety net.

We know what the American Dream is. It sells pens, plane tickets and Pontiacs. Fly American, the pride is back. There is also the American night terror haunting the middle class: on the street corners ahead is a bag lady and a bag gentleman waiting to be you. It happens, you read about it, middle-class families in the shelters . . . traditional family gets its nucleus busted . . . lives in a 1976 Cadillac Eldorado and showers in a church. It's a nightmare ride in lunatic park, families zipping up and down, sliding smaller past the dot where you can stay in the neighborhood, past where you would feel right about staying in touch. Homelessness, property-lessness, the pain and penury of cancer, these are the cares that mark the onset of middle age, when youth is done and you must admit the future, the much talked about future, the one which was to be planned with the help of a registered financial adviser, with your independent insurance representative, that future, that one in the commercials and the frightmares, it has arrived.

† One percent of the households own sixty percent of all the privately held stock in American business; the top ten percent of American families own ninety percent of those shares owned by individuals.

These fears were not Malcolm's. From first to last he was too well moneyed to worry about how he was going to pay for the kids' college or patch together retirement, but he wasn't Tisch or Trump, one of those past-macho, stick-it-in-your-ear types who win themselves man-without-mercy reputations. All his life Malcolm did nice things for people.[14] Fifty years after the fact, one of his comrades-in-arms in World War II's Company D, 334th Regiment of the Railsplitter Division, remembered his kindness: "There was many times in the States, we had men—it seemed like they were mostly the uneducated—that come out of the south for some reason, I don't know why. But anyhow, he would help them write letters and help them spell words that some of them couldn't write or didn't know how to spell very well . . . He always had time for them and then those that wanted to, he would take his own time and try and teach them to read. He was very much out of place, he was a well-educated man. I don't know whether it was Harvard or what college out of the east he come from . . ." If Malcolm was a social climber who couldn't resist a rusty European title, he wasn't a snob. People of every station remembered him with affection like his buddy in Company D: "His mother took us out—about three days before we shipped overseas—she took us honky-tonkin' around New York. Which—we's from—Pete was from Kentucky and I was from Indiana, Southern Indiana—took us into some restaurants which we'd never been in before, of course. Pretty fancy. Wasn't used to having your glass filled up every time you took a sip out of it."[15]

Malcolm was used to having his glass filled and with the best wine. By the standards of his fellow Americans he was fantabulously rich. Thus, although he did many kindnesses, past a certain point he knew little about the millions who lived around him. Like his brother millionaires he did not concern himself about how financially tenuous life is for others, how dangerous it is for democracy to have tens of millions whose material interest in the society jumps back and forth between narrow and none.

We are not a nation of shopkeepers, nor yeomen. We are a nation of employees. Yet the nation was constructed by political architects who presumed that most of the voters would be owners of the dominant form of productive property, farms. What-

ever Hamilton and Jefferson disagreed on, each believed the best way to bind people to the republic was by giving them a chance to have a stake in it. Men would not join mobs because they would own property; mobs in the street break windows and mobs in the legislature confiscate property.

In lieu of owning farmland, it is assumed that today's responsible citizen can own a share of productive America by buying stock, being a capitalist instead of an employee. Yet we have a couple of hundred million people living in the United States who lack the capital to become owners and take up the responsible citizenship the authors of the *Federalist Papers* had in mind.

Not surprisingly, government is under pressure from the property-free middling millions to provide them what they are powerless to provide for themselves. It moves, in its glacial way, in on business, making more rules and adding more costs for everything from crippled workers to maternity leave. Managers cry that such matters should not be settled by government, but by whom? Rare is the worker who can bargain on terms approaching equality with the corporate employer. Unions are all but gone, thanks to the corruption, arrogance and incompetence of their officials, and the torpor of the ordinary members, but also thanks to hundreds of millions, perhaps billions, of dollars spent over the years to destroy them. Management might have thought twice, because now those whom it preferred not to bargain with via a union, professional association or some other collectivity come back to business cloaked in the power and clumsiness of government authority. Much of the regulation, which it quite rightfully detests, is the result of business's unwise use of its own strength. It employed and still does employ the power to crush any private sector, non-governmental effort to make it behave responsibly. The public relations people may becloud what's going on with facile lies, but the underlying attitude isn't much different from the one attributed to Commodore Vanderbilt, who at least had the grace not to hire a swarm of wasp-waisted bullshit artists, but spat it out plain when he said: "Law! What do I care about the law? Hain't I got the power?"

Business people are mistaken to believe they can get away without regulatory retribution when Continental Can rigs its computer to dump thousands of longtime employees out the

door just before they become eligible for their pensions. Management called it the Bell Program, a reverse acronym for "Let's Limit Employee Benefits."[16] And five will get you three that the executive who devised the scheme grumps around the golf course flaying the air with his mashie and denouncing the Social Security System. Well, business will get its bell rung and its neck too, if it thinks in the post-union era, it is free to pull tricks like that. Business, take warning, white collar wrath may be as terrible as blue collar anger. The middling millions, or some large chunk thereof, are close to becoming an untethered mass, unweighted by the conservatism which comes with having property to conserve. Politically, they are underorganized and underexperienced, and haven't, therefore, learned to practice self-discipline in vexatious times. The trouble will come if there are too many people on the skids to keep medicated, distracted by prurient TV docudramas, politically quieted by tranquilizers, stifled, tamped down and self-absorbed in the twisted individualism fostered by therapists, gurus, aerobic salons or cults.

Business may not take warning. A New York State woman, who organized candlelight vigils and circulated petitions against the developers' intention to cut down a stand of oak trees, found herself being sued for six and a half million dollars for defaming the company's character. Ordinary people have no money to defend against suits. They bite their tongues and mark the consequences of free market dogmatics as they are lived out on the "even playing field." A corporation lawyer, engaged in the work of curbing other people's tongues, warns: "Your freedom of speech stops at the point where you libel or defame our product."[17]

That may be, but corporate freedom of speech is unstoppable. How extraordinary corporate power is. For more than a century it has been able to market tobacco poison unhindered, as the tobacco industry has scythed down one generation after the next. Tobacco's dangers were known for a long time, but the industry has been able to proselytize against the knowledge that the stuff kills from the last century forward.

In 1828 the *Journal of Health* declared tobacco "an absolute poison."[18] By the 1890s some states were trying to ban the manufacture or import of cigarettes, but fat chance.[19] Even the moneyed and powerful were defeated by the corporation using

its constitutional right to persuade young people to buy something that would kill them. Thomas A. Edison and Henry Ford joined forces in 1914 for their "The Cigarette Must Go" crusade, printing a million copies of a pamphlet called, "The Case Against the Little White Slaver," to what effect we know.[20]

Bull Durham tobacco was spending a hundred thousand dollars a year on advertising in the early 1880s. Given the shrinkage in the purchasing power of the dollar, and the opportunities of the time, the sum is roughly equal with what is spent to support a cigarette brand in the 1990s. "A machine can make the cigarette," a student of the industry wrote in 1906, "but advertising must make the market."[21] The glamorizing and exploitation of athletic heroes to sell cigarettes to kids was underway by the turn of the century when the American Tobacco Company hired James Hogan, Yale '05, to peddle coffin nails. He got a commission on every package sold in New Haven.[22]

For more than a century we have been helpless against corporate entities which have been endowed with the privileges of a human being and with special protections—notably limited liability—which people don't have. In American law a corporation gets the same protection citizens get under the Constitution and the Bill of Rights. Since it is legally a person, a corporation has free speech, and since it has free speech, it can use its freedom to peddle poison to children. It was the Supreme Court which made the corporation into a human being, as God the Father made Jesus into one. Jesus' sojourn in human form was short, a corporation's is forever.

Thurman Arnold was railing about the consequence of making corporations into people in 1937, when he wrote, "The Supreme Court of the United States, because it could express better than any one institution the myth of the corporate personality, was able to hamper Federal powers . . . This court invented most of the ceremonies which kept the myth alive and preached about them in a most dramatic setting. It dressed huge corporations in the clothes of simple farmers and merchants and thus made attempts to regulate them appear as attacks on liberty and home."[23]

Since Arnold the corporations have begun to privatize, as they like to say, the Constitution, to make the Bill of Rights an

asset. The *New York Times*[24] was moved to protest in an editorial, under the head of "THE BILL OF RIGHTS, FOR RENT: Join Philip Morris and the National Archives in celebrating the 200th anniversary of the Bill of Rights. . . . The big cigarette maker has paid $600,000 for the right to link itself in televised and printed promotions with the official custodian of America's historic documents. The United States has allowed itself to get taken by the producers of Marlboro cigarettes, Kool-Aid, Miller Beer and Jell-O. Philip Morris is spending $60 million for a two-year image-lifting campaign. For a mere 1 percent of that, it was able to rent the Bill of Rights. It's a shabby transaction at any price . . ." The paper was mistaken, Philip Morris didn't rent the Bill of Rights, it bought it outright, it has got it in fee simple.

Citizen action to turn the on-charging corporate steer in a different direction takes forever when it can be done at all. Until young black men began to torch the cities in the 1960s, nothing anyone could think of doing could get the big companies to hire on merit. For decades bankers made bad loans here and abroad on a scale so large it requires scientific notation to write the numbers, and at home, a belated Federal Reserve Board Report acknowledged the same bankers were turning down thousands of credit-worthy African-American home mortgage applicants. No amount of pleading or picketing could make these loans.[25] Attempts to organize shareholders to make officers of major corporations rein in have failed. Everything has been tried and everything fails. Some of the efforts are ingenious and valiant, such as getting people to confine their buying of securities and products to companies which conduct their business with decency and honor.[26]

Scandal does succeed. When people like Ralph Nader are able to nail a company like General Motors doing something like manufacturing an unsafe car, which he did and they did, then things happen. Laws are passed, regulations are put in place and business hates them, often with good reason. Government has not learned how, and may not even care to try, to draw up and enforce regulations without doing expensive damage. The moral is that bad private sector managers are rewarded with bad public sector managers.

If self-regulation, every trade association's nostrum, is a trick, then we shall have to learn to regulate well. Some things can't

be accomplished by outside public action. Though we can cry shame, bang spoons on pots and do our best to treat piratical business people as anathema, we can't go in and run people's businesses. However, the tax system can be used to discourage Wall Street's destructive speculations. From Dan Drew to Henry Kravis there have been one hundred and fifty years of this nonsense. End it with a few, simple, nicely designed tax disincentives. As for the bankers, they have been pulling the same catastrophic number ever since Andrew Jackson killed off America's first and best central bank. Because it seems to be deep within the character of certain types of American bankers to go hog happy in bad loans, we need a two-tier banking system. Tier one is heavily regulated and insured. Tier one depositors will get a lower return on their money, but they will get their money. With tier two banks, anything goes, but they are not insured, and when they crash at the end of the next decade of greed, well—happy landings.

From the start America was unprepared for the coming of the corporate form of organization, or the Bill of Rights would have contained an Eleventh Amendment putting some kind of bridle on massed corporate power. But when the corporate form introduced itself into the national life, the country wasn't ready for it, couldn't control it and crumpled under it. Henry Adams, bowled over, complained, "Power such as this has never in the world's history been trusted in the hands of mere private citizens."

"The impact of the newborn corporation on American society was almost cataclysmic," wrote John Tipple in *The Gilded Age.* "There was no place for it among existing institutions and no sanction for it in traditional American values. . . . There was no ready place for the large industrial corporation which was neither an individual nor a natural manifestation. As an artificial person created by charter and comprising many individuals and their wealth, the corporation was infinitely greater in size and power than the isolated individual about whom American society had been conceived . . . guaranteed immortality by the society which fathered it. . . . Freed from death, and incidentally from death dues and inheritance taxes, the corporation waxed strong upon accumulated lifetimes and earnings of many individuals."[27]

Until the invention of business, factories were tiny places, little riverside mills, employing a couple of dozen people, establishments whose only noise was the creak of the waterwheel driving simple, wooden machines. Ownership was personal; there was no limited liability and certainly no labor force as we know it. People had not yet been converted into personnel. More often than not, the mill owner didn't hire individuals, but households. The household rented its house from the mill owner, who paid the head of the household, man or woman, for the totality of its labor as this entry into an old rent book shows:

"Oct'r 1–1853 I have rented to Joseph Wright the house lately occupied by Alexander Crozier on the following Conditions. Joseph Wright Agrees to keep 2 Hands working in the factory at all times While he occupies the House, (sickness of the Hands excepting) and that he will give 2 weeks notice of his intentions to leave the house and of the hands to quit work (under all Circumstances) if required and at the expiration of the 2 weeks notice to give up peaceable possession of the House or forfeit the lying times of the hands or in case of removal the hands will forfeit without a regular notice being given. [signed] Joseph Wright"[28]

The mill owner lived nearby in the same hamlet and, as often as not, was a prominent layman in the same church the mill hands went to. The owner was almost invariably in politics, and not as a distant, semisecret campaign contributor, but, as the old records make clear, as an elected official.[29] Yes, the mill owner was powerful, but there were hard and fast limits to his power because he was contained by a thousand-and-one community, religious and familial crisscrosses. Precorporate society bears almost no resemblance to what we live under.

The American system was put together with the small-scale commercial endeavor in mind, a world in which the predominant form of manufacture was the mill in the hamlet. It didn't occur to the people of two centuries ago that those whom they would have called men of affairs would grow so mighty, so unconstrained, that they could pit sovereign states against each other for their own purposes. But they do as these boasting remarks by Lee Iacocca, the Ludwig of the Chrysler Corporation, reveal clearly enough:

"Ford, when I was there, General Motors, Chrysler, all over the world, we would pit Ohio versus Michigan. We'd pit Canada versus the U.S. We'd get outright grants and subsidies in Spain, in Mexico, in Brazil—all kinds of grants. With my former employer (Ford), one of the last things I did was, on the threat of losing 2,000 jobs in Windsor, I got $73 million outright to convert an engine plant . . . I've had great experience in this. I have played Spain versus France and England so long I'm tired of it, and I have played the states against each other over here."[30]

The coming of massed corporate power blew the society's ancient system of control and accommodation to kingdom come. Theodore Roosevelt and William Howard Taft, possibly because they were born closer to the corporation's advent, closer to the mill in the hamlet, and could better appreciate what had happened, both wanted the federal chartering of corporations. They saw that the system of state chartering, which continues on to this day, permitted corporations to run loose unchecked or unsupervised by anyone.‡ It wasn't done and these organizations, not unlike the religious orders in Europe before the Reformation, grew to independent power, some say even international power, under the control and oversight of no one.

Federal chartering is not going to solve our problems. It will not make for new managers, it will not create an educated work force, it will not lessen the number of street criminals and white collar crooks, it will not stop businessmen from cradle robbing children into the commercial society by the time they can toddle, it will not make the wealth we need. It is one small step we might take, but we have to take steps in the business realm as well as the other. We must act. Perpetual chartering should end. Corporate charters should be for stated periods of time, renewable if the terms of the charter are adhered to; corporate charters should limit the lines of business the company is allowed to conduct. Enough of these jack-of-all-trades-master-of-none corporations getting their snouts into everything and doing nothing well.

Business can't take more regulating, even that arising from

‡ States fight for corporate business just as communities fight each other to get a company to locate in their areas.

federal charters. Yet on the bias, it is a device which might be used to make business stick to its own business. These organizations are too valuable to the society to be sent hither and thither according to the egomaniacal whims of the local corporate Ludwig. In an earlier period when corporations had to be chartered by a state legislature they were granted the privileges of incorporation to go into a certain line of work. No more moseying from the steel business to the oil business to the investment business.

A corporation which must apply for rechartering every so often is a company more likely to be dissuaded from destroying the culture to sell sneakers. Without new regulation, but by the power of a general, non-specific menace, corporate executives must learn that, if they are going to continue to have the power to create the glamour examples and shimmering celebrities for our young people to model themselves on, those examples may no longer be men and women who are at their best stark naked or when they are jumping and shouting on stage or in an athletic arena. The new heros must be men and women who use their brains. We need active people, not entertainment-dependent bottle babies. The United States, a nation of a quarter of a billion people, has come close enough to turning itself into a huge Kuwait, a place populated by people who have so much money they can hire others to maintain their society.

We don't have to go back to the Puritan age, but we have got to go back to work and that necessity cannot be sabotaged by business sociopaths who will sell their blue jeans and their beer even if it means their own grandchildren will be in the streets begging for a night's lodging. We need the nurses, the biologists, the engineers, the mechanics, the competent, pro-society business executives. The plug must be pulled on the all-entertainment society. Turn the elevator music off. If the society no longer allows a mining or logging company to go where it will and turn the terrain into something that looks like the landscape of a planet photographed by a passing space probe, then companies must stop turning the children into tubers. As it is now, when the yellow buses stop in front of the school in the morning, they're delivering sacks of potatoes.

The legal sophistries making corporations people should be done away with. People are people, nobody else is. Limited lia-

bility should be modified. If an oil company's stockholders knew that they would have to pay a portion, not all, but a portion of the damage done to a seacoast by a negligently maintained tanker, there would be fewer accidents.

The manna from heaven, nature will take care of our nation approach must be discarded. Neither the free market, nor human nature, nor evolution, nor dumb, automatic progress nor any other hypothetical construct will take care of our country. That's our job, and we must do it by deliberate and thoughtful action. We are not doomed, we are not predestined to decline, to fail, to grow ever weaker, to die on the vine of history. That is not written anywhere. If it happens, and it might, it will be our fault. Only the past is inevitable, the future we make for ourselves.

We are a species of toolmakers, and our greatest tool is human society. We Americans should know that better than any other people. We are a consciously, deliberately made nation. We are a man-made nation. We believe that China was always there, that England was always there, but we know that America was made by people whose names we can recite. It was planned out and written down; it was not something inherited from the time of kings and cavemen; it was invented by a group of people. Our capital, the city of Washington, wasn't something which rolled out of the Middle Ages, immemorially old and accepted. Hamilton and Jefferson agreed on where it was to be and then it was planned, laid out and built, the deliberate work of the thinking hand. America was consciously invented, and then reinvented again and again, in peace and war, by genius and industry, reinvented by new people coming and giving of their ideals, and their hopes, their thoughts and talents. It is time for us to make our country yet again.

# APPENDIX

---

# Malcolm
# the Politician

TEN YEARS of Malcolm's life were dedicated to his political vocation. It is not treated in the body of the book because it is not germane to business themes. For the curious, the high points are touched on below.

Back from the war, Malcolm married a pretty young woman who'd grown up almost around the corner from the Forbes' house in Englewood. She was a stockbroker's daughter, which may explain how the newly married couple could afford to move to Far Hills, New Jersey, a ritzy and leafy section of New Jersey far from the oil refineries off Cancer Boulevard in Bayonne.

By 1949 Malcolm had dug himself in deeply enough to be elected to the Bernardsville Borough Council. The next year he began to run for the Republican nomination for the state Senate, a seemingly impossible job because the seat was held by a

man who got there shortly after 1776 and, with the help of the Republican organization, had held it ever since.

Malcolm won the primary, he said, by ringing eighteen thousand doorbells, and he may have. The *Somerset Messenger-Gazette,* the local newspaper, wrote, in explaining the upset victory, that, "Time and again during the closing weeks of the campaign scores of voters were heard to comment on the 'folksy' vote-getting methods the victor employed from the day he started, in addition to chatting with housewives on their front porches and attending church suppers. They remembered Forbes as 'the man who came to call,' always bareheaded and often soaking wet from the rain, who could talk about apple pie or taxes." The general election was a foregone conclusion.

A young state senator in a hurry to get to the White House, Malcolm got behind the effort to get Dwight Eisenhower into the building first. One of a continuing pilgrimage of politicians who visited Ike in Paris, where he was running NATO, Malcolm got the franchise to run the New Jersey Eisenhower for President operation, thereby giving him a means to make friends and contacts across the state for his next move, getting the Republican nomination for governor.

The first time he took a shot at it, he missed, but the second time he won the primary. But the governor's chair was not to be his. "In the 1957 New Jersey gubernatorial campaign," his campaign manager, Ray Batemen wrote, "the G.O.P. candidate, Senator Malcolm Forbes, set off on an ambitious and newsy summer trip to visit the state's 567 municipalities. Early in the tour a wire-service photographer snapped his picture wading through water, pants baggy and rolled up to his knees, to hand out pamphlets to a group of ladies on the other side. At that moment he looked like a clam digger—not like a Governor. The picture hit every paper in the state."

Malcolm also got outfoxed. Having bought the time for a twenty-four-hour telethon which was to begin at midnight, his opponent, incumbent Robert Meyner, bought time earlier in the evening before Malcolm's show was to begin. "We arrived at the decision," Meyner said some years later, "that we would conclude our program at about twenty minutes of twelve. I gave my final speech and we wound up at about ten minutes of

twelve. And they played 'the star spangled banner.' Then for the next eight minutes they had scenes of Crete, and Greece and Turkey, and soft music."

Malcolm was so badly whipped it seems unlikely the TV incident had much to do with his losing, but it has gone into the treasury of New Jersey political lore. The following year, Malcolm resigned his state senate seat and thoughts of greater things, although it was said that the reason he wrote so many valentines to politicians in his "Fact & Comment" column was in hopes that an ambassadorship or even a seat on a commission might come his way. It never happened. He was a delegate to the 1960 Republican National Convention, but his political career was over.

# NOTES

**PREFACE**

**1.** as quoted in *Bunny: The Real Story of Playboy* by Russell Miller, Holt, Rinehart and Winston, New York, 1984.

**2.** A readable roundup of this kind of distressing statistic is to be found in the current edition of *The State of Working America,* by Lawrence Mishel and David M. Frankel, Economic Policy Institute, M. E. Sharpe, Inc., Armonk, New York.

**3.** *Forbes,* March 2, 1918. B. C. Forbes' estimate of Rockefeller's net worth was disputed but when it comes to such fortunes, estimates of their dollar value are something of a theoretical game. In the practical realm such gigantic properties can't be brought to market quickly without forcing down the price they might fetch.

**4.** As quoted in *The Prize: The Epic Quest for Oil, Money, and Power,* by Daniel Yergin, Simon & Schuster, New York, 1991.

**5.** "Forbes's 50," *Time,* November 17, 1947.

## ONE: **The Business of Booze and Schmooze**

**1.** *New York Times,* October 23, 1977.

**2.** *People,* September 4, 1989.

**3.** *Los Angeles Times,* December 5, 1985.

**4.** Fred Bruning in *New York Newsday,* September 11, 1989.

**5.** Leonard E. Larsen in *New York Newsday,* August 23, 1989.

**6.** *The New Republic,* September 11, 1989.

**7.** *New York Daily News,* August 24, 1989.

**8.** *New York Times,* August 24, 1989, via the Associated Press.

**9.** Jim Hoge, Interview.

**10.** Ibid.

**11.** *Washington Post,* August 16, 1989.

**12.** *On with the Show!* by Robert C. Toll, Oxford University Press, New York, 1976.

**13.** *Pills, Petticoats & Plows: The Southern Country Store,* by Thomas D. Clark, University of Oklahoma Press, Norman, 1964.

**14.** Ibid.

**15.** November 8, 1873.

**16.** The material on the mail order houses was drawn from *Catalogues and Counters: A History of Sears, Roebuck and Company*, by Boris Emmet and John E. Jeuck, University of Chicago Press, Chicago, 1950.

**17.** *More Than I Dreamed*, by Malcolm Forbes, edited by Tony Clark, Simon & Schuster, New York, 1989.

**18.** *America's 60 Families*, by Ferdinand Lundberg, Vanguard Press, New York, 1937.

**19.** ABC News Show: Show #104, Diane Sawyer and Sam Donaldson Hosts, August 24, 1989.

**20.** *People*, September 4, 1989.

**21.** Jim Hoge, Interview.

**22.** "Road to Morocco," by Liz Smith, *New York Daily News*, August 22, 1989.

**23.** Ellis Henican in *New York Newsday*, August 17, 1989.

**24.** "Health-benefit Pledges Broken," by Michael Tackett and Christopher Drew, *Chicago Tribune*, December 5, 1989.

**25.** Joann S. Lublin in *The Wall Street Journal*, April 22, 1991.

**26.** Eugene Carlson in *The Wall Street Journal*, June 6, 1989.

**27.** For a list of who all came, consult Ellis Henican, "Forbes to Celebrate 70th in Style—'Flying nearly 600 close pals to Tangiers for casbah bash,'" *New York Newsday*, August 17, 1989.

**28.** *The Japan That Can Say No—The Decline of An America Which Can Only See 10 Minutes Ahead*, by Akio Morita, unpublished. A version of this book, without Morita's contributions, was published by Simon & Schuster in 1990.

**29.** Jim Hoge, Interview.

**30.** *The Wall Street Journal*, July 2, 1991.

**31.** "The Vendetta—How American Express Orchestrated a Smear of Rival Edmond Safra—Top Aide to James Robinson Oversaw Two Who Spread False Stories World-Wide—Officers Deny Doing Wrong," *The Wall Street Journal*, September 24, 1990.

**32.** "American Express—The Failed Vision," by John Meehan, Jon Friedman and Leah J. Nathans, *Business Week*, March 19, 1990.

**33.** *The Wall Street Journal*, September 24, 1990.

**34.** "Up, Up and Away with Malcolm Forbes," by Suzy, *New York Daily News*, June 17, 1984.

**35.** "Top Bankers Received Healthy Bonuses, Despite Firms' Record Losses in 1987," by Jeff Bailey and Robert Guenther, *The Wall Street Journal*, March 29, 1988.

**36.** "Notable & Quotable," *The Wall Street Journal*, March 20, 1987.

**37.** "It's a Stronger Bank That David Rockefeller Is Passing to His Successor," by Carol J. Loomis, *Fortune*, January 14, 1980.

**38.** "Chase: Can Labrecque Turn It Around?" by Peter Lee, *Euromoney*, September 1, 1990.

**39.** Ibid. "Chase management has not changed its performance targets— 15% return or higher on equity, and 0.75% return on assets—for a decade. Nor has it met them. The feeling persists that Chase is a company always about to turn the corner but not quite making it."

**40.** "Chase Manhattan Corp. Increases Loan-Loss Reserves by $1.15 Billion," by Robert Guenther and Peter Truell, *The Wall Street Journal,* September 21, 1989.

**41.** "Chase Reports 3rd-Period Loss Of $1.11 Billion," by Robert Guenther, *The Wall Street Journal,* October 12, 1989.

**42.** "Chase Manhattan Cuts Dividend, Staff Presaging More Bad News in Banking," by Fred R. Bleakley, *The Wall Street Journal,* September 24, 1990.

**43.** Henican, "Forbes to Celebrate 70th in Style."

**44.** Thomas B. Rosensteil in *Los Angeles Times,* October 19, 1986.

**45.** Phillip H. Dougherty in *New York Times Sunday Magazine,* September 17, 1967.

**46.** Lundberg, op. cit.

**47.** *The Life of J. Pierpont Morgan,* by Andrew Sinclair, Little, Brown and Company, Boston, 1981.

**48.** This picture by Chris Welles, "Is the Forbes Money Balloon About to Burst?" printed in *MORE,* April 1977, could be everybody's composite description of Malcolm's use of hospitality to make a sale: "Ritually enacted in Malcolm's sumptuous Greenwich Village townhouse amid selections from Malcolm's extensive—and expensive—art collection—it is usually attended by Malcolm, Dunn, several Forbes editors and the chief executive and advertising manager of a large corporation. Following an impeccably appointed meal, fine wine (served in personally inscribed silver goblets), and an off-the-record conversation enlivened by questions from the editors and by the chief executive's own curiosity about Malcolm's lifestyle (which is usually far more grandiose than his own), the editors retire as Malcolm, Dunn [*Forbes* publisher James Dunn] and the corporate guests repair for coffee in Malcolm's office. There the subject shifts smoothly to the corporation's ad schedule for the next quarter."

**49.** Wayne Welch, Interview.

**50.** Norman Pearlstine, Interview.

**51.** Ibid.

**52.** Welles, op. cit.

**53.** For straight skivvy on the subject, you may consult *Hit Men,* by Frederic Dannen, Times Books, New York, 1990.

**54.** *The Big Spenders,* by Lucius Beebe, Doubleday & Company, Garden City, New York, 1966.

**55.** *Diamond Jim: The Life and Times of James Buchanan Brady,* by Parker Morell, Simon & Schuster, New York, 1934.

**56.** Ibid.

**57.** *The Greatest-Ever Bank Robbery: The Collapse of the Savings and Loan Industry,* by Martin Mayer, Charles Scribner's Sons, 1990.

**58.** *The Predators' Ball: The Inside Story of Drexel Burnham and the Rise of the Junk Bond Raiders,* by Connie Bruck, Penguin Books, New York, 1989.

**59.** *Bartlett's Familiar Quotations,* by John Bartlett, fourteenth edition, Little, Brown and Company, Boston, 1968.

**60.** The Mellon quote comes from Dwight McDonald in " 'Fortune' Magazine," *The Nation*, May 8, 1937.

**61.** Bruck, op. cit.

## TWO: **Clear Cutting the Mind**

**1.** "Eating Out with Malcolm Forbes—Uncommon Tastes of a Passionate Man," by Bryan Miller, *New York Times*, April 19, 1989.

**2.** "Malcolm Forbes Preserves a Bit of His Scottish Heritage," by Muriel Freeman, *Somerset Courier-News*, October 17, 1988.

**3.** Ibid.

**4.** " 'Bury Me with My Fathers,' Jacob Said to His Sons," by Malcolm Forbes, *Forbes*, October 17, 1988.

**5.** Psalm 104, verses 21, 23.

**6.** Genesis, Chapter 3, verse 19.

**7.** Entitled "Toil and Truth," it was "Specially written for *Forbes*," by Lilburn Harwood Townsend and appeared in the April 15, 1925, issue.

**8.** *Malcolm Forbes: Peripatetic Millionaire*, by Arthur Jones, Harper & Row, New York, 1977.

**9.** Ibid.

**10.** Scots had a history in American printing and publishing. George Bruce had introduced the stereotype process to the industry, and Adam Ramage had made important contributions to printing technology, but the most important Scotsman was James Gordon Bennett, the founder of the *New York Herald*, a newspaper of power and major importance in shaping the mass culture which emerged in the second half of the nineteenth century.

**11.** *Forbes*, September 29, 1917.

**12.** As quoted by Jones, op. cit.

**13.** *Rockdale: The Growth of an American Village in the Early Industrial Revolution*, by Anthony E. C. Wallace, Alfred A. Knopf, New York, 1978.

**14.** *Henry Varnum Poor: Business Editor, Analyst, and Reformer*, by Alfred D. Chandler, Jr., Arno Press, New York, 1981.

**15.** "In the Days of B.C. Forbes," by Lucien O. Hooper, *Forbes*, September 15, 1977; *Malcolm Forbes: The Man Who Had Everything*, by Christopher Winans, A Thomas Dunne Book, St. Martin's Press, New York, 1990.

**16.** *The James Gordon Bennetts, Father and Son: Proprietors of the New York Herald*, by Don C. Seitz, Bobbs-Merrill Company, Indianapolis, 1928.

**17.** *America's 60 Families*, by Ferdinand Lundberg, Vanguard Press, New York, 1937.

**18.** "Fortune Magazine," by Dwight Macdonald, *The Nation*, no. 144, May 8, 1937.

**19.** Seitz, op. cit.

**20.** *American Journalism, a History: 1690–1960*, by Frank Luther Mott, Macmillan Company, New York, 1962, third edition.

**21.** "Greater Expectations—How Forbes Magazine Got the Way It Is—and by Whom," *Forbes*, September 15, 1977.

**22.** *Citizen Hearst: A Biography of William Randolph Hearst*, by W. A. Swanberg,

Collier Books, New York, 1986, originally published, 1961. Unless otherwise noted the Hearst material is drawn from this source.

**23.** James Gordon Bennett, Jr., was a genius at newspapering, but not at socializing. New Year's Day 1877 found Bennett fils visiting the Manhattan home of the very social Miss Caroline May, his intended, but drunk as a skunk, the gentleman did, in full view of the company assembled, unbutton his fly, withdraw his member and relieve himself in the fireplace. That a) ended his betrothal, b) got him physically thrown into the street, and c) challenged to a duel by Miss May's brother. The two met on the field of honor, discharged their weapons in the air and entered social history as the last occurrence of formal dueling in the United States.

**24.** Seitz, op. cit.

**25.** *Looking Backward: 2000–1887* by Edward Bellamy, New American Library, New York, 1960, originally published in 1888.

## THREE: "Rich Men Who Are O.K. and Others Who Are Not"

**1.** Edwin Markham entry, *Dictionary of American Biography*, second supplement.

**2.** *Forbes*, May 15, 1927.

**3.** *The Money Game in Old New York: Daniel Drew and His Times*, by Clifford Browder, University Press of Kentucky, Lexington, 1986.

**4.** *Sparrow Point: Making Steel—The Rise and Ruin of American Industrial Might*, by Mark Reutter, Summit Books, New York, 1968; *Grover Cleveland: A Study in Courage*, by Allan Nevis, Dodd, Mead & Company, New York, 1933; *Eugene V. Debs: A Biography*, by Ray Ginger, Collier Books, New York, 1962; *A History of the United States Since the Civil War*, by Ellis Paxson Oberholtzer, Macmillan, New York, 1937; *Emma Goldman: An Intimate Life*, by Alice Wexler, Pantheon Books, New York, 1984.

**5.** In 1870 the steel production in the United States was 77,000 tons. Ten years later it had grown, unbelievably, to 1,397,000 tons. Source: Historical Statistics of the United States, Bureau of the Census.

**6.** As quoted in *The Rise of American Civilization*, by Charles A. Beard and Mary R. Beard, Macmillan, New York, 1937.

**7.** *Steel Titan: The Life of Charles M. Schwab*, by Robert Hessen, Oxford University Press, New York, 1975.

**8.** *Forbes*, December 1, 1932.

**9.** Frick bought Fragonard's *Progress of Love* from J. P. Morgan, the younger, and in other ways did his part to turn the graphic arts into a free market speculation. He is credited with one *mot* in his lifetime. "Railroads," he said, "are the Rembrandts of investment."

**10.** *Malcolm Forbes: Peripatetic Millionaire*, by Arthur Jones, Harper & Row, New York, 1977.

**11.** Jacob Schiff, 1847–1920, beloved for his benefactions, was a major figure in the financing of the railroads and enormously rich.

**12.** Russell Sage, 1816–1906, had a reputation which would make a Michael Milken look good. The reputed inventor of "puts and calls," a vicious stock

market game now played on a vast scale by computer, Sage was as rich as he was miserly, so cheap he would haggle over the price of an apple. There isn't space enough to list his plunderings.

**13.** *Forbes,* October 16, 1920.

**14.** Jones, op. cit.

**15.** *The Life and Times of Golden Rule Jones,* by Harvey S. Ford, unpublished Ph.D. dissertation, University of Michigan, 1953.

**16.** *Our Times: the United States, 1900–1925, The War Begins, 1909–1914,* Volume IV, by Mark Sullivan, Charles Scribner's Sons, New York, 1932.

**17.** *Fit for America: Health, Fitness, Sport and American Society,* by Harvey Green, Pantheon Books, New York, 1986.

**18.** Horace Fletcher hit the American scene in 1903 with publication of his book *The New Glutton.* His impact was as great as the Hula Hoop fifty-five years later. Businessmen besides Patterson took his idea up. John D. Rockefeller himself pronounced, "Don't gobble your food. Fletcherize or chew very slowly while you eat." There were contests to see how slowly a person could eat a cracker and clubs were started where people forgathered to eat slowly and chant:

> I choose to chew
> Because I wish to do
> The sort of thing that
> Nature had in view,
> Before bad cooks invented sav'ry stew;
> When the only way to eat was to chew! chew! chew!

### FOUR: Getting the Goods

**1.** *Constructing the Corporate Image: Architecture, Mass Media and Management in the Early Multinational Corporation, a Case Study of the National Cash Register Company, Dayton, Ohio, U.S.A., 1884–1906* by Janet Yvonne Abrams, unpublished Ph.D. dissertation, Princeton University, 1989.

**2.** *Forbes,* November 10, 1917.

**3.** *Think: A Biography of the Watsons and IBM,* by William Rodgers, Stein and Day, New York, 1969.

**4.** *Catalogues and Counters: A History of Sears, Roebuck and Company,* by Boris Emmet and John E. Jeuck, University of Chicago Press, Chicago, 1950.

**5.** *The Expansion of Everyday Life: 1860–1876,* by Daniel E. Sutherland, Harper & Row, New York, 1989.

**6.** *Victorian America: Transformations in Everyday Life, 1876–1915,* by Thomas J. Schlereth, HarperCollins, New York, 1991.

**7.** *Middletown: A Study in Modern American Culture,* by Robert S. Lynd and Helen Merrell Lynd, Harcourt, Brace & Jovanovich, New York, 1929.

**8.** *The Coming of Managerial Capitalism: A Casebook on the History of American Economic Institutions,* by Alfred D. Chandler, Jr., and Richard S. Tedlow, Irwin, Homewood, Illinois, 1985.

**9.** *Pills, Petticoats & Plows: The Southern Country Store,* by Thomas D. Clark, University of Oklahoma Press, Norman, 1964.

**10.** The material on Sears is drawn from Emmet and Jeuck, op. cit.

**11.** *Malcolm Forbes: The Man Who Had Everything,* by Christopher Winans, St. Martin's Press, New York, 1990.

**12.** *American Genesis: A Century of Invention and Technological Enthusiasm, 1870–1970,* by Thomas P. Hughes, Penguin Books, New York, 1990.

**13.** Hughes, op. cit.

**14.** Although a Russian émigré, Sikorsky, 1889–1972, did his most important work in the United States.

**15.** Goddard's patents and his work generally make him the parent of everything from bazooka-type antitank weapons to the Boeing 747 and moon travel.

**16.** It was Armstrong's inventions of a new kind of vacuum tube which allowed Americans of the 1920s to throw away their headsets and listen to their radios through loudspeakers, theretofore impossible. His work was important to the development of radar, and to him goes the credit for inventing stereophonic and multiplex broadcasting.

**17.** *Armstrong's Fight for FM Broadcasting: One Man vs Big Business and Bureaucracy,* by D. H. V. Erickson, University of Alabama Press, University, Alabama, 1973.

**18.** *Father Son & Co.: My Life at IBM and Beyond,* by Thomas J. Watson, Jr., and Peter Petre, Bantam Books, New York, 1990.

**19.** See the first issue of *Forbes.*

**20.** Professional photographers did not take to the new film, so Eastman developed the inexpensive Kodak—a word apparently of his invention—containing a hundred exposures per camera load. After use the customer sent the camera back to the factory where the film was developed, the camera reloaded and both were returned. A long way from the Polaroid, also invented by a lone genius.

No self-advertiser like Hearst or Malcolm, he gave the enormous sum of two and a half million dollars to Massachusetts Institute of Technology in 1912 under the name of "Mr. Smith." It was but one of a number of gifts to several schools, the total amounts of which were nothing short of stupendous.

**21.** *Adventures of a White-Collar Man,* by Alfred P. Sloan, Jr., in collaboration with Boyden Sparks, Doubleday, New York, 1940.

**22.** Ibid.

**23.** As quoted by Hughes, op. cit.

**24.** *Inside Media,* June 12, 1991.

## FIVE: Loss Leaders

**1.** *America in the Gilded Age: From the Death of Lincoln to the Rise of Theodore Roosevelt,* by Sean Dennis Cashman, New York University Press, New York, 1984.

**2.** Ibid.

**3.** As quoted in *The Coming of Managerial Capitalism: A Casebook on the History*

*of American Economic Institutions,* by Alfred D. Chandler, Jr., and Richard S. Tedlow, Irwin, Homewood, Illinois, 1985.

**4.** *Andrew Carnegie and the Rise of Big Business,* by Harold C. Livesay, edited by Oscar Handlin, HarperCollins, New York, 1975.

**5.** As quoted in Livesay, op. cit.

**6.** *Forbes,* November 1, 1932.

**7.** *Managing,* by Harold Geneen with Alvin Moscow, Avon Books, New York, 1984.

**8.** November 24, 1917.

**9.** *Steel Titan: The Life of Charles M. Schwab,* by Robert Hessen, Oxford University Press, New York, 1975.

**10.** As quoted in *Forbes,* June 1, 1934.

**11.** *Forbes,* October 15, 1930.

**12.** Hessen, op. cit.

**13.** Hessen, op. cit.

**14.** *New York American,* July 2, 1936.

**15.** *Luce and His Empire,* by W. A. Swanberg, Charles Scribner's Sons, New York, 1972.

**16.** *Newsweek,* November 7, 1988.

**17.** *The Wall Street Journal,* August 18, 1988.

**18.** *The Wall Street Journal,* April 15, 1991.

**19.** *Business Week,* April 1, 1991.

**20.** *The Visible Hand: The Managerial Revolution in American Business,* by Alfred D. Chandler, Jr., Belknap Press of Harvard University Press, Cambridge, Massachusetts, and London, England, 1977.

**21.** Livesay, op. cit.

**22.** Peter F. Drucker in *The Wall Street Journal,* November 20, 1990.

**23.** *America by Design: Science, Technology, and the Rise of Corporate Capitalism,* by David F. Noble, Alfred A. Knopf, New York, 1977.

**24.** *Forbes,* September 15, 1917.

**25.** *Forbes,* January 1, 1932.

**26.** *Forbes,* April 16, 1921.

**27.** Livesay, op. cit.

**28.** Livesay, op. cit.

**29.** *Business Week,* March 19, 1990.

## SIX: **Ludwig's Castle**

**1.** *America in the Gilded Age: From the Death of Lincoln to the Rise of Theodore Roosevelt,* by Sean Dennis Cashman, New York University Press, New York, 1984.

**2.** *Victorian America: Transformations in Everyday Life, 1876–1915,* by Thomas J. Schlereth, HarperCollins, New York, 1991.

**3.** *The Scientific American,* July 20, 1895.

**4.** *America Adopts the Automobile, 1895–1910,* by James J. Flink, MIT Press, Cambridge, 1970.

**5.** *The American Automobile,* by John B. Rae, University of Chicago Press, Chicago, 1965.

**6.** *Middletown: A Study in Modern American Culture,* by Robert S. Lynd and Helen Merrell Lynd, Harcourt, Brace & World, New York, 1929.

**7.** *Forbes,* November 1, 1930.

**8.** The Department of Commerce records show five thousand fridges were sold in 1921, two years after Malcolm's birth; in 1930 the year he celebrated his eleventh birthday, almost nine hundred thousand of them were sold, the last year sales were ever to be under a million.

**9.** *My Years with General Motors,* by Alfred P. Sloan, Jr., Doubleday, New York, 1990.

**10.** *Henry Varnum Poor: Business Editor, Analyst, and Reformer,* by Alfred D. Chandler, Jr., Arno Press, New York, 1981.

**11.** Of the three leading business magazines, *Forbes* is the most likely to raise questions about the rationality of some of the more notorious of the reigning CEOs. *Business Week* is seldom there first, but it will pop a story about gross misconduct in the executive suite from time to time. *Fortune* is the Shih Tzu of business publications, a creature whose little red tongue will lick any executive's fingertip.

The periodical press is no worse than the business rating services. Outfits like Standard & Poor's and Moody's, which make their livings assigning credit ratings to companies and governmental entities which sell bonds to the public, and which are supposed to be early warning systems for investors or depositors, seldom do more than confirm that a disaster has already occurred.

**12.** Ludwig II, 1845–86, one of the better known and crazier members of the Wittelsbach family, spent money on a scale which outdid anything an American CEO has yet tried. The King was addicted to Richard Wagner and building enormous dream palaces. His most famous, and most fantastic artifact being Neuschwanstein. This fairy tale castle seems to have inspired the one which serves as the logo for Disneyland. Mad Ludwig drowned himself, but in American business circles suicide is an act CEOs make others commit.

**13.** *Ramparts,* October 1973.

**14.** *Business Week,* April 1, 1991.

**15.** "The World of Business—Undoing the Eighties," by Connie Bruck, *The New Yorker,* July 23, 1990.

**16.** *Fortune,* June 18, 1990.

**17.** *New York Times,* April 27, 1978.

**18.** *A Life of James Fisk, Jr., Being a Full and Accurate Narrative of all the Enterprise in Which He Has Been Engaged,* by Marshall P. Stafford, Polhemus & Pearson, New York, 1871.

**19.** *Jim Fisk: The Career of an Improbable Rascal,* by W. A. Swanberg, Charles Scribner's Sons, New York, 1959. Swanberg includes this description of Fisk's digs: "It was a great hall, entered through carved oak doors that led into an anteroom protected by a bronze gate guarded by ushers. In the inner sanctum Fisk sat enthroned in a huge chair studded with gold nails, before a broad desk raised on a dais, surrounded by mirrors and silken hangings. The cerulean ceiling was splashed with crimson ovals emblazoned with the word

'Erie' in gold. A gold-and-brown rug sank under the feet. Even the wash stand in the corner was a $1000 affair of marble and porcelain, a reporter noted, 'the bowl being tinted with rose and gold, and displaying the figures of lovely nymphs in disporting attitudes.' "

**20.** *New York Times,* July 15, 1991.

**21.** *The Wall Street Journal,* June 26, 1991; and also see *In Search of Excess: The Overcompensation of American Executives,* by Graef S. Crystal, Norton, New York, 1991.

**22.** Other businessmen have become popular heroes of sorts. Henry Ford almost made it to demigod status with the five-dollar-a-day pay; Charlie Schwab became one because of his feats of production in World War I, the same with Henry J. Kaiser in WWII. Samuel Insull and A. P. Giannini in the 1920s, both to be discussed later, Robert Young of the New York Central Railroad in the 1930s, even J. P. Morgan, the elder, when he stopped the Panic of 1907, but none of these men won for themselves the Robin Hoodish aura of Big Jim Fisk, none had barroom ballads composed in his honor.

**23.** *The Gilded Age:* Revised and Enlarged Edition, H. Wayne Morgan, editor, Syracuse University Press, Syracuse, N.Y., 1970.

**24.** *The Fall of the House of Hutton,* by Donna Carpenter and John Feloni, Harper & Row, New York, 1989.

**25.** *Malcolm Forbes: The Man Who Had Everything,* by Christopher Winans, A Thomas Dunne Book, St. Martin's Press, New York, 1990. Winans describes a long, uncomfortable evening with Forbes during which a male magazine staff member rejected the publisher's advances, going on to say this had no pejorative effect on the young man's standing at the office. Interviews with other *Forbes* staff people confirm that sex with Malcolm neither helped nor hurt an employee.

**26.** *America's 60 Families,* by Ferdinand Lundberg, Vanguard Press, New York, 1937.

**27.** *Three Plus One Equals Billions: The Bendix—Martin Marietta War,* by Allan Sloan, Carroll & Graf, New York, 1983.

**28.** Occasionally a CEO will get the gate for conduct unbecoming or some such. Standley H. Hoch was forced out of the top job at General Public Utilities Corporation, the outfit which owns the Three Mile Island atomic electrical plant, which almost melted down. The board acted against Hoch after a local government regulatory agency received an anonymous letter saying Hoch was having an affair with Susan Schepman, the vice president of communications, whom he'd hired. It is said that both parties to this office romance were good at their work and hardly behaving in the true CEO ethos tradition. But there is politics at work here. This is a much troubled company in a heavily regulated industry so that it appears that a terrified Board of Directors did the unthinkable and moved against its CEO, very possibly when it shouldn't have. See *New York Times,* June 13, 1991.

**29.** *Forbes,* August 1, 1930.

**30.** *The House of Morgan, An American Banking Dynasty and the Rise of Modern Finance,* by Ron Chernow, Atlantic Monthly Press, New York, 1990.

**31.** *Enterprise Denied: Origins of the Decline of American Railroads, 1897–1917,* by Albro Martin, Columbia University Press, New York, 1971.

**32.** *Forbes,* November 10, 1917; also see *The Robber Barons: The Great American Capitalists, 1861–1901,* by Matthew Josephson, a Harvest/HBJ Book, Harcourt, Brace, Jovanovich, San Diego, New York, London, 1934, reprint 1962.

**33.** *The Predators' Ball: The Inside Story of Drexel Burnham and the Rise of the Junk Bond Raiders,* by Connie Bruck, Penguin Books, New York, 1988.

**34.** *Business Week,* October 27, 1986.

**35.** *Chicago Tribune,* December 4, 1989. *Business Week,* October 27, 1986, said of what it called "the Danville disaster," that ". . . Icahn earned a $8.5 million profit on his $14 million investment. But now Dan River is burdened with debt and has slashed 2,000 local jobs. Plummeting retail sales have decimated the downtown area, says Mayor C. Miller Vernon."

**36.** Taken from an article appearing under Mr. Icahn's byline in *Business Week,* October 27, 1986.

**37.** As quoted in Bruck, op. cit.

**38.** *The Wall Street Journal,* April 29, 1991.

SEVEN: **The Great Begatsby**

**1.** *E. H. Harriman, a Biography,* by George Kennan, two volumes, Boston, 1922. Reprint, Books for Libraries Press, 1969.

**2.** John Bigda, Interview.

**3.** *Forbes,* December 16, 1985.

**4.** Robert Kiley, Interview.

**5.** *Steel Titan: The Life of Charles M. Schwab,* by Robert Hessen, Oxford University Press, New York, 1975.

**6.** *The Life and Legend of Jay Gould,* by Maury Klein, The Johns Hopkins University Press, Baltimore, 1986.

**7.** *The Visible Hand: The Managerial Revolution in American Business,* by Alfred D. Chandler, Jr., Belknap Press of Harvard University Press, Cambridge, Massachusetts, and London, England, 1977.

**8.** *The House of Morgan, An American Banking Dynasty and the Rise of Modern Finance,* by Ron Chernow, Atlantic Monthly Press, New York, 1990.

**9.** Hessen, op. cit.

**10.** Ibid.

**11.** *More Than I Dreamed,* by Malcolm Forbes, edited by Tony Clark, Simon & Schuster, New York, 1989.

**12.** George Shultz, Interview.

**13.** John Naeglin, Interview.

**14.** Mrs. Peggy Escher, Interview.

**15.** *Andrew Carnegie and the Rise of Big Business,* by Harold C. Livesay, edited by Oscar Handlin, HarperCollins, New York, 1975.

**16.** Chernow, op. cit.

**17.** *The Seven Fat Years; Chronicles of Wall Street,* by John Brooks, Harper & Brothers, New York, 1958.

**18.** *Once in Golconda: A True Drama of Wall Street, 1920–1938,* by John Brooks, Harper & Row, New York, 1969.

**19.** Escher, Interview.

**20.** Roger von Rath, Interview.

**21.** Ibid.

**22.** *Malcolm Forbes: Peripatetic Millionaire,* by Arthur Jones, Harper & Row, New York, 1977.

**23.** "Physical Culture—Ill-Physician, Heal Thyself," by Robert Lewis Taylor, *The New Yorker,* October 28, 1950.

**24.** *Bunny: The Real Story of Playboy,* by Russell Miller, Holt, Rinehart and Winston, New York, 1984, and also, *Hefner,* by Frank Brady, Macmillan Publishing, New York, 1974.

**25.** *Cornflake Crusade,* by Gerald Carson, Rinehart & Company, New York, 1957.

**26.** Parenthetically we can thank this same remarkable man (1852–1943), whose interesting story has no place in this book, for the word granola. Gorp, however, is of a different coinage.

**27.** "Physical Culture—Weakness Is a Crime," by Robert Lewis Taylor, *The New Yorker,* October 21, 1950.

**28.** As quoted in *Body Love: The Amazing Career of Bernarr Macfadden,* by William R. Hunt, Bowling Green State University Popular Press, Bowling Green, Ohio.

**29.** Taylor, "Physical Culture—Weakness Is a Crime."

**30.** "Bernarr Macfadden," by William H. Taft, *Missouri Historical Review,* October 1968.

### EIGHT: The Mumbling Millions

**1.** October 7, 1905, as quoted in *Fit For America: Health, Fitness, Sport and American Society,* by Harvey Green, Pantheon Books, New York, 1986.

**2.** Ibid.

**3.** "Physical Culture—Weakness Is a Crime," by Robert Lewis Taylor, *The New Yorker,* October 21, 1950.

**4.** *Magazines in the Twentieth Century,* by Theodore Peterson, University of Illinois Press, Urbana, 1964.

**5.** *Bunny: The Real Story of Playboy,* by Russell Miller, Holt, Rinehart and Winston, New York, 1984.

**6.** "Physical Culture—Ill-Physician, Heal Thyself," by Robert Lewis Taylor, *The New Yorker,* October 28, 1950.

**7.** *Body Love: The Amazing Career of Bernarr Macfadden,* by William R. Hunt, Bowling Green State University Popular Press, Bowling Green, Ohio.

**8.** Taylor, "Physical Culture—Ill-Physician, Heal Thyself."

**9.** "Exploiting the Health Interest–Type of Advertising That Makes 'Physical Culture' Commercially Profitable," *Hygeia,* November 1924.

**10.** Hunt, op. cit.

**11.** Taylor, "Physical Culture—Ill-Physician, Heal Thyself."

**12.** Working for the paper was at least as much fun as writing for it. Bernarr

had invented a method for what he called "brain breathing." It involved, according to his biographer William Hunt, "a series of exercises of the neck to induce more active cerebration. The neck movement had to be coordinated with inhaling through one nostril only. Newsroom staffers, who tried the exercises out at the desks, reported wonderful recoveries from their hangovers. When Macfadden brought in a man who had cured himself of the drug habit through physical culture methods and had the paper announce free consultations to all addicts, [managing editor Emile] Gauvreau was less amused. 'That evening our editorial rooms were turned into a raving asylum by all manner of terrifying, shaking creatures who crawled with pawing hands over shuddering copy readers, climbed on chairs and finally had complete possession of the place.' "

**13.** *Now the News: The Story of Broadcast Journalism,* by Edward Bliss, Jr., Columbia University Press, New York, 1991.

**14.** Taylor, "Physical Culture—Ill-Physician, Heal Thyself."

**15.** "An American Idealist," by H. L. Mencken, book reviews of: *The True Story of Bernarr Macfadden,* by Fulton Oursler; *Bernarr Macfadden: A Study in Success,* by Clement Wood; *Chats With the Macfadden Family,* by Grace Perkins, *The American Mercury,* May 1930.

**16.** *The General: David Sarnoff and the Rise of the Communications Industry,* by Kenneth Bilby, Harper & Row, New York, 1985.

**17.** *A Tower in Babel: A History of Broadcasting in the United States,* Volume 1— to 1933, by Erik Barnouw, Oxford University Press, New York, 1966.

**18.** The Chicago information is all taken from *Making a New Deal, Industrial Workers in Chicago, 1919–1939,* by Lizabeth Cohen, University of Cambridge Press, Cambridge, 1990.

**19.** Ibid.

**20.** Barnouw, op. cit.

**21.** Bilby, op. cit.

**22.** *In All His Glory: The Life of William S. Paley, The Legendary Tycoon and His Brilliant Circle,* by Sally Bedell Smith, Simon & Schuster, New York, 1990.

**23.** Peterson, op. cit.

**24.** Although we are taught that Teddy Roosevelt was a "trust buster," and that business people sometimes violate the "antitrust laws," we moderns have little, up-close and personal experience with the word. Under a trust, all the stock in a group of companies was traded for shares in a new single company called a trust. Although now under the same corporate ownership, the companies composing the trust continued to do business as independent organizations, except that they did not compete with each other in any way. The trust was fashionable among businessmen at the turn of the century and unfashionable among the rest of the population, which abominated them. So unpopular were they that companies not part of one would put on their billboard advertising "Not Made by a Trust."

**25.** Memo written by AT&T executive Lloyd Espenschied, as quoted in Barnouw, op. cit.

**26.** Naomi Fein, Interview.

**27.** *Forbes,* "Fact & Comment," December 1, 1967.

**28.** *Forbes*, "Fact & Comment," September 18, 1989.

**29.** *Forbes*, "Fact & Comment," August 15, 1963.

**30.** "Biography—Malcolm Forbes," prepared by Malcolm Forbes and submitted to Princeton by Malcolm Forbes, December 1989.

**31.** Fein, Interview.

## NINE: The Music Never Stops

**1.** *A Question of Character: A Life of John F. Kennedy*, by Thomas C. Reeves, Free Press, New York, 1991.

**2.** *Never Done*, by Susan Strasser, Pantheon Books, New York, 1982.

**3.** *Catalogues and Counters: A History of Sears, Roebuck and Company*, by Boris Emmet and John E. Jeuck, University of Chicago Press, Chicago, 1950.

**4.** *Pierre S. DuPont and the Making of the Modern Corporation*, by Alfred D. Chandler, Jr., and Stephen Salsbury, Harper & Row, New York, 1971.

**5.** *The Morality of Spending: Attitudes Toward the Consumer Society in America, 1875–1940*, by Daniel Horowitz, The Johns Hopkins University Press, Baltimore, 1985.

**6.** *Middletown: A Study in Modern American Culture*, by Robert S. Lynd and Helen Merrell Lynd, Harvest/HBJ Book, San Diego, New York, London, originally published 1929.

**7.** *Culture, Inc.: The Corporate Takeover of Public Expression*, by Herbert I. Schiller, Oxford University Press, New York, 1989.

**8.** *The Shaping of the American School, 1920–1941*, by Edward A. Krug, University of Wisconsin Press, Madison, 1972.

**9.** Lynd and Lynd, op. cit.

**10.** *Einstein: the Life and Times*, by Ronald W. Clark, Avon Books, New York, 1984.

**11.** Ibid.

**12.** Based on National Academy of Science figures, discussed later.

**13.** *New York Daily News*, December 20, 1986.

**14.** *Summary Report 1989: Doctorate Recipients from United States Universities*, conducted by the National Science Foundation, U.S. Department of Education, etc., Delores H. Thurgood, research associate, National Academy Press, 1990.

**15.** *Foreign and Foreign-born Engineers in the United States: Infusing Talent, Raising Issues*, Committee on the International Exchange and Movement of Engineers, National Research Council, National Academy Press, Washington, D.C., 1988.

**16.** *Friday Night Lights: A Town, a Team, and a Dream*, by H. G. Bissinger, Addison-Wesley, Reading, Massachusetts, 1990.

**17.** *City Games: The Evolution of American Urban Society and the Rise of Sports*, by Steven A. Reiss, University of Illinois Press, Champaign, 1989.

**18.** Bissinger, op. cit.

**19.** School board budget advisory committee member—interview.

**20.** *College Sports Inc.: The Athletic Department Versus the University*, by Murray Sperber, Henry Holt and Company, New York, 1990.

**21.** "The Art of Big Business," by Brian Willis, *Art in America,* June 1986.

**22.** *Selling Culture: Bloomingdale's, Diana Vreeland, and the New Aristocracy of Taste in Reagan's America,* by Debora Silverman, Pantheon, New York, 1986.

**23.** As quoted in "New York's Party Palace—The High Life at the Gilded Metropolitan Museum," by John Taylor, *New York,* January 9, 1989.

**24.** From the Special Advertising Supplement on Business and the Arts, *Forbes,* May 1, 1989.

**25.** *Forbes,* May 15, 1960.

**26.** *People,* July 19, 1982.

**27.** *Mellon's Millions: The Biography of a Fortune—The Life and Times of Andrew W. Mellon,* by Harvey O'Connor, John Day Company, New York, 1933.

**28.** *The Money Lords: The Great Finance Capitalists, 1925–1950,* by Matthew Josephson, Weybright and Talley, New York, 1972.

**29.** *American Business in the Twentieth Century,* by Thomas C. Cochran, Harvard University Press, Cambridge, 1972.

**30.** *The Money Game in Old New York: Daniel Drew and His Times,* by Clifford Browder, University of Kentucky Press, Lexington, 1986.

**31.** *Forbes,* October 15, 1927.

**32.** *Forbes,* December 1, 1927.

**33.** *Once in Golconda: A True Drama of Wall Street, 1920–1938,* by John Brooks, Harper & Row, New York, 1969.

**34.** *Forbes,* November 15, 1929.

## TEN: Nutmegs and Dynamos

**1.** Malcolm Forbes in *Forbes,* September 15, 1967.

**2.** *Malcolm Forbes: Peripatetic Millionaire,* by Arthur Jones, Harper & Row, New York, 1977.

**3.** Last Will and Testament of Bertie Charles Forbes, April 2, 1952.

**4.** Last Will and Testament of Malcolm S. Forbes, signed the eighth day of July, 1988.

**5.** *Forbes,* October 15, 1932.

**6.** *Insull,* by Forrest McDonald, University of Chicago Press, Chicago, 1962.

**7.** Ibid.

**8.** Ibid.

**9.** *In One Man's Life: Being Chapters from the Personal & Business Career of Theodore N. Vail,* by Albert Bigelow Paine, Harper & Brothers, New York, 1921.

**10.** *The Years of Lyndon Johnson: The Path to Power,* by Robert A. Caro, Alfred A. Knopf, New York, 1982.

**11.** Theodore Vail, the founder of the American Telephone & Telegraph, possessed of the same vision as Insull, expressed the idea in his AT&T slogan, "One Policy, One System, Universal Service." Universal electric service preceded universal phone service by several generations, however.

Vail's dream for a nation interconnected through the telephone undoubtedly came from his years with the Post Office Department where he played an

important role in bringing about a universal and efficient mail system. (Yes, it once was very good.)

The work of both men may have contributed to the modern politics of entitlement in ways not yet studied. It is safe to say that if such things as phone and electrical service are regarded as a quasi right, Vail's and Insull's labors, though unintentionally, helped make it so. If the consumer society traces some of its beginnings to the egalitarianism of Andrew Jackson's time, the commercial missionary work of mass distribution in the 1890s opened the door to political promise and entitlement. A chicken for every pot, a car in every garage, promised Herbert Hoover in 1928. He was giving political articulation to values and viewpoints injected into the culture the previous generation by men like Vail and Insull.

**12.** *A Streak of Luck: The Life and Legend of Thomas Alva Edison*, by Robert Conot, Seaview Books, New York, 1979.

**13.** McDonald, op. cit.

**14.** Surprisingly few major figures in business history have had biographies written of them which do them justice. Forrest McDonald's *Insull*, the University of Chicago Press, does right by the old boy, who, with his short stature and his white, whoopsy mustaches, looked like the little man on the Monopoly game cards. Since he was at the height of his fame when the game made its debut, he may have been the silly chap cavorting through Community Chest and mortgaging Reading Railroad.

**15.** *American Genesis: A Century of Invention and Technological Enthusiasm*, by Thomas P. Hughes, Penguin Books, New York, 1990.

**16.** *Victorian America: Transformations in Everyday Life, 1876–1915*, by Thomas J. Schlereth, HarperCollins, New York, 1991.

**17.** "Clash of the Titans—Kohlberg vs. Kravis, Roberts," by Christopher Byron, *New York*, September 25, 1989.

**18.** Profile of Walter Sherman Gifford, by Jack Alexander, *The New Yorker*, June 12, 1937.

**19.** *The Money Lords: The Great Finance Capitalists, 1925–1950*, by Matthew Josephson, Weybright and Talley, New York, 1972.

**20.** Milton Friedman, *The Wall Street Journal*, August 28, 1991.

**21.** In modern money, this has got to be the equivalent of a couple of million dollars, and all to one candidate running in a primary.

**22.** *George W. Norris: The Persistence of a Progressive, 1913–1933*, by Richard Lowitt, University of Illinois Press, Urbana, 1971.

**23.** *Forbes*, May 1, 1934.

**24.** *Forbes*, January 15, 1931.

**25.** There is a large Warren Buffett cult. He is regarded as the good speculator, the one who does not bring death and destruction with his arrival on the scene. In addition investment nerds worship Buffett as the man who studies and analyzes companies with such care, knowledge and detachment that he invariably finds the best ones to buy into. The Buffett aura has been buttressed by publicity for his lifelong residence in Omaha, Nebraska, where he lives a simple, down-home life which is as celebrated in its own way as Donald Trump's rococo extravagances are celebrated in theirs. Of late, how-

ever, the good speculator may have been spending too much time in dinner jackets in the back of the pridemobiles, the long power-car limousines, which is not a good a place for the quiet study of investment value. In recent years he has invested large amounts in Jimmy Robinson's operation at American Express and in Salomon Brothers. After John Gutfreund, (he will slap your hands unless you pronounce it Goodfriend), the CEO at Salomon Brothers, was forced to confess he had put company above country in the government bond scandal and resigned, Buffett who, like most speculators, has never run anything in his life, rushed in to take Goodbuddy's job in order to save his investment.

**26.** McDonald, op. cit.

**27.** *Business Week* March 18, 1985.

**28.** *Business Week,* January 16, 1989.

**29.** *Business Week,* March 4, 1985.

**30.** One source, *The Robber Barons: The Great American Capitalists, 1861–1901,* by Matthew Josephson, A Harvest/HBJ Book, Harcourt, Brace, Jovanovich, San Diego, New York, London, 1934, reprint 1962, says that the redoubtable Jay Gould was paid a tidy premium for relinquishing his stock after failing to capture the Albany & Susquehanna Railroad. If true this 1869 coup might qualify Gould for the honor of being the first greenmailer but his two biographers don't think he made a profit on the deal. See *Jay Gould, His Business Career, 1867–1892,* by Julius Grodinsky, University of Pennsylvania Press, Philadelphia, 1957, and *The Life and Legend of Jay Gould,* by Maury Klein, The Johns Hopkins University Press, Baltimore, 1986.

There is no figure in business history who has a more divided jury. Modern scholars see him as a major figure in the building and perfecting of the railroad system, a business visionary of sorts. On the other hand, Henry Adams, no mean scholar himself, and a contemporary, regarded him as scarcely more than a corruptionist and a pig.

**31.** "Old Master or Gray Predator?" by Jonathan R. Laing, *Barron's,* July 4, 1988.

**32.** *Forbes,* October 23, 1989.

**33.** Laing, op. cit.

**34.** *Business Week,* July 2, 1984.

**35.** Ibid.

**36.** William H. Vanderbilt.

**37.** "MSF's children talk of 'Pop'—Thanks for the memories," by Jean Whiston, *Hills-Bedminster Press,* March 8, 1990.

**38.** Laing, op. cit. Unless otherwise noted the material on Lindner comes from this article.

**39.** "Taking in Each Other's Laundry," by Allan Sloan and Howard Rudnitsky, *Forbes,* November 19, 1984.

**40.** *The Wall Street Journal,* April 12, 1991.

**41.** Sloan and Rudnitsky, op. cit.

**42.** McDonald, op. cit.

**43.** *Forbes,* June 1, 1934.

**44.** Grodinsky, op. cit., and Klein, op. cit. Both of Gould's biographers

demonstrate that Gould, the Wall Street demon personified, was also a productive and far-seeing businessman.

## ELEVEN: "The Play-things of Speculators"

**1.** *Forbes*, September 29, 1917.

**2.** *The Speculator: Bernard M. Baruch in Washington, 1917–1965*, by Jordan A. Schwartz, University of North Carolina Press, Chapel Hill, 1981.

**3.** They are, should anyone care to know, *Somerset Messenger-Gazette, Middlesex Chronicle, Bound Brook Chronicle, Piscataway-Dunellen Review, Metuchen-Edison Review, South Plainfield Reporter, Green Brook-North Plainfield Journal, Highland Park Herald, Hills-Bedminster Press, Franklin Focus, Scotch Plains-Fanwood Press, Somerset County Shopper* and *Middlesex County Shopper*.

**4.** *Adventures of A White-Collar Man*, by Alfred P. Sloan, Jr., in collaboration with Boyden Sparks, Doubleday, New York, 1940.

**5.** *Andrew Carnegie and the Rise of Big Business*, by Harold C. Livesay, edited by Oscar Handlin, HarperCollins, New York, 1975.

**6.** Steel Titan: The Life of Charles M. Schwab, by Robert Hessen, Oxford University Press, New York, 1975.

**7.** *Pierre S. DuPont and the Making of the Modern Corporation*, by Alfred D. Chandler, Jr., and Stephen Salsbury, Harper & Row, New York, 1971.

**8.** *In One Man's Life: Being Chapters from the Personal & Business Career of Theodore N. Vail*, by Albert Bigelow Paine, Harper & Brothers, New York, 1921.

**9.** *Father Son & Co.: My Life at IBM and Beyond*, by Thomas J. Watson, Jr., with Peter Petre, Bantam Books, New York, 1990.

**10.** *The Wall Street Journal*, July 15, 1991.

**11.** *In All His Glory: The Life of William S. Paley, The Legendary Tycoon and His Brilliant Circle*, by Sally Bedell Smith, Simon & Schuster, New York, 1990.

**12.** *Three Blind Mice: How the TV Networks Lost Their Way*, by Ken Auletta, Random House, New York, 1991.

**13.** *The Wall Street Journal*, January 24, 1991.

**14.** *Forbes*, August 1, 1932.

**15.** *Forbes*, June 15, 1932.

**16.** Unpublished paper entitled *Estimates of Personal Wealth, 1986*, by Marvin Schwartz and Barry Johnson, Foreign Special Projects Section, Internal Revenue Service.

**17.** *The Concentration of Wealth in the United States—Trends in the Distribution of Wealth Among American Families*, by the Democratic Staff of the Joint Economic Committee, Based on Data, Analysis and Additional Assistance Provided by James D. Smith, July 1986. Ordinarily I suspect anything prepared by the Democratic Staff of any public body, but Smith, not part of the staff, is regarded as preeminent in the little-known field of who owns how much of what.

**18.** An observation first made by Woodrow Wilson in regard to the members of the United States Senate but a good wisecrack may have more than one application.

**19.** *Making A New Deal: Industrial Workers in Chicago, 1919–1939,* by Lizabeth Cohen, Cambridge University Press, Cambridge, 1990.

**20.** *Forbes,* October 31, 1931.

**21.** *The Presidency of Herbert C. Hoover,* by Martin L. Fausold, University of Kansas Press, Lawrence, 1984.

**22.** *Herbert Hoover: A Public Life,* by David Burner, Alfred A. Knopf, New York, 1979.

**23.** *Forbes,* October 1, 1929. B.C. wrote that, "Mussolini has transformed Italy. That is what most impresses one who has not visited that land for years . . . Whereas Italian cities used to be overrun with every conceivable variety of beggars, none are to be found to-day. Whereas dirt used to abound, the chief cities are now remarkably spruced up. Whereas loafing and laziness used to be everywhere in evidence, most of the people are now working . . . But the relative few who voiced criticism declared that it was utterly unsafe to utter one word publicly against the Fascisti . . . The utter loss of freedom of speech, of freedom of the press, and the arrogance of Mussolini's cohorts were dwelt upon bitterly. One thing which struck me was the amazing prevalence of military and police . . . I was told that there were even more spies in plain clothes than military uniform. And this also constituted a serious grievance among the limited number who dared to speak their minds freely."

**24.** *Forbes,* April 1, 1933.

**25.** *Forbes,* July 1, 1930.

**26.** *Forbes,* June 1, 1932.

**27.** *Forbes,* January 15, 1932.

**28.** *Forbes,* September 1, 1930.

**29.** *Forbes,* November 1, 1932.

**30.** *Forbes,* November 15, 1932.

**31.** *Forbes,* October 15, 1931.

**32.** *Forbes,* September 1, 1930.

**33.** *Forbes,* September 15, 1931.

**34.** *Forbes,* April 1, 1933.

**35.** *Forbes,* October 15, 1930.

**36.** Hessen, op. cit.

## TWELVE: **The Platinum Pickle**

**1.** *The Wall Street Journal,* June 21, 1991.

**2.** *The Wall Street Journal,* April 17, 1991.

**3.** *Business Week,* August 11, 1986.

**4.** *The Emergence of Multinational Enterprise: American Business Abroad from the Colonial Era to 1914,* by Mira Wilkins, Harvard University Press, Cambridge, 1970.

**5.** "International Harvester's Story: How a Great Company Lost Its Way," by Barbara Marsh and Sally Savile, *Crain's Chicago Business,* November 8, 1982 and November 15, 1982. An outstanding reportorial job which closely describes how IH slipped downward over the decades.

**6.** *More* magazine, April 1977.

7. *Manhattan Passions*, by Ron Rosenbaum, Penguin, 1988.

8. Marsh and Savile, "International Harvester's Story: How a Great Company Lost Its Way."

9. *The Wall Street Journal*, April 3, 1991.

10. This number comes from *Newsweek*, January 20, 1986. Journalism is full of goofy numbers like this one, which may or may not be based on some unknown slavey going through I know not what set of records. Nevertheless, no doubt exists that many companies changed their name, often at frightening cost and sometimes for questionable gain, as was the case with the various old Standard Oil companies, which annealed to each other under the banner of Exxon. As a collection of apparently unconnected companies like Esso and Standard Oil of New Jersey, they were low profile and low target. Exxon quickly become a synonym for the biggest, baddest oil company on the planet.

11. *Gurus in the Boardroom*, by Sharon Churcher, unpublished monograph, September 1991.

12. *Pierre S. DuPont and the Making of the Modern Corporation*, by Alfred D. Chandler, Jr., and Stephen Salsbury, Harper & Row, New York, 1971.

13. *The Visible Hand: The Managerial Revolution in American Business*, by Alfred D. Chandler, Jr., Belknap Press of Harvard University Press, Cambridge, Massachusetts, and London, England, 1977.

14. F. Donaldson Brown seems to have been the inventor of flexible budgeting, a procedure for allocating different levels of outlays depending on the volume of business the company might be doing. Again, an obviously necessary tool in hindsight, but not before it was devised. In large organizations, choosing the right information and knowing what to do with it to arrive at a useful budget demands much knowledge, skill and ingenuity.

15. *Rude Awakening: The Rise, Fall and Struggle for Recovery of General Motors*, by Maryann Keller, HarperPerennial, New York, 1990.

16. *Relevance Lost: The Rise and Fall of Management Accounting*, by H. Thomas Johnson and Robert S. Kaplan, Harvard Business School Press, © 1987, 1991 by the President and Fellows of Harvard College.

17. *My Years With General Motors*, by Alfred P. Sloan, Jr., edited by John McDonald with Catharine Stevens, with a new introduction by Peter F. Drucker, Doubleday Currency, paperback, New York, 1990.

18. As quoted in Sloan, op. cit., a 1924 memorandum, entitled "Pricing Policy in Relation to Financial Control," by Brown spells it out clearly enough if you are hip to business language: "A monopolistic industry, or an individual business under peculiar circumstances, might maintain high prices and enjoy a limited volume with a very high rate of return on capital, indefinitely, at the sacrifice of wholesome expansion. Reduction of price might broaden the scope of demand, and afford an enlargement of volume highly beneficial, even though the rate of return on capital might be lower. The limiting considerations are the economic cost of capital, the ability to increase supply, and the extent to which demand will be stimulated by price reduction.

"Thus it is apparent that the object of management is not necessarily the highest attainable rate of return on capital, but rather the highest return consistent with attainable volume, care being exercised to assure profit with

each increment of volume that will at least equal the economic cost of additional capital required. Therefore the fundamental consideration is the economic cost of capital to the individual business."

**19.** *The Seven Fat Years: Chronicles of Wall Street,* by John Brooks, Harper & Brothers, New York, 1958.

**20.** My analysis here leans on the work of H. Thomas Johnson and Robert S. Kaplan, who have written about the technical incompetence of the finance and accounting people in corporate America and the blockhead schools of business which are run by airy-fairy theoreticians who have never, if I may be pardoned the use of that tough guy cliché, met a payroll in their lives.

**21.** Johnson and Kaplan, op. cit.

### THIRTEEN: **King Harold and the G-Theory**

**1.** *Zeckendorf: The Autobiography of William Zeckendorf,* Holt, Rinehart and Winston, New York, 1970.

**2.** "Man in a $100-Million Jam," by Gilbert Burck, *Fortune,* July 1960.

**3.** Zeckendorf, op. cit.

**4.** This example of how Zeckendorf did it appeared in Burck, op. cit.: "Let us suppose that Zeckendorf undertook to acquire for $10 million a building that was earning $1 million a year, but could earn $1,300,000 through increased rents, and was being depreciated at $300,000 a year. To begin with, he borrowed $9 million through a first and second mortgage, so that his actual cash outlay was only $1 million. Thereafter he sold a leasehold on the building for $5 million ($1,500,000 in cash and a $3,500,000 mortgage) and $600,000 rent. Then he sold his remaining equity in the structure for $1,200,000. All told, through three complex deals, he received $15,200,000 for a building that he bought for $10 million. Of the $5,200,000 profits, $3,500,000 was in the form of a leasehold mortgage."

**5.** Zeckendorf, op. cit.

**6.** Over the decades Rohatyn metamorphosed into the big-time businessman who could "write." At any rate his byline popped up in *The New York Review of Books,* as elsewhere he was hailed as a business statesman who had risen above money to save New York City from bankruptcy and do other high-minded things. Earlier, in the time of the Nixon administration, he was known to operate less publicly, in the dark marches between politics and business, that no-good-man's-land of access, dubious campaign contributions and favors.

**7.** *Financier: The Biography of André Meyer, A Story of Money, Power, and the Reshaping of American Business,* by Cary Reich, William Morrow and Company, New York, 1983.

**8.** Ibid.

**9.** *In All His Glory: The Life of William S. Paley, The Legendary Tycoon and His Brilliant Circle,* by Sally Bedell Smith, Simon & Schuster, New York, 1990.

**10.** *The General: David Sarnoff and the Rise of the Communications Industry,* by Kenneth Bilby, Harper & Row, New York, 1986.

**11.** The application of the word to an agglomeration of functionally unrelated enterprises may have first been made in the pages of *Forbes* by Jim Cook.

**12.** Reich, op. cit.

**13.** Charles P. Alexander and Adam Zagorin, *Time*, January 28, 1985.

**14.** *Fortune*, November 11, 1985.

**15.** "What We Learned from the Great Merger Frenzy," by Lewis Beman, *Fortune*, April 1973.

**16.** January 12, 1987.

**17.** *Newsweek*, October 9, 1967.

**18.** October 28, 1985.

**19.** *The Wall Street Journal*, November 20, 1990.

**20.** *The Wall Street Journal*, February 20, 1991.

**21.** *Beatrice: From Buildup Through Breakdown*, by Neil R. Gazel, University of Illinois Press, Urbana, 1990.

**22.** *The Wall Street Journal*, November 21, 1988.

**23.** *Forbes*, March 18, 1991.

**24.** *The Wall Street Journal*, April 9, 1991.

**25.** *The Wall Street Journal*, May 16, 1990.

## FOURTEEN: Honky Tonkin'

**1.** Keeping the Corporate Image: Public Relations and Business, 1900–1950, by Richard S. Tedlow, JAI Press, Greenwich, Connecticut, 1979.

**2.** *The Idea Brokers: Think Tanks and the Rise of the New Policy Elite*, by James Allen Smith, Free Press, New York, 1991; Tedlow, op. cit.

**3.** Kravis comes from great wealth, having been sent to the best schools and having had all the large, carved, double-doors opened for him. In *The Money Machine: How KKR Manufactured Power and Profits* (Time Warner Books, New York, 1991), Sarah Bartlett describes how Henry's father, Ray, an oil geologist, made a fortune by doing such things as striking up a profitable relationship with Joseph Kennedy, father of the President. Ray Kravis was a friend of the father of President Bush, who called up to ask him to give boy George his first grown-up job. Ray is also famous as golf's first circumnavigator. In the company of Salim "Cy" Lewis, a well-known stock jobber at Bear Stearns, he took eight weeks in 1954 to circle the globe, playing a round of golf at every stop. If people with that kind of background lack so much as a modicum of *noblesse oblige*, Middle Americans had better look to their own resources.

**4.** "Where are the Shareholders Yachts?" by Benjamin Stein, *Barron's*, August 18, 1986. The exact quote is: "John W. Kluge made a profit of about $3 billion on an investment in which he had to put down no cash at all. The profit was made entirely by paying the stockholders of the formerly public Metromedia about one-sixth of what their company was worth. To be more precise, John W. Kluge paid his own stockholders, roughly one-sixth or less what their equity ownership in Metromedia turned out to be worth."

**5.** *Forbes*, March 2, 1918.

**6.** Jonathan Greenberg, Interview; Paul Sturm, Interview.

**7.** *New Light on the History of Great American Fortunes: American Millionaires of*

*1892 and 1902*, edited with an introduction by Sidney Ratner, Augustus M. Kelley, New York, 1953.

**8.** *Forbes*, October 1, 1984.

**9.** Jay Gissen, Interview, May 17, 1990.

**10.** *Philadelphia Inquirer*, October 7, 1990.

**11.** *Trump: The Deals and the Downfall*, by Wayne Barrett, HarperCollins, New York, 1992.

**12.** See, if you're a masochist, *Statistics of Income and Related Administrative Record Research: 1984*, by Mary F. Bentz and Marvin Schwartz, Internal Revenue Service Document, October 1984; *Improving Wealth Estimates Derived From Estate Tax Data*, by James McCubbin, Internal Revenue Service Document, undated.

**13.** These numbers are derived from *Estimates of Personal Wealth, 1986*, by Marvin Schwartz and Barry Johnson, Foreign Special Projects Section, Internal Revenue Service; *The Concentration of Wealth in the United States—Trends in the Distribution of Wealth Among American Families*, by the Democratic Staff of the Joint Economic Committee, Based on Data, Analysis and Additional Assistance provided by James D. Smith, July 1986. Much other information suggests there have been no permanent shifts in the distribution of wealth in the United States in this century, so while inflation and the rises and dips of the business cycle may move the numbers around a little, the percentages don't change much.

**14.** His charities were as diverse as giving millions to Princeton University and eight hundred dollars for a plaque marking the New Jersey birthplace of the man who, to some at least, is a hero—the African-American, quasi-Communist, Paul Robeson. He also gave a million dollars for AIDS research, which took a degree of courage, in as much as he was being blackmailed because he paid men to have sex with him. "News from Princeton University," a press release from the office of Communications/Publications, January 21, 1984; *(Somerville, New Jersey) Courier-News*, March 1, 1990; Muriel Freeman, Interview. Robeson was also included in *They Went That-a-Way: How the Famous, the Infamous and the Great Died*, by Malcolm Forbes with Jeff Bloch, Ballantine Books, New York, 1988; *New York Daily News* and an interview with George Warnock.

**15.** John Naeglin, Interview.

**16.** *The Wall Street Journal*, January 3, 1991.

**17.** *The Wall Street Journal*, July 9, 1991.

**18.** *Fit For America: Health, Fitness, Sport and American Society*, by Harvey Green, Pantheon Books, New York, 1986.

**19.** *Affairs of State: Public Life in late Nineteenth Century America*, by Morton Keller, Belknap Press of Harvard University Press, Cambridge, Massachusetts, and London, England, 1977.

**20.** *Our Times: The United States, 1900–1925—The War Begins, 1909–1914*, Volume IV, by Mark Sullivan, Charles Scribner's Sons, New York, 1932.

**21.** *The Development of National Advertising, 1865–1920*, by Daniel Andrew Pope, unpublished Ph.D. dissertation, Columbia University, New York, 1973.

**22.** *Sports & Freedom: The Rise of Big-Time College Athletics,* by Ronald A. Smith, Oxford University Press, New York, 1988.

**23.** *The Folklore of Capitalism,* by Thurman W. Arnold, Yale University Press, New Haven, Connecticut, 1937.

**24.** November 19, 1989.

**25.** *Charity Begins at Home: Generosity and Self-Interest Among the Philanthropic Elite,* by Teresa Odendahl, Basic Books, New York, 1990; *The Wall Street Journal,* October 21, 1991.

**26.** See *The Better World Investment Guide: One Hundred Companies Whose Policies You Should Know About Before You Invest Your Money,* by Myra Alperson et al., Prentice Hall, New York, 1991; *Shopping for a Better World: A Quick and Easy Guide to Socially Responsible Supermarket Shopping,* by Ben Corson et al., Council on Economic Priorities, Ballantine Books, New York, 1989.

**27.** "Big Businessmen and a New Economy," by John Tipple, in *The Gilded Age,* Revised and Enlarged Edition, H. Wayne Morgan, editor, Syracuse University Press, Syracuse, N.Y., 1970.

**28.** *Rockdale: The Growth of an American Village in the Early Industrial Revolution,* by Anthony E. C. Wallace, Alfred A. Knopf, New York, 1978.

**29.** Ibid.

**30.** As quoted in *Poletown: Community Betrayed,* by Jeanie Wylie, University of Illinois Press, Urbana, 1989.

# INDEX

# Index

# Index

# Index

# Index